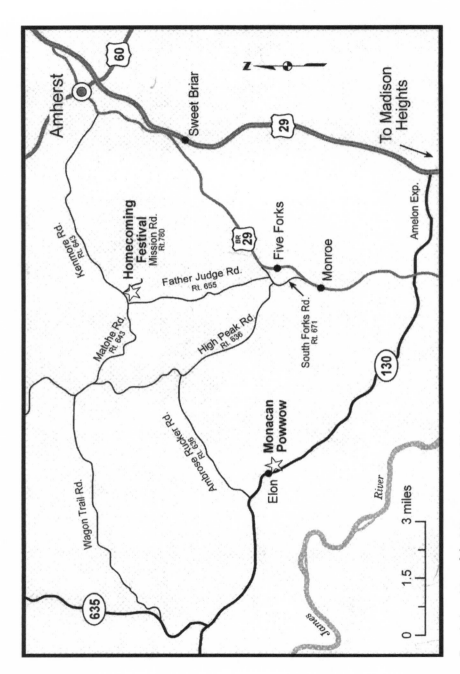

Frontispiece. Map of the Monacan region in Virginia.

THE MONACAN INDIAN NATION OF VIRGINIA

The Drums of Life

ROSEMARY CLARK WHITLOCK

with a Foreword
by J. ANTHONY PAREDES
and an Introduction
by THOMAS J. BLUMER

THE UNIVERSITY OF ALABAMA PRESS
Tuscaloosa

CONTEMPORARY AMERICAN INDIAN STUDIES
J. Anthony Paredes, *Series Editor*

Copyright © 2008
The University of Alabama Press
Tuscaloosa, Alabama 35487-0380
All rights reserved
Manufactured in the United States of America

Typeface: Bembo

∞
The paper on which this book is printed meets the minimum requirements of American National Standard for Information Sciences-Permanence of Paper for Printed Library Materials, ANSI Z39.48-1984.

Library of Congress Cataloging-in-Publication Data

Whitlock, Rosemary.
    The Monacan Indian Nation of Virginia : the drums of life / Rosemary Clark Whitlock.
        p. cm. — (Contemporary American Indian studies)
    Includes bibliographical references and index.
    ISBN 978-0-8173-1615-0 (cloth : alk. paper) — ISBN 978-0-8173-5488-6 (pbk. : alk. paper) — ISBN 978-0-8173-8113-4 (electronic) 1. Monacan Indians—Virginia—Amherst County—Interviews. 2. Monacan Indians—Virginia—Amherst County—Social conditions. 3. Monacan Indians—Virginia—Amherst County—Government relations. 4. Amherst County (Va.)—Race relations. 5. Amherst County (Va.)—Ethnic relations. I. Title.
    E99.M85W55 2008
    305.8009755'496—dc22

                                                                    2007048092

Contents

Illustrations

Foreword

This is not the usual book from an academic press. It makes no pretense of scholarly analysis, intellectual discourse, or defense of a thesis. The author is one of the people of whom she writes, the Monacans. In a sensitive introduction, scholar Thomas J. Blumer, Ph.D., provides illuminating background on the author and situates the book's significance by way of comparison with his own work with the Catawba. Blumer correctly identifies the work as "folk history" and makes clear the importance of such works not only for the Monacans but also for many other similar groups in the eastern United States. Similarly, the book can also be considered a kind of auto-ethnography in which a people tells their own story through one of their own without theoretical or interpretive embellishment—"just the facts" as they see them.

There have been very few scholarly studies of the Monacans. They have been on the periphery of anthropological awareness of Virginia Indians since the days of Frank Speck (Cook 2003: 195). Recently, however, the Monacans have come to the general attention of scholars through the work of a few anthropologists, most notably a prize-winning book by Samuel R. Cook (2000). The interested reader can turn to this and other works for objective analyses of Monacan history and society. By contrast, in Whitlock's volume, scholars have a gem of a subjective sourcebook, a close-up and down-to-earth recounting of the experiences of Monacans past and present plus a couple of outsiders who played important roles in modern Monacan history.

This is a sourcebook not only on Monacans *per se,* but also on their perceptions and reactions to external forces that have shaped their destiny. Especially noteworthy in this respect are commentaries and accounts of the activities of Walter Plecker. He was registrar at the Bureau of Vital Statistics of the Virginia Board of Health during the heyday of enforcement of Virginia's infamous anti-miscegenation, racial purity, and forced sterilization laws and policies during much of the first two-thirds of the twentieth century (for which the Virginia legislature formally apologized in 2001).

Again, there are numerous works where the reader can find scholarly treatment of the history of Virginia's race laws and the widespread eugenics movement that was a driving force for Plecker and others of his era. Particularly useful in this regard are the writings of University of Virginia professor Paul Lombardo (e.g., 2003). Cook (2000) provides a straightforward outsider's account of the impact on the Monacans of Walter Plecker and the laws he enforced. In this book, however, insider accounts give readers at least a glimpse of the personal anguish caused by Virginia's race policies among the Monacans, a group whose very identity as Indians was being erased by governmental fiat.

All of that was to change in the latter half of the twentieth century as Virginia Indians got "on the move" (Rountree 1992). Consequently, Indian identity in Virginia came to be celebrated, and the Commonwealth officially recognized eight Virginia Indian groups, the last being the Monacans in 1989 (ibid.). Notwithstanding Virginia's "state recognition," none of these groups are officially acknowledged as Indian tribes by the United States with a "government-to-government" relationship with the federal government. As of this writing, however, there is a bill moving through Congress for federal acknowledgment of six Virginia groups as Indian tribes, including the Monacan Nation, a bill that is attracting considerable attention in "Indian Country" (e.g., *Indian Country Today,* Wednesday, May 16, 2007, pp. A1, A4).

Regardless of the eventual outcome of the Monacans' quest for federal recognition as an Indian tribe, they are a distinct ethnic group and a people. This book does much to document from the inside details of Monacan life, past and present, historic and quotidian, public and private. Whatever might be the objective validity of statements made by Whitlock and her interviewees, their accounts stand as valuable information for scholarly comparisons with other "unrecognized" groups currently asserting their Indian identity in the East. Beyond Indian comparisons, the Monacan customs and practices detailed in these personal narratives are useful counterparts for examining much wider similarities in the ways of other rural southern folk cultures, white and African American as well as Indian. Likewise, the Monacan materials presented here are a valuable data-point for anthropological understanding of the rapid spread and elaboration in eastern North America of a quasi-religious complex of "Indian culture" manifest in powwows, sweat baths, "seventh-generation" rhetoric, and other beliefs and practices (cf. Cook et al. 2004; Paredes 1995, 1999).

Rosemary Whitlock's book is, yes, a celebration and tribute to her people, which will, no doubt, be enthusiastically received as such. It is also a valuable corpus of data in the very human stories told that will enrich scholarship on the Monacans and more.

J. Anthony Paredes, series editor

References Cited

Cook, Samuel R.

2000   *Monacans and Miners: Native American and Coal Mining Communities in Appalachia.* Lincoln & London: University of Nebraska Press.

2003   Anthropological Advocacy in Historical Perspective: The Case of Anthropologists and Virginia Indians. *Human Organization* 62: 191–201.

Cook, Samuel R., John L. Johns, and Karenne Wood.

2004   The Monacan Nation Pow Wow: Symbol of Indigenous Survival and Resistance in the Tobacco Row Mountains. *Southern Anthropologist* 30 (2): 1–19.

Lombardo, Paul A.

2003   Taking Eugenics Seriously: Three Generations of ??? Are Enough? *Florida State University Law Review* 30: 191–218.

Paredes, J. Anthony

1995   Paradoxes of Modernism and Indianness in the Southeast. *American Indian Quarterly* 19(3): 341–360.

1999   *Review of* Ritual and Myth in Odawa Revitalization, by M. Pflug. (U of Oklahoma Press, 1998). *Journal of Anthropological Research* 35:305–7.

Rountree, Helen C.

1992   Indian Virginians on the Move. In *Indians of the Southeastern United States in the Late 20th Century,* edited by J. Anthony Paredes. Tuscaloosa: University of Alabama Press.

Acknowledgments

I am grateful to Thomas Blumer, author of a pictorial book on Catawba Indian pottery. He is also the Catawba Indian historian and has other books to his credit. Thank you, Tom, for recommending The University of Alabama Press.

I am grateful for the guidance of J. Anthony Paredes, who not only provided the Preface to this work in order to set the Monacan experience in context, but who aided in numerous ways with his thorough understanding of the American Indian experience.

My thanks and gratitude to the two unidentified readers who reviewed this manuscript and offered wise suggestions, which I have endeavored to incorporate into this work.

I am indebted to Roger Nuckles, Monacan. Roger was my gracious guide in Amherst County. He rode with me and introduced me to many of the Monacan people who kindly consented to interviews for this book. A couple of times when I ventured out at night alone to interview someone, I returned to Parish Hall to find Roger standing at a rail in misty rain to make sure I returned safely. Roger didn't want to be interviewed for this book, but despite his shyness, he is very much a part while standing in the shadows. Thank you for your many hours of patience.

My eternal thanks to Paulette Avant, who took over a handwritten manuscript and typed all those pages onto a computer. Paulette is fast and efficient. This book would have remained a pile of papers stacked on a work table in my home office had Paulette not come to the rescue. How does one thank an angel of mercy?

I also owe a debt of gratitude to Lancaster County (South Carolina) librarian Richard Band. Richard talked to Paulette Avant and called to tell me Paulette's help was on the way. Richard has encouraged me through the years and has helped with researching hard-to-find information on this book as well as previous ones.

Thank you with love and a hug to my daughter, Sherry Knight. Sherry has been severely pushed to meet her own obligations of an active schedule as a church pianist, hospital volunteer, and a wife to give this manuscript countless hours of editing and revisions as well as suggestions and the use of her computer. Thank you, Sherry, for your patience and your eagle-eye for errors to help ready it for publication.

I am indebted to the *Monacan News,* a nonprofit publication. My hope is that with the help of some pages of Monacan history included in the appendix, this book will be a steppingstone toward Virginia legislators bringing to fruition the granting of federal recognition to the Monacan Indian Nation of Virginia.

Thanks to Marilyn Root, my cousin on the Branham side, for help in the beginning.

Thanks to Gerald Townsend, retired photographer, who salvaged some old beat-up pictures for me.

There are so many people who have helped and encouraged me, and I hope I have not left out any contributor to the cause, for all your time and effort was greatly appreciated.

Introduction

My tenure among the Catawba Indian Nation of South Carolina began in the summer of 1970. Although I did some related work among the Eastern Band Cherokee and spent a year or so studying the Pamunkey Indians of Virginia, I had no real intention of broadening my knowledge beyond my friends, the Catawba. Over the years and as splinter Indian groups surfaced throughout Dixie, I learned something of the Monacan tribe of Virginia. I knew their approximate location west of Lynchburg but never expected to make any meaningful contact, until I relocated in Lancaster, South Carolina, to spend my remaining years closer to the Catawba.

During a workshop organized by Professor Steven Criswell, the director of the fledgling Native American Program at the University of South Carolina, Lancaster, I was approached by a lady who introduced herself as Rosemary Whitlock, a professional writer and a member of the Monacan Indian Nation of Virginia. She clutched in her hands part of a manuscript she was working on with her people. Rosebud—I prefer to use her Monacan name given to her at birth—asked me to look at what she had produced. I agreed, not really knowing what I faced.

That night at home I began to read "Drums of Life." Here I had in my hands a book written by a Monacan and telling of their story just prior to recognition by the Commonwealth of Virginia. This is the very thing that I had pleaded with the Catawba to produce. My thesis had from the beginning been that the much-needed Catawba history would not be totally authoritative until some enterprising Catawba would do research on his or her people and put pen to paper. How lucky, I thought, the Monacan have skipped much of what I had attempted to do in numerous articles and three books on the Catawba and was ready to present the academic world with their history as only the Monacans themselves know it. My first chore was to convince Rosebud that she had a publication. My second chore was to do researchers and library catalogers a favor and present them with a helpful title. We made a compromise: *The Monacan Indian Nation of Virginia: The Drums of Life.* I convinced my new friend that her book would be published or would be the death of me. The University of Alabama Press was my first and only suggestion.

Although Mrs. Whitlock's study only covers a century of Monacan history, the twenty eight interviews with Monacans and friends of the Monacan make the volume nearly impossible to put down once the reader has begun. Of course the volume covers quite well the racial terrors created by Walter Plecker and the Virginia law of racial integrity. The sorrows of not being allowed to put their race down as "Indian" are amply covered by most of Mrs. Whitlock's informants.

But this history contains more than sorrow, for the Indians speak freely of finding joy in their hearts and lives despite their poverty. They made do with what they had, but in the meantime slowly lost their land base on their sacred Bear Mountain through an inability to pay taxes. They were caught in a world that would not allow them an education until the Episcopal Church stepped in and built a rudimentary log schoolhouse, grades 1–7. Good paying jobs were closed to the uneducated or partially educated Indians. Many tribal members took the avenue of escape to Maryland and a better life with more educational opportunities. Life had been so hard in Virginia that many were not told they were Monacans until adulthood. Many returned to the area around Bear Mountain to revive the opportunities of their people. The eventual recognition of the Monacan Nation by Virginia and their current hope of federal recognition are fully discussed.

The book abounds with sincerity and honestly speaks of sorrows and the joys related to growing up in close family groups in substandard housing. Feed bags were saved for clothing and bedding which sufficed in cabins heated by wood gathered for the stove. The entire family worked in the fields and they managed on the meager returns of sharecropping for white landowners who had purchased Monacan land. In off times the women made baskets of honeysuckle and split oak which they sold to local store owners. Although life was hard, it was complete, and Mrs. Whitlock leads us with great tenderness into life as only she and her people knew it.

It is only natural that a woman of Rosemary (Rosebud) Whitlock's superlative people and English language skills would write a monumental book about her people, the Monacan Indians of Virginia. The Monacan people are truly fortunate that Mrs. Rosemary would come along at this important juncture in their long but little-documented history. She has gathered a masterpiece of folk history that will provide Indians and scholars alike with the core of Monacan history as only the Indians themselves have experienced it. My wish is that every one of the over one hundred small Indian nations scattered across Dixie would come upon a resource such as that provided here by Mrs. Whitlock.

Mrs. Whitlock was born Rosebud Clark in Selma, Virginia, in 1926. Her parents were Frank C. and Dora Branham Clark. She grew up with eight brothers and sisters. She attended school in Covington and Craigsville, Virginia, but quit school in the fourth grade and went to work. In 1944, she married Kenneth Whitlock and they settled in Lancaster, South Carolina, where they raised four children: Sherry Whitlock Knight, Katherine Whitlock Thompson, Dr. Gregory Whitlock, and Brent Whitlock.

After her children were raised, Mrs. Whitlock realized an old dream and returned to school. The year was 1971. She began this project with the encouragement of her husband and her four children. She attended night classes in Lancaster High where she became an honor student and a substitute teacher. At the age of forty-eight, she graduated. She asked Greg, who was also graduating that year, if he would be embarrassed to walk across the stage in the same ceremony as his mother. His response was quick: "Mama, I will be the proudest one there."

Mrs. Whitlock's writing journey began as a machine operator at the Lancaster, South Carolina, plant of the Mallory Battery Company. In December 1979, she submitted a short piece to the company's work-related newsletter entitled *The Lancaster Reporter.* The piece is entitled "It could happen just the way it reads . . . who knows" and relates the fictional conversation between two batteries named Dura and Celle before they bed down for the night. A company official by the name of John Bergman spoke to Mrs. Whitlock about the piece and said, "The two cells come alive. If you can do that with two batteries, you can write a book." A woman of action, Mrs. Whitlock took the man seriously and began to write with great determination and published her efforts.

The result is that Mrs. Whitlock, a writer of great skill, has left an amazing paper trail for people to follow for many years to come. She is a published poet and the author of four books: *Makin' Do* (1983); *Mountain Home* (1987); *After Tomorrow* (1990); and *Golden Nuggets* (1993). She also received a host of writing and public service awards to name a few: World of Poetry, Silver Poet Award, 1986; the Southern Writers' Guild Third Place Award for an article, "What is Truth," 1986; World of Poetry Golden Poet Award, 1989; American Rosie the Riveter Association Award, 2004. Before Mrs. Whitlock began to publish book-length efforts, she submitted her work to literary publications and produced a storm of successes, including contributions to *Modern American Lyrics* (1963); *Melody of the Muse* (1964); *Versatility in Verse* (1965); *A Burst of Trumpets* (1966); *Yearbook of Modern Poetry* (1971); *Lyrics of Love* (1972); *Melody of the Muse* (1979); *Lyrical Voices* (1979); *Poetic Treasures* (1980); and *The American Poetry Anthology* (1983).

Mrs. Whitlock's interests go beyond the art of writing prose and poetry to a profound civic awareness. Her awards also reveal this interest: Red Rose Winner, Letters to the Editor of the Lancaster News, Lancaster, South Carolina, July 1984 and June 1988; The Community Playhouse of Lancaster County, 1991, Certificate of Appreciation, Lancaster County Council of the Arts, 1995; and a Certificate of Appreciation, Veterans of Foreign Wars of the United States, 2002. She is currently a member of the Lancaster County Sheriff's Department Advisory Board and is a former member of the Strategic Task Force on Education, also in Lancaster.

Aside from her book-length efforts, some of her poems have appeared in anthologies including the Young Publication of Appalachia, Virginia. For several years, she has written occasional guest editorials for the *Lancaster News,* Lancaster, South Carolina. For a number of years, she was a member of the Lancaster Council of the Arts. She received an award for the most volunteer hours for the year 1993–1994. In 2003 she was voted Top Board Member for the Lancaster Public Library. In 2002, the U.S. Veterans of Foreign Wars gave Mrs. Whitlock a certificate of appreciation for her service at the Quantico Marine Naval Base.

The idea for the volume being published here on Mrs. Whitlock's tribe, the Monacan Indians, was talked about and thought over during a long period of time. Both of her parents were Monacan Indians. The actual firm inspiration for *The Monacan Indian Nation of Virginia: The Drums of Life* came to the author during the dedication of a memorial at a Monacan cemetery, located behind the long-gone Crawford's Store.

The memorial had been a topic of discussion among the Indians for a long time and it includes all the surnames of those Indians known to be buried there. Mrs. Whitlock had to go. Her daughters Sherry and Katherine made the long trip from Lancaster, South Carolina, to Virginia. During this visit, Mrs. Whitlock told her daughters, "I feel the book on my people is something I have to do." The girls were unanimous in their response: "What's stopping you?"

Some months later her son Brent took his mother back to Virginia. Her grandson Griff Thompson followed with her car so she would have some method of transportation in a very rural area. She stayed in Virginia three months interviewing the Indians, resulting in the comments memorialized in this book. For further information, she visited local libraries such as that at Sweet Briar College; at the older churches she checked records; and she searched newspaper files at the county courthouse.

While *The Monacan Indian Nation of Virginia: Drums of Life* is basically the work of many people, either Indians or those who had a unique opportunity to know and come to love the Monacan people, Mrs. Whitlock's writing skills dominate every page. The people who were interviewed in the course of researching this volume tell their stories with great sincerity. She simply told each:

"Just tell me what is in your heart," and they did just that. Through the writing skills of Mrs. Whitlock, the reader is ushered from one topic to another in an artful way. In producing this volume, Mrs. Whitlock ventured into uncharted ground and just followed her heart.

In short, Rosemary Whitlock was well prepared to do the Monacan research and writing. She came to the project with four books to her credit and tremendous people skills. Her dedication to the Monacan people is profound. These talents helped her take the idea to the next step. The book itself is divided into twenty-eight interviews or chapters and some very important historical appendixes. The people Mrs. Whitlock interviewed opened their hearts and exposed their memories with great sincerity. The results are very sad, indeed, when the Indians talk about the use of the term "issue" and other degrading comments and acts. The book weeps when Mrs. Whitlock's informants told of the hurt surrounding Virginia's racial integrity law and Plecker's interpretations of the law. In the interviews, we see the Monacan fleeing Amherst County for areas where they would not be looked at as "odd" and treated with contempt at unexpected times. We see the Monacan people taking the situation in hand and getting the education denied them for so long. We see them coming home and helping to organize the tribe, a tribe that had not been organized in a very formal way since the Colonial period. At times, we break out into laughter at their experiences, but the laughter is with them not directed at them. Such is Mrs. Whitlock's skill in telling a tale. One example was when a young Monacan man came home from college and had to explain to his mother why a red light was not quite appropriate on their front porch. The story of this small Indian community is sometimes sad, often uplifting, and at times hilariously funny. Mrs. Whitlock has made her mark on the history of her people and will always be remembered for her efforts. The Monacan people can thank the Great Creator above that Rosebud Whitlock has come along at this point in their history.

Thomas J. Blumer, Ph.D.
Lancaster, South Carolina

THE MONACAN INDIAN NATION OF VIRGINIA

Virginia Monacan Indians

Federal Recognition Past Due

Within the confines of the Racial integrity Act of 1924 (Appendix J), the state of Virginia recognized only two races—white and colored—and legislated against mixed-race marriages. The law required that a racial description of every person be included on birth certificates and prevented marriages between white and nonwhite persons. The law is widely accepted as the strictest ban on miscegenation in the United States, a law that remained in force until 1967 when it was overturned by the United States Supreme Court in *Loving v. Virginia.*

In the pages of this book, Monacan Indians will tell of their personal holocaust brought about by the Eugenic Control Law and magnified by the hatred of Dr. Walter Ashby Plecker (1861–1947). Plecker earned his medical degree in 1885 from the University of Maryland and moved to Hampton, Virginia, in 1892, becoming its public health officer in 1902. When Virginia's Bureau of Vital Statistics was established, Plecker became the first state registrar, serving from 1912 to 1946 until he retired at age eighty-five.

But life itself is never all bad all the time. The Monacans will describe the wigwams of yesteryear. They will explain the outside and inside of sweat lodges. They will speak of the interesting meaning of some numbers. They will pull up a chair and chat awhile about the gathering of herbs, basket weaving, and quilting. They will share with you the meaning of tribal dances and recall some family superstitions, especially the conjure ball.

The Monacan Indians are a people of inherent wisdom, endurance, and a sense of humor.

The Monacan Indians of Virginia reside mostly in Amherst and Rockbridge counties, and the frontispiece of this book shows the direct route to the Monacan Mission Center from Lynchburg, Virginia. Take Route 29-N to just before the town of Amherst; the Amherst County Library is on the left. At the library, take a left onto Kenmore Road, Route 643. Travel approximately eight miles out

1. Rosemary Clark Whitlock on the bridge over Falling Creek at the Monacan Mission Center in 1998.

Kenmore Road to the Monacan Center on your left. You will see a small sign at the edge of the road reading "Mission."

The shortest way is to take Route 29 from Lynchburg to S-5 Forks, Route 671 to Father Judge Road, Route 655. At the end of Father Judge Road take a right onto Kenmore Road. The Mission Center will be on your right on Kenmore Road. The Mission Center is where the Monacan Museum is located and also where the October annual Homecoming is held.

The map points out the routes from all directions to the tiny place of Elon, Virginia, where the Monacan Powwow is held in May of each year.

Some of the interviews I had with the Monacans took place in Parish Hall at the Mission Center on Kenmore/Mission Road. Some interviews took place in interviewees' homes in surrounding areas. Diane Shields and Karenne Wood were interviewed in the *Monacan News* office in Madison Heights, Virginia (at that time in 1998). The *Monacan News* office is now at the Mission Center. The former clerk of court of Amherst County, William E. Sandidge, was interviewed at his office in the Shrader J. Thompson & Associate Law Offices in Amherst, Virginia. I also interviewed George Branham Whitewolf at his Indian jewelry workshop in Madison Heights.

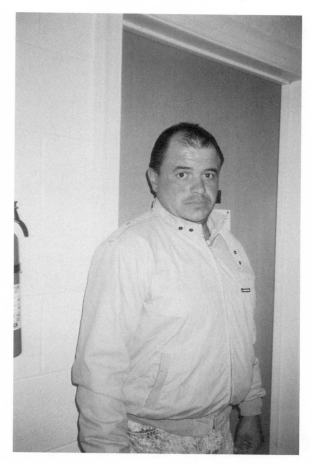

2. Roger Nuckles, author's patient Monacan guide and
friend, who accompanied the author during the interviews and additional research in Amherst and Lynchburg.

The Monacan Nation has approximately fourteen hundred registered Monacans as of 2006. Some of them live in the Lynchburg, Madison Heights, Amherst,
Virginia, area. Others have scattered into other states or other parts of Virginia.

According to Monacan chief Kenneth Branham, Republican senator George
Allen, who used to be governor of Virginia, and Democratic senator Jim Moran
are sponsoring a bill through the Senate for Monacan federal recognition. Republican senator John Warner, West Virginia, is cosponsoring the bill.

The six Virginia nations, the Chickahominy, Eastern Chickahominy, Nansemond, Rappahannoc, Upper Mattaponi, and Monacan all have lawyers representing them.

I interviewed twenty-six Monacans, one Episcopalian minister to the Monacans, and one former clerk of the court for Amherst County, Virginia. Then I added a chapter of my own family, a self-interview. I'll try to explain that odd happenstance.

I, too, am of Monacan descent, but I grew up in other areas of Virginia and knew nothing about the Amherst County region. I first knew my maternal grandparents' side of the family as living in Big Island, Virginia. Then they lived in Baltimore, Maryland. I lived with my parents in Longdale and then Covington, Virginia. My mother never mentioned the Amherst area of Virginia to me. I grew up being taught I had some Cherokee Indian blood on my dad's side of the family. My mama never told me anything about where she grew up or who her ancestors were other than her parents and one uncle. I had no idea there were even any Indians known as Monacan Indians.

I knew nothing of where my parents married. I knew nothing of Dr. Plecker, the state birth registrar, until the court trial I write of when I was nineteen years old. This discovery will be in the self-interview and some of the court documents are in the appendices.

In the beginning the Monacans were reluctant to share with me from their hearts about growing up Monacan Indian in Amherst County. In the past they had been disillusioned by newspaper reporters and authors who claimed they would write beneficial articles if they would share their story. The resulting articles, however, were derogatory.

I met with some of the Branhams, Hicks, Johns, and others at St. Pauls Episcopal Mission Church on a Sunday morning in 1998. I spoke with them of the learning experiences when I became aware of my mother's Monacan genealogy and some of the hurtful experiences she had endured, as had a few of my older siblings. This came to light in the court trial. I told the Monacans present that I would share my learning experience from the trial as understanding from my heart their trauma of growing up in Amherst County where Dr. Plecker had made frequent visits. This was in response to their questions as to why I wanted to write the story of the Monacans by the Monacans. Bless their hearts. In response to my answer they came forward with handshakes, trusting me to tell their story in sincerity and truth.

The majority of those interviewed would seem to become a little tense when they spied the cassette recorder and my notebook and ink pen at the ready. Therefore, I asked each interviewee to begin by telling me the names of their parents and grandparents. I would jot down those names in my notebook and, while doing so, quietly turn on the recorder. Usually by the time they named their immediate ancestors and told me the correct spelling of names, their fear of the recorder had been forgotten. That's why each chapter starts with a very scanty genealogy.

In Appendix K, the reader will find a list of the questions I asked in the interviews; some of which were generally asked of all interviewed and some of which were asked of particular persons who were more knowledgeable or more discerning of some subjects. Also, there were some communications by this interviewer such as nods of my head, meaning "continue, please," because I didn't want to interrupt their train of thought. Sometimes I was busy wiping at tears in my eyes. Sometimes there was a burst of shared laughter. At times there were moments of silence to give the interviewee a moment to collect their thoughts and memories or to settle their emotions.

I learned long ago when interviewing people, especially older people, the more often one interrupts the interviewee with rapid-fire questions, the less meat of the subject one garners. Just sit back and listen and allow their thoughts and memories to take form and paint a picture for you. Only interrupt with a question when absolutely necessary.

As I began to write this story, reviewing my notes and listening to the recorded interviews, I realized that some experiences were so similar I would have to attribute those to one or two interviewees in order not to be excessively repetitive. There are also experiences not universal to all and research by some Monacans and positions of offices held not common to all. Those experiences are told by those particular persons.

To my knowledge from my research, the Monacans were in Virginia in the late 1500s. According to McLeRoy and McLeRoy (1995), in the late 1500s, the Algonquins drove the Iroquois into the Great Valley of Virginia and the Piedmont. The Iroquois in turn captured the native Monacans, then killed some Monacans in Virginia. By the 1700s, the Confederacy's numbers were greatly reduced to an estimated fifteen thousand Monacans. Many of those Monacans were rounded up by Virginia authorities early in the eighteenth century and held for "safe-keeping" at Fort Christianna in Brunswick County.

The recorded encounter by Captain John Smith took place in 1607 when his map of Virginia identified five Monacan villages along the James River, plus other villages (Cook 2000; Houck and Maxham 1993; Wood and Shields 1999).

When Dr. Walter A. Plecker became state registrar of Vital Statistics of Virginia in 1912, he made war on the Monacan Indians by falsifying records and by claiming that the Monacans were Negroid free issue, especially in Amherst County. He also ordered other people in responsible positions to falsify Monacan records (Smith 1993).

From 1912 until his 1946 retirement, Plecker spent those thirty-four years in office venting his hatred of anyone he considered of impure blood line. He tried to achieve his impossible dream of a pure white race.

The word "issue" was a degrading word used against Monacans for many years in Amherst County. Because no one has ever seemed to know just what the word meant in that usage, it has become a word of interest over time. Some historians and authors have tried to research the word, but it remains more or less a mystery word taken out of its normal usage.

Cook (2000) wrote that in the late 1800s the census enumerators decided to quit using the term "mulatto" for race and to use instead "black." Cook says it was probably during that period of time the term "issue" became used for reference for the Monacans. Dr. Walter A. Plecker used the word "issue" in some of his correspondence in referring to the Monacans.

Estabrook and McDougle (1926) claim the word was derived from the term "free-issue," which developed about January 1, 1863, the date the black slaves were freed.

Another reference to "issue" was in a letter from Estabrook to Dr. Charles Davenport: "My dear Dr. Davenport, Dr. W. A. Plecker's offer to make copies of the Ishy manuscript is due to the fact that he, himself, desires a copy to use, not only in checking his own records, but in the various cases now appearing in the Virginia courts where some of the Isshies are filing suits to compel the County Clerk to issue either white or Indian registration cards" (Smith 1993).

Debra Bogdon, a student at Sweet Briar College, in her thesis in May 1973, gave her interpretation of the word "issue": "Research in the 1920s concluded that the tribe evolved from four fountain heads: a white man named Johns and three Indians—Redcross, Evans, and Branham. According to the legend, the Indians were moving up from the Carolinas and stopped in Amherst. The initial mixture of white and Indians caused those offspring to be socially separated from the rest of the community, resulting in further segregation and thus, the 'issue' identity as a separate group" (Bogdon 1973). Bogdon never uses the Indian name Monacan in her thesis.

When I asked all those I interviewed what the word "issue" meant as directed at them by white people, some of them said that during the 1900s, the word had been defined as having different spellings and pronunciations such as issue, issy, ishy, hue bangies, white nigger, yellow, and free issue.

The Monacans said it was not so much the word itself that mattered. It was the contemptuous look that accompanied the word. The look itself was why they came to dread the word. It cut to the Monacans' hearts in any of the forms mentioned because of the "look."

When I inquired of the younger Monacans at one of their youth meetings as to their interpretation of the word "issue," they all said they have never known. Occasionally, some of their white friends use it in a joking manner, but they say they don't know what it means either. It's just a word they've heard their parents or grandparents use for the Monacans. They say that if they ask their elders what the word means, the answer is usually, "We don't know. We do know it was once a fighting word between Indians and white folks."

Some young people say, "It hurt our people a long time ago, so the word sucks."

In this new millennium the word "issue" is being returned to its proper usage. The era of Dr. Walter A. Plecker's destructive reign of hate in his search of a pure white race is now nothing but dark history. The Monacan Nation can take their rightful place in the mainstream of Americans.

2
Chief Kenneth Branham

I am Kenneth Branham. When my cousin, Ronnie Branham, was chief of the Monacan Indian Nation from 1989 to 1994, I was the assistant chief. When Ronnie resigned because of health problems, I was elected chief in 1995 when I was forty-one years old.

My dad was Rufus Branham and my mom is Lacy (Johns) Branham. My maternal grandparents were Luther and Cammie (Branham) Johns. My paternal grandparents were Harry and Edith (Johns) Branham. Harry was the unofficial chief of our people for many years prior to Ronnie being elected.

I've been fortunate in having the pleasure of growing up with both sets of my grandparents still living. I even had the joy of growing up with my great-grandparents on my dad's side of the family. They were Walter and Delia (Terry) Branham. I knew my great-grandmother on my mom's side, Kate Johns.

I have two children by my first marriage, Timothy, who is twenty-one, and a daughter, Jody, who is eighteen. Then I was divorced for several years until in 1990 I met and married Judy Frances Ferguson from Lynchburg, Virginia. She has two teen-aged sons, Mark and Travis.

I've lived in Amherst County all my life. I grew up knowing I was Indian. I attended the mission school at St. Pauls Mission Center on Kenmore Road through the third grade. In 1963 we were admitted into the public schools from which Indians had been heretofore barred.

In 1964 the mission school closed its doors forever. Some of us went to school at Elon, some to Amherst, and some to Madison Heights and Monroe. The irony of the whole thing was that Monacan children in all other counties other than Amherst County had always been accepted in the public school system.

I'll admit that for many years while growing up, I did harbor bitterness in my heart for the way my people were rejected by the white and black folks of this county. It wasn't until I grew up and married Judy that I really began to deal with

3. Kenneth Branham enjoying a light moment with Dena Branham. The reader will meet Dena in chapter 7.

my feelings of being rejected, finally realizing that it had affected my interaction with other people to some extent. My wife, Judy, has helped me a lot. One of the first really serious things she said to me after a few dates was, "We've got to work on your attitude. You need to knock that chip off your shoulder. It's heavier than you think and it's interfering with the good person you really are."

But I want to get back to when I was a young boy and leaving the shelter of the mission school. The Saturday before we were to enter the public schools on Monday, my dad took me to visit the man who would be driving the school bus on our route. Now, my dad was a big man. He stood six feet and two inches tall and weighed 240 pounds. He called the bus driver to his front door and said, "Mr. Rucker, this is my son, Kenneth. He will be riding your bus beginning on Monday. You will stop and pick him up."

I didn't understand at the time why my dad did what he did. I didn't know that some of the bus drivers had made the statement they would not pick up Monacans. I soon learned some of the children on other routes had been passed by.

The first few weeks in public school in the fourth grade were really good. I made friends quickly. Then, after those few weeks I noticed my new friends were shying away from me. I asked some of them why they were shunning me—what had I done? They shuffled their feet and mumbled, "We told our parents about you, our new friend, and they said we were not to play with you because you are different from us."

That revelation from my new friends hurt me. It took me a period of time before I understood it wasn't the kids themselves, kids are kids, skin color is no big deal to kids. These were adults who had said to their kids, "You can't associate with that boy. He's different from you. He's an 'issue.' If you know what's good for you, you'll avoid him."

It's sad when adults harbor prejudice, because kids are like sponges. They need to trust in adults. They look to adults for guidance; they learn from their wisdom, their experience, and their common sense, but some adults fail in some or all of these areas and teach much like the Pharisees.

In school whenever we were asked to fill out official forms, on the blank space to be filled in as to race, we Monacans would pencil in the word white. It wasn't that we were ashamed of being Indian, but we had quickly learned if we wrote down Indian, the teachers would mark through it and write down colored or issue or mixed. Virginia's law didn't allow Indian as a recognized race on any legal document. A few teachers tried to help us out by standing up for us, but most of them were afraid of Walter Plecker's wrath.

One of my new friends ignored his parents' warnings and remained my friend and asked me to join the Boy Scout troop of which he was a member. I thought about it and decided I would like that, so I went home and asked my parents' permission to do so. They became very quiet and stood near the kitchen stove, just looking at each other. I could see the worry in their expressions, but they had never tried to hold us back in any endeavor that was worthy. Slowly, they nodded their heads at each other and then turned towards me. My dad said, quietly, "All right, Son, you can join, but how will you get to the meeting?"

"That's easy, Dad, my friend's mom picks him up from school and he said I could ride with them. His dad is the Scout leader. They live only a couple of miles from us. You've known his mom all your life."

The next day, I attended the meeting with my friend. There were four other boys in attendance, too, wanting to join. The leader of the troop gave us papers to take home and fill out. After our parents signed them, we were to bring back the completed forms to the next meeting. I was so excited I thought I could hardly wait for the next meeting, but the very next day at school, my friend who had asked me to join told me his dad said they weren't going to add any new members at this time. A few days later I learned the other four boys who had applied had been accepted as new members. I never held any ire towards my friend who had asked me to join. He had been sincere. It was the prejudice of his dad that denied me the right to be a Boy Scout of America.

When I entered high school I was very active in sports. My dad told me, "Son, if you make the Little League team, I'll buy you a glove."

I knew my dad was proud of me. I also knew it would be a monetary sacrifice of one or more needs in order to buy me a glove. Also, I was left-handed, which made a glove more expensive. I didn't think of my family as poor, not really poor. We had an abundance of love. We had plenty to eat. There were always clean clothes for us to wear. I knew, too, my grandmother made our clothes and we raised all our food-stuff that could be raised. I knew that both my parents worked really hard to provide for us, but money was a different commodity.

I borrowed a glove from a left-handed friend and I made the team on the tryouts. On the following week, on the day of the first game, I was dressed and I had my friend's glove. I was standing on the porch waiting for my ride, when my dad arrived home. He came up the steps and handed me a bag. Inside were a brand-new glove and a brand-new pair of cleats. I found out later from my mother, my dad had gone to the bank and had borrowed one hundred dollars to buy what I needed to play ball. As I sit here recalling days of old, it is now 1997, I am forty-two years old; and I still have that glove packed away with the memory of my dad and his love for me.

I played baseball and football all through high school. If it hadn't been for sports I might have been a dropout. I didn't really care for subjects. I guess most boys don't. I kept my grades up because I had to in order to play ball. I made a lot of new friends. I became aware that most sports-minded people play this game called life by a different set of rules than most other people. The fellows on our ball teams didn't care that I was Indian. They didn't care that my skin color was of a darker hue. They didn't care that their homes had indoor plumbing and mine didn't. Some of those guys often came home with me on Friday from school to spend the night with me and they always seemed to enjoy being in my home with my people.

I loved sports so much that in my senior year I told my coach if he could arrange it, I'd come back to high school next year and play ball! My coach laughed a belly laugh and said, "The thought is tempting, but I couldn't live with myself and neither could you and you know it as well as I do."

I was also into wrestling and it was through wrestling I won a scholarship and my parents were so proud that now I could go to college. Even when good things happen, one's dreams don't always come true. Tragedy came to call instead, one hot summer day. My father was killed in the month of May. He was working in the Montrose Orchards. The land was very hilly. He was driving a tractor, and those working near him said later they didn't know exactly what happened. They thought the brakes may have failed. At any rate he lost control of the tractor. The tractor struck a tree and the impact threw him head first from the tractor and the tractor ran over him. Dad never regained consciousness.

How many times while growing up had we heard Dad say, "My dream is that all four of you, my children, will have the good fortune to graduate from college."

I went away to college that autumn and I finished my first year with good scores, but my heart was heavy and I knew I had a serious decision to make that summer. My mom was struggling very hard trying to make a living all alone. I had three sisters younger than I. I knew I must return and get a job to help my family. The following year my sister, Marilyn, graduated from high school. The next year, the middle sister, Carolyn Sue, graduated. When my younger sister, Edith, walked across that stage two years later, I felt my heart would burst. One of my dad's dreams was on the way to coming true. Things may have been better for me had I graduated from college, but *if* is an unknown. I believe I did what God wanted me to do and that's enough for me.

Indians really are regular people with hopes and dreams and minds and hearts. We weren't a savage people even when the Europeans arrived, not until we were forced into becoming savage. If we had been savages when the Europeans landed, I can guarantee you the Europeans would have had a really hard time getting off the boat! Instead, we welcomed them and helped them adjust to this land. Fifty years later, they wrested the land from us and forced most Indian nations onto small nonproductive tracts of land.

We are now teaching young people when we are invited to speak at schools that scalping did not originate with the Indians. There is proof of that fact. Scalping was first introduced in this land by the incoming French.

The Constitution of the United States was based almost entirely on the Iroquois Indian Law in upstate New York. The Iroquois had their laws written down and they called it the Great Book of Laws. One can look at a copy of those laws and compare it with a copy of the Constitution and one will see I speak truth. George Washington supervised the writing of the Constitution. Benjamin Franklin and Thomas Jefferson wrote amendments to it. One thing they ignored when they wrote the Constitution based on the Great Book of Law of the Iroquois was the part which stated that women own everything, not men. They sort of left that part out when they brought their finished draft to the Congress. I always tell the students this part of the Great Book of Law because it's true. The men hunted and provided food, but the women did all the day-to-day work. They prepared the food and made the clothing for all. They nursed the ill. They kept the home fires burning. They even had the vote of whether men went to war or not. For if men go out to fight a war and are killed, who is the hardship on—the wives, the mothers and the kids. So the women even had the authority to make those decisions: to war or not to war.

The white people refused to accept us as Indians or white and said we had to be black. The black race said we weren't black and not to try to shove us off on them. They both said we couldn't be Indian because there were no Indians in Virginia. In denying our existence, they were, in essence, insisting we were a nonpeople. It was hard for us to understand how other people could be looking directly at us while saying, "You do not exist." I've often wondered how they would have felt if they had walked in our shoes for a day.

If it hadn't been for St. Pauls Church we would not have survived as a Monacan Nation. The Episcopalians taught us to hang onto and be proud of our God-given heritage. God made all of us as descendants of one man and one woman: Adam and Eve, according to the Bible of God-inspired Scriptures. God didn't mention color, so who can really know what color Adam and Eve were? I believe any of us should think long and hard before any man thinks of condemning any phase of God's creation.

The log cabin that was the original Episcopalian Mission School has been in existence since the 1860s. For many years the log cabin was the school, the church, and the social hall. Later on, a new school was built beside the log schoolhouse. I attended the new school through the third grade. That school is now the Monacan Museum. We've recently spent sixty thousand dollars to renovate it. The separate church was built in 1908. In 1996 Bishop Light presented the deed to us, restoring seven acres of ancestral land to the Monacan Tribe. They retained the church and the parsonage. Those two buildings and the portion of land they occupy still belong to the Southwest Diocese of Virginia.

We have applied for a grant to help us restore the log schoolhouse. The log schoolhouse means so very, very much to our people, especially the senior ones. In those days of long ago that little building was the site of the activities that was their salvation in more ways than one. That was where they gathered to renew their courage and to keep hope alive. That was where they endeavored to obtain an education. That was where the teachers and priests encouraged them to believe in God and to hold their heads high and to believe in themselves.

Now, thank God, we are officially recognized by the state of Virginia. We are now not only included as students in all schools, we are invited by teachers and professors to speak in elementary, high schools, and colleges to students. They are in essence saying, "Come and teach us the part of history of which we are relatively ignorant because it was mainly left out of our history books. Now we are all free to learn from one another and we want to learn the Indian culture, too."

We don't mean to harp on the past, no one can turn back the pages of time and change anything. We can use the past, though, as a learning tool for all of us; Caucasian, African American, and Indian. The past can act as a springboard to know what to incorporate and what not to incorporate. Past experiences can help lead us into a more corporate future for all races. This world is getting to be more like next door to all, as travel is now so accessible to and from all parts of the earth, even to the moon.

We strive to share with students attitudes of a positive nature. We often use an illustration about two fellow prisoners. These two men were thrown together into a dungeon with only one tiny window to give light. One prisoner looked out and down through the barred window. All he saw was the brown hard-packed earth. The other prisoner, who was St. Paul of the Bible, looked out the same window, but he looked up and saw the blue sky and the golden sun. Life is never all bad if we can see the good things, too.

When we held our first powwow, I was a little hesitant because some of the older people weren't enthused about it. They said we were bringing back old ways and we would only get hurt all over again. I took my grandma, Cammie Johns, by the arm and walked her around the circle. As we walked, I asked, "Grandma, you are a wise woman and I value your opinion. What do you personally think about having a powwow? Please, tell me." She looked up at me and her eyes filled with tears. She said, "Keep on doing the things you are doing, Kenneth. If I were fifty years younger, I'd be helping you. This will prove to be a good thing to do."

Needless to say my eyes filled with tears, too. I loved my grandma and her valued opinions came from living a long life in very tough times. She attended every powwow with me as long as she lived. She was in a wheelchair in the last two powwows, but she was there with me and for me. I had made a necklace for her and had given it to her at the first powwow. She always wore it. When she became very ill, I sat beside her bed one night. She said to me, "Kenneth, if the good Lord is willing I want to go to the next powwow with you, but He knows best."

Two weeks later, in the wee small hours of night, she had a hemorrhage and died late that afternoon. I wore the necklace I had made for her at the next powwow. It felt as though she was walking around the circle with me.

Sometimes when our family gets together for a time of fellowship, my three sisters—Marilyn, Carolyn Sue, and Edith—insist on taking trips down memory lane, despite my objections. They always drag up my escapades as a boy and laugh uproariously. I'll share a few because I know they'll tell all anyway. One of their favorites to tell is about my rock-throwing career. I was a master at it and I was also mean at the age of thirteen. I don't mean being "mean" like stealing or fighting or things like that, but I was restless and energetic. I wanted to hunt but my dad said I wasn't old enough yet to have a gun. I improvised. I did my hunting with rocks as my rifle. I could knock rabbits over like tenpins with a blow to their heads. I'd take the rabbits home and prepare them and Mom would cook them.

Rabbits weren't the only object of my rock forte. I'd throw at anything that moved, excluding people and cars. I'd throw at chickens, not aiming directly at them, but close enough to make them run. The day came, though, when I was off my aim and I hit a rooster and nearly knocked his head off. He fell over and I knew before I got to him he was dead. I was scared and could envision myself being restricted for the rest of my life over this deed. I looked around and made sure no one was looking and I picked up that dead rooster and threw him in the chicken house. I was in hopes my dad would think the rooster had just up and died of natural causes. It didn't work. The next day, my dad said, "Son, something has killed my best rooster. Do you have any ideas as to what it might have been?"

I said, "It must have been an old fox."

My mom always did the switching of us kids whenever we got too out of hand, but I didn't get a switching this time. For some reason Dad never did say anything about the rooster to anyone besides me.

I hadn't really learned my lesson, though, as apparently he had hoped I would. One day, that same summer, I saw one of our two milk cows grazing near the house. I threw a rock the size of a baseball and hit that cow squarely between the eyes. That cow went down on her front knees and she was bawling, moo-oo-oo. I thought, Oh, Lord, I've killed that cow and I can't throw her anywhere. I ran into the house and up the stairs and hid. I could see that old cow through the window and she had her feet stuck up in the air and I threw myself on the bed and hid my face in the pillow. Finally, I realized I didn't hear her bawling and I dredged up enough nerve to look out the window. That old cow had gotten to her feet and was staggering along the fence row. I ventured outside after awhile and went down to the pasture to check on her. She looked all right and was munching grass. She lifted her head and just looked at me. I was glad all she knew to say was moo and she'd already said that.

That just about cured my rock throwing, but not quite. I did make a vow to myself I would never throw rocks at an animal again and I didn't. But that didn't keep me out of trouble. I still had a way to go for the final cure.

We always had a big woodpile even in the summer because we must have firewood for the big stove. On this day, Carolyn and I had been sent to gather wood for Mom in preparation for cooking supper. Near the woodpile was a pole with a guy wire. I threw a rock and hit the guy wire. The rock ricocheted and hit Carolyn Sue in the head. Her head started bleeding and she started crying and ran to find Mom. I knew there was no way out this time, but I thought I might be able to make it a little easier on myself. I voluntarily cut my own switch and I cut a big one. While Mom doctored on Carolyn's head I cut a slit in the switch down low. I cut it only about halfway through the stem. I knew the switch would break after Mom gave me a couple of whacks with it. I outsmarted myself. I had cut the slit too far down. Mom grasped that thing up near the top and started with a strong whack across my legs. That big switch was doing a real number on my legs and backside. I took off and jumped over the bed and Mom was right behind me, still whacking.

I wonder why my sisters remember these things and never remember any of the good things I did at age thirteen. I must have done something good. If I can recall what it was I'm going to ask them why they never talk about the good things.

I do remember one of the good deeds I tried to do. Carolyn Sue had a baby tooth that was wobbling around in her gum. It was that loose. She refused to stand still and let me grasp it with my fingers and pull it out. So, one day, I talked her into letting me tie a string around the tooth and I tied the other end to the door-knob. I used the kind of string bologna came tied up with in those days. The rest should have been easy, but every time I attempted to shut the door, Carolyn Sue ran forward to give the string plenty of slack. She was crying and I was mad. Edith came in through the opened doorway just when Carolyn Sue was crying and I was fussing and trying to make her promise to stay put. Edith just looked at us and apparently decided she didn't want to inquire as to what we were fussing about. Humming a tune softly and not knowing what we were trying to do, Edith shut the door and pulled Carolyn Sue's tooth.

This is one trip down memory lane all four of us like to take and recall a happening with our beautifully innocent Mom. I arrived home from college one night and the porch light had been turned on to light my way. It was a red light! I burst through the doorway and didn't even bother to greet anybody. Instead, I roared, "Mom, what are you doing burning a red light on the front porch?"

Mom said, "Son, it's springtime and the bugs are really bad this year on the farm. That's called a bug light. The red glare keeps the bugs away."

I said, "Mom, that bulb is coming out right now."

She said, "Kenneth, with Rufus dead and you in college, it's hard enough to spare money for a light bulb. I need to use this bulb until it burns out. Besides, what's wrong with a red light?"

I said, "Mom, you and my sisters are here alone in this house with no man living here and that red light is dangerous. In the city, if a red light is turned on at a house, that means that house is a house of ill repute!"

"Whatever does that mean?" Mom asked.

"It means it's an advertisement that a prostitute lives there, or, to put it as mountain folks would say it, it means a no good woman," I answered.

Mom looked astounded and then she became disquieted as she said, "You mean you're working your way through college to learn such stuff as that?"

Like I said and still say, life can never be all bad where there are love and laughter to share with one another. I thank God for my family.

3
George Branham Whitewolf

I am George Branham Whitewolf. My great-grandparents were Richard Branham and Christina Wise Branham on the paternal side. My maternal great-grandparents were Elisha B. Willis and Ella Adcock Willis. My grandfather was Abraham Branham and his first wife was Anna Elizabeth Willis. In 1895, she died in childbirth at the age of fifteen years old, leaving behind their firstborn, Clarence. Now, here was Abraham with a newborn baby to care for all by himself. He soon did the typical thing in those days. He married Anna's sister, Willie Ann Willis, who was helping him care for the baby. Together, they had fifteen children of their own. Their middle son, George Albert Branham, married Dorothy Detloss, a German girl. I am their firstborn son, George Jr. I'll explain my surname of Whitewolf as we go along.

At one time my father owned four or five hundred acres on Bear Mountain here in Amherst County, Virginia. He gradually lost the land for lack of funds to pay taxes. There were other Monacan landowners who lost their land under the same circumstances. In Amherst County, the Monacans were refused a proper education which could have fitted them for wage-earning jobs. Because of lack of education they were pushed into menial jobs and paid with foodstuff they raised themselves and with log cabins to live in consisting of one or two rooms rather than with monetary wages.

After having to forfeit their land, my parents moved to Glen Burnie, Maryland. There my father got a decent job and I was born in a Baltimore hospital in 1942. I grew up in Glen Burnie. I learned from my dad that my granddaddy had also left Amherst in 1926 at the age of fifty-two. This was a couple of years after the Virginia Racial Integrity Act was passed into law. The state of Virginia planned to accomplish what legislators fondly referred to as enabling Virginia to bring into being a eugenically pure race defined as strictly upper class, pure Caucasian. In light of Virginia's persecution of Indians, I guess Glen Burnie, Maryland, became a refuge for hurting Indians from Virginia.

In 1960 and just out of high school, I left home and wandered all over the country. I spent a lot of those years out west living with and learning from other Indians more about Indian culture. While there with the Lakotahs in 1972, I changed from being filled with alcohol to being filled with the spirit of God, my Creator. The Lakotah medicine men say, "Nagi." That means filled with God's Spirit. This was my second birth so I changed my surname from the English name of Branham to the Indian name of Whitewolf.

In 1991 I came to Amherst County to try and help my people, the Monacans. The spelling of the name, Monacan, has changed. A long time ago it was spelled Mahnee-chan. I learned of the original spelling in my extensive research. At one time there was an area on top of Bear Mountain that was bare of vegetation. The Mahnee-chans gathered there to fast and to pray, to hold their ceremonies seeking visions from the Creator for guidance.

While researching the everyday lives of our people, I inquired, why did the Monacans choose such a little mountain such as Bear Mountain to call home? Surrounding this little mountain there is the range of Tobacco Row Mountains and Davis Mountain; Jones Mountain and High Peak Mountain. All of these are big mountains. Why then did the Monacans choose a little mountain such as Bear Mountain? Mah-toe-EE means bear and is correctly spelled Matohe. Why did Will Johns choose Matohe, pronounced Mah-toe-EE, to buy up land while dreaming of making his mountain home for all Monacans? I think it's because this mountain is believed to be sacred ground, dating back four thousand years as a place of prayer. It's kind of like the Jews feel about Israel. Why do the Jews insist on going back to Israel each time they've been driven out or subjected to other rule? They go back because they believe it is the Promised Land. They want to be there when God, the heavenly King, comes for them. And so with the Monacans, gradually, they are returning from being scattered into all states. They are coming home.

The cruel names once used by some people in this area with the intention of being hurtful to the Monacans are used no more. Hopefully, those names will soon be forgotten by all concerned. Names like Issue, Mixed, Colored, Red Nigger, Trash—these wounding names were caused by Dr. Walter A. Plecker's vendetta against Indians. He spent a lot of his time in Amherst County nurturing the destructiveness of a people his heartless soul feared and hated. Yes, Plecker was filled with the brand of poison Satan thrives on.

The state of Virginia finally gave us state recognition in 1989 and now we are working toward federal recognition as a Monacan Nation. We're buying back our land. We have used the profits made at powwows held for the last six years to buy back 118 acres of Bear Mountain. We are proud of what we are trying to accomplish. We are one of only a few eastern tribes that own land without having federal recognition. There are only eight tribes owning more land than we own. I'm not speaking of federally recognized tribes that have been given reservations by the government. We have never had a reservation and we don't want one. We are the only nation I know of who are buying back land we once owned and were cheated out of as a result of inability to pay taxes stemming from inability to hold wage-earning jobs because we were not afforded an education.

We are working together now, all the residents of Amherst County. We all want to put the past behind us and live in today and on into tomorrow with all of us giving 100 percent in our sincere efforts to be a community of neighbors. All of us have heard the old saying that a marriage has to be fifty/fifty. That's a lot of baloney! If each marriage partner gives only 50 percent of themselves to make a marriage work well, then each partner is getting cheated out of 50 percent. Don't give half of yourself. Give all of yourself. Then you can't fail. True, none of us can keep score on any given day because percentages tend to vary from day to day and one or the other of us is going to fall short from time to time. But if each of us is sure he's doing his level best all the time to give 100 percent, then he knows it will balance out to that for a twosome, a family, or a community of people. An Indian chief once put it this way, "Life is never meant to be played at. Life is meant to be lived and living requires hard work."

To go back to the land, let me explain what Mother Earth means to Indians. Even our name has to do with the earth. The word Monacan comes from the Algonquin Indian language and means "Earth People" or "Diggers in the dirt."

Indians live seven generations into the future. This means one must use his time on earth to try to make the world a better place for future generations by taking care of the earth and all the earth nurtures. Then the earth will still be good for generations to come—even for great-grandchildren seven generations removed.

The white man doesn't always live by this rule. They live by the rule of, when I'm 76.04 years old (according to insurance companies' calculations, that's the average life span), someone else can worry about the environment. Why should I care just so it serves me 76.04 years?

To prove I'm not just whistling Dixie, let's take a look back. When the white man came to America from Europe, Europe was a devastated land. Diseases were rampant. There were plagues of all kinds, too numerous to go into. In fact, the white man brought a lot of diseases into America that Americans had never been subjected to. Until the white man arrived in this bounteous land, America was like living in paradise. Ah, this country was so very beautiful and lush with an abundance of forests, animals, fowls of the air, sea life, sand dunes, and clean waters. Indians never attacked anything of nature's bounties just for the sport of it or to get rich financially. Indians only cut a tree when it became necessary to build a boat or a dwelling. They only hunted when food had to be provided for their families and then only animals good for food. To the Indian the earth itself is their mother and one never abuses their mother.

When we began going into schools and colleges as guest speakers, I soon learned the students wanted to know more about the sweat lodges. The lodge itself is made up of a wooden frame with wood stripping or of a wooden frame covered with blankets or quilts. Let me explain that even for a sweat lodge a strong, healthy tree is never cut down and used to make a lodge. Instead, we search for a dying tree and put it to good use without robbing the environment of a productive tree. My sweat lodge is covered with old blankets given to me as throw-a-ways. Therefore, I call it my $1.98 church.

Anytime from two to six hours before the sweat is to take place, I build an open fire, again using dead wood with which to heat twenty-eight stones which are native rocks. It takes more stones in the wintertime than it does in the summertime, and it takes two hours in the summer and about six hours in the winter to get the stones red hot. Once the sweat begins it lasts four hours, so the entire process takes six to ten hours.

To the Indians rocks are sacred. In fact, everything in God's creation is relative to each other, so to speak. The Creator created many, many things before he created man, therefore, these other things are his created children, too. I spoke on this subject recently in a small church and a man came up to me afterwards and said, "I can believe what you said because I remember reading in the Bible in Luke 19:40, and also in Habakkuk 2:11, 'if we keep silent about our Creator even the stones will cry out.'"

Even the open air fire to heat the stones has meaning. Fire is the Creator's special gift to mankind. Think about it. Only human beings need fire. We need fire over which to prepare food. We need fire to keep ourselves warm. We need fire to forge our tools. We could go on and on of ways in which we need fire. Even for pleasure we need fire. Think of the flickering flames from a burning log to dream by. Nothing else in all of God's creation has need of fire.

Many people don't realize one can abuse a fire. When we're on location tending the fire to heat the stones, we are there several hours and so we often munch on goodies or read throw-away types of articles. Therefore, we have burnable trash, but we never place trash on the stone heating fire. We build a separate fire some distance away for the trash fire. All fires have a purpose. For example, there is a ceremonial fire and there is a war fire. There is a signal fire and the other fires I've already spoken of. We can see every fire has a reason for being. Not us for the fires, but the fires for us. It is our responsibility and our duty to keep these fire functions separate and never take advantage of any fire for the wrong purpose.

I need to point out that there is a ring of separate stones surrounding the open fire bed with an opening which represents an exit from the fire to enter the sweat lodge. That ring of stones represents the war bonnet because the fire is the chief. We carry the red-hot fire stones into the lodge and place them in a prepared center pit and pour water over them. The water on the hot stones creates steam, which represents the breath of life.

There is sometimes confusion on the part of some of our guests on Homecoming Day. One or another guest will peep inside an empty lodge and observe the charred pit. They will assume a fire has burned inside the lodge and wonder what kept the lodge from catching on fire. This illusion is just that—an illusion. It is caused when the hot stones from outside are brought inside with the outdoor fire's ashes still clinging to them. Then, when the water is poured over the hot stones; the heat, the clinging ashes, and the steaming water create the charred appearance in the earthen pit.

The first time one enters a sweat lodge, it can be a frightening experience. The quarters are very close for six or seven adults. It's very dark inside and it's so hot, so steamy, and so smoky—one feels one can't breathe. We begin to sweat like rivers of water and the sweat is absorbed into the earth, making us one with the earth. We pray to God as we share with Him and with one another the perplexities and frustrations of our everyday lives. It seems as though the sweat is draining all we don't want from our minds and bodies, and cleansing takes place. As we share in prayer we begin to realize that none of us have to carry life's load alone, we can be there for each other. We gain insight into our inner beings. We come out of the sweat lodge after four hours feeling closer to God and to one another in a way that no other experience can afford us.

A Note from the Interviewer

That lovely September afternoon as we sat in George's workshop, while he shared from his life's experiences, he had kept very busy creating necklaces. The last one he made by first sizing a soft leather strip. Then he threaded onto it a white tooth, which was a black bear's tooth. On either side of the tooth George placed four golden-colored beads. Then he placed the necklace in my hands. He said, "The first four beads, two on each side, represent the four directions. The last four beads represent the four seasons. The black bear's tooth represents Bear Mountain, Matohe. This is my gift to you and it is blessed of God to keep you safe on all your journeys."

This interviewer shall treasure this special necklace always.

4
Danny Gear

I am Danny Pultz Gear. My great-grandparents were John and Sarah Clark Pultz. My grandparents were Rufus Coolidge Pultz and Beverly Shifflett Pultz. My parents were Rufus Coolidge Pultz Jr. and Elizabeth Wilhelm Pultz. My mother, Elizabeth, was a Mississippi Choctaw. I knew there was Indian blood on my dad's side, too, but I didn't know which nation.

My parents had moved to Maryland from Irish Creek in Rockbridge County, Virginia, when I was still a young lad. I knew George Branham in Maryland, and after he moved to Amherst he began urging me to visit him and meet with the Monacans. George said, "I have learned my people need help. Please come and help."

While I was visiting George, I learned I was also related to the Monacans on the Pultz side. I've been in Amherst several years now. My wife, K. Lynn, and I are buying a house and we're expecting a son to be born any day now.

I didn't become involved in research or leadership roles until some of the leaders invited me to do so. I now sit on council and I'm one of the drummers. I am spending every moment I can spare on research. Research is very difficult. Our language is Tutelo. It's Siouan based. This language doesn't mean we are Lakotahs or Dakotahs. We aren't a branch of the Sioux out west. Siouan based is like putting a group of Latin-speaking people in a room together. Just because their language is Latin based doesn't mean the South Americans, Mexicans, Spaniards, and the Italians are going to understand each other's language, because they aren't. Siouan based just means that some of our words are very similar. For the most part, words are not of particular Indian nations, but instead are regional to each tribe according to locations. I'll give an example: two words may have the same spelling, yet contain a different meaning from one another, depending upon the stressed syllable—for instance, TAH-pah means ball; tah-PAH means buffalo head.

There are actually very few Indians of any nation who can speak their complete tongues anymore. Many years ago the United States Government forbade the Dakotahs to speak their particular tongue. Is it any wonder dialects are all but dead?

The Monacan Indians are part of a group of Indians that make up a Confederacy of five consisting of the Mowhencho, Massinack, Rossawek, Monasukapanough, and Monahassanugh. These five groups spoke Tutelo; therefore, the United States Government, using the European method of configuration, lumped these five nations together forming one Confederacy. When I first began researching Monacans, I was able to find very little information, but when I recalled how the Europeans grouped Indian nations together according to their dialects, I began looking under Tutelo and boom! I found ceremonial histories, all kinds of useful information. I have received from Kansas (which is a Siouan name) and Philadelphia museums some copies of recordings recorded onto beeswax saucers on which our ancestors were singing in Tutelo. Curators from these two museums were kind enough to make cassettes of these recordings for me. I mention these few examples to help you understand that Monacans didn't exist according to European history, but Tutelos did exist.

When I first came to Amherst County there were some residents who told me, "These people around here who claim to be Indian don't know the first thing about being Indian. Most of these so-called Indians have never been out of this county, much less this state."

Once upon a time we occupied land in West Virginia and into both North and South Carolina.

Not just Monacan Indians, but many, many Indians inhabited American land before Europeans even knew this land existed. God chose Indians to be the caretakers of this land he created. The reason he chose us to be his janitorial caretakers is because Indians have always had a sense of kinship, an understanding of the relationship between earth and mankind. We feel this kinship far more deeply than do Europeans and we don't take advantage of the land in a destructive way as they soon began to do after their arrival.

When the Pilgrims first arrived in what, to them, was this New World, we shared our food with them. We taught them which wild-growing plants were safe to eat and which were not safe. As I said earlier, Indians have a sense of kinship with the earth and all God's creatures. We instinctively have always known to observe the wild animals and which plants they eat. This is something Europeans didn't know as they believed wild animals were dumb beasts of the field and forest. Animals are born knowing which plants are safe for food and which are not. They know which plants are poisonous. We know that whichever plants are safe for animals are also safe for mankind.

We also taught the Pilgrims how to plant crops suitable to our climate and earth. As I explain to the students when I am invited to speak at various schools, I tell them the Pilgrims would have soon starved to death after landing at Pilgrim Rock had we not been there to help them. We were the first to reach out to meet their needs by providing for them with food lines, the first soup kitchens and the first super bars and we didn't charge a dime for those Thanksgiving feasts.

In the late nineteenth century, people are becoming better educated as a whole and learning more about what kind of people Indians actually were in the sixteenth century. There are still a minority, though, who have some misunderstanding about Indians. At the powwows, there are still a few people who will approach us and with an all-knowing grin upon their faces say, "How."

I'm always tempted to ask, "What do you mean when you greet me with, 'How'? If you think How is my given name, then you've greeted several of us by the same name. If you're asking how in general, you need to be more specific."

Concerning our regalia, people will come up to us and say, "You didn't make these garments by hand. This attire was sewn on a sewing machine. Real Indians didn't use sewing machines."

I'm standing there and thinking, the first machine was marketed in 1851 and had Indians been able to afford those marvels of industry, we would have thanked our Creator for that great invention by a gifted inventor and gladly have sewn our regalia on those marvelous stitching machines.

Sometimes, we'll hear one lady whispering to another lady, "I've always been scared of Indians. They have to be kind of wild people or they wouldn't wear that scary paint on their faces, and feathers on their heads and those strange clothes."

I feel like whispering back, "Hey, Lady, dressing up has always been for ceremonial purposes for our people. White people do it, too, for different reasons, so, you see, it doesn't have anything to do with whether one is Indian or not. Have you never dressed up for Halloween? How about New Year's parties? How about if you act out a part in a community play or in the movies or other types of drama?"

I realize there are still some people who think we're out of Hollywood, like in *Dances with Wolves*. Once upon a time we did use bows and arrows to hunt with. Only white people were allowed to use guns.

I've been called "issue" a few times since I moved to Amherst County. The reason these things still take place is very simple and age old. Let me give you an example. A mother is teaching her daughter to cook. The mother prepares a ham and brushes it with a glaze for baking. Then the mother cuts the ham into two halves and places one half in an iron pot and the other half in a separate iron pot. Then she places both iron pots in a large oven. The daughter watches her mother in order to learn from her, but she is now perplexed. She asks, "Mama, why did you divide the ham? Why didn't you put the entire ham in the large roasting pan?"

The mother answers, "I don't know, daughter. You'll have to ask your grandmother. She taught me to do it this way."

The girl walks into an adjoining room where her grandmother is seated at her quilting frame. She asks her grandmother about the ham and the two pots. The grandmother answers, "The reason is simple enough. I never owned a large roasting pan and none of my iron pots were big enough to hold a whole ham. Besides, my mother baked ham that way, too."

This little story, handed down through a lot of generations, illustrates how customs are handed down and most people never question the reason behind a particular custom. This daughter did question, not out of humorous curiosity, but seeking knowledge and wisdom and understanding of the reasons why, which, of course, was the intent of this old wives' tale.

Some of our customs are different from the white man's customs. Let's talk about one custom in particular. The Monacan Indian ladies in this area down through the ages have made baskets from split oak, honeysuckle vines, and pine straw. [Basket weaving is fast becoming a lost art among the Monacans.] The ladies make these baskets for functional purposes. Large ones are to hold dirty laundry, others of a different shape or size are meant for mending/sewing supplies or fruit. Still others are to hold floral arrangements. One can see these baskets are created to be used.

I've noticed when white ladies purchase these baskets from the Indians, they tend to place them out of harm's way and show them off to their guests as conversational pieces and beam with pleasure as their guests exclaim, "Aren't they beautiful?"

The baskets are becoming more expensive as conversational pieces tend to do. They also become useless vessels.

Another custom is noteworthy and now becoming more a custom of the past. The Monacans are a real community of people, ready and willing to help each other. Until recent years, if the man of a household died, he was in many ways replaced. There was a ceremony that made the pact official. It was called a redressing ceremony.

The Indians never had a widow in their midst to struggle along all alone. There was never such a person as an orphaned child being ignored. Whenever the husband/father died, a brother or a sister would move into his home and assist the bereaved family until the family had time to learn to cope and found ways to provide. Until recent years families were so large there was never a problem of not having an unmarried brother or sister that could move in and be a source

4. Split-oak basket, handmade by Bertie Duff Branham's mother, the late Dessie Johns Duff. The basket is aged and not really kept outside.

of help and comfort. Without fail some man in the tribe would assume the responsibility of becoming the father figure to the orphaned children as long as the widow remained a widow. This duty of a man accepting the role of a male authority was recognized as a need in helping raise those children and giving the family proper balance.

Here it is the year of 1997 and prejudice can still raise its ugly head. At this time we have a civil rights case pending in court against the school board in Amherst County for discrimination against Indians and blacks. The principal of a particular school has resigned since the suit was filed and a personnel director's contract was not renewed.

We have Monacans in this area born with blond hair and blue eyes and some born with red hair. Sure, there are mixed marriages just as it is with any nation of people. There are still a few people in this area, mostly among older, "set-in-their-ways" people, who will look at a blond with blue eyes and if that child's name is associated with the old hit/hate list of Dr. W. A. Plecker, then the child is to them mixed, colored, or "issue," the last being used with the misunderstood meaning.

There is the matter of alcohol being known as fire water for Indians. This is true, but does the white man understand why it is so? Before the Europeans came, the Indians made a wine with wild grapes and dandelions. These were very mild wines made only twice a year: in the springtime the dandelion wine and in the autumn the wild grape wine. Therefore, we were not acquainted with the strong stuff until nearly four hundred years ago when the invading Europeans introduced us to strong alcohol. The Europeans and Oriental peoples had been inundated to strong alcohol entering their bodily systems for thousands of years and so it wasn't a great shock to their systems for the most part. Whereas medical scientists assert that our people are not genetically geared to alcohol because our digestive systems have not been so attuned over thousands of years and our systems do not adjust.

I've had my share of problems with both alcohol and drugs. I'm very glad to say somehow, someway, some common sense was finally knocked into my stubborn head and I've been my own man, totally free of both alcohol and drugs for the past eight years. I was twenty-three when I stopped messing with that stuff and I'm thirty-one now and I intend to stay on this far better road of life.

I don't intend for what I'm about to share with you to be an excuse for my troubles as a young man. I could have made better decisions. My family life was terrible as a child. I could tell you horror stories about drugs, alcoholism, prostitution, beatings, and divorce; about being left alone over and over again, scared and hungry. At the age of nine years old, I ran away from home. I ran to a schoolteacher who had been very kind to me. She and her husband took me into their home and their hearts. They went through the proper channels and adopted me. My parents didn't care. They were only too glad to be rid of me.

Let me share with you a story about choices from an illustration told to me many times. The story tells of two canoes. The canoes are traveling down the river side by side. One canoe is built to ride out rough waters along its passageway. The other canoe is built for beauty. Can you choose which canoe you want to ride in if you have had no experience with canoes? Still and all one must make a choice. Everyone must decide which canoe is the best one in which to travel the river called life. Some people have told me the sturdy canoe represents Jesus Christ.

Let's talk about belief in God. I have so many questions. I can believe in God as Creator, but I can't really believe in Jesus except as a wise prophet. Let me share with you my reasoning and the reasoning of some others I've discussed religion with. To begin with, I believe we've been on earth fifteen thousand years and Jesus Christ was on this earth two thousand years ago. How could mankind have believed in him thirteen thousand years before he appeared on earth? Some people say we can believe by reading and studying the Bible. Some people have told me God walked with Adam in the Garden of Eden and promised Adam the Savior would appear on earth in due time and from that time on man did believe in a Son of God as the Savior. But that brings another question to my mind. The Europeans didn't arrive in America until 1621, bringing their form of religion. The Indians were already here, and since belief in Christianity arrived in America with the Europeans, therefore, it didn't exist past four hundred years ago in America. Then there are those who say the Indians believed in the Great White Father as the one and only Creator. What the Europeans didn't understand is the Great White Father is the Indian's name for God.

We know God is the Creator. This universe is far too complex to exist through or by happenstance. The Indians have always known this because long ago they lived almost as one with the earth. They knew everything on this earth—the rocks, the trees, the waters—are all equal to mankind who was created after all these necessities and after all the animals of every species, also.

Now we arrive at the important point of God as the all-wise Creator. If the trees vanished tomorrow, we would all very soon die. Why? The trees provide much of our oxygen. Of course, there are other sources of oxygen, but the trees also provide mankind's shelter from the elements. The rocks provide minerals much needed by mankind, especially by those oils impregnating our water supplies. If the waters disappeared today from all the earth, in seven days, we would die. In fact, the whole world would die without water. If all the animals would disappear, mankind would die. Mankind is dependent upon animals not alone for food (meat is expendable), but for clothing, medical discoveries, and on and on. Mankind could not survive without animals, trees, rocks, and water. But, hey, listen up! If mankind disappeared today this world would flourish! Yes, the world would be a much better place without mankind.

To get back to the subject of man's religion, the history books tell us the Europeans left England to escape religious persecution. They were not allowed to worship as they pleased in their own country, so they came in search of a land where they could be free to make their own choices.

Now let me share with you what the Europeans proceeded to do in this, their new land. They very soon proceeded to insist that the Indians practice the European's religion as the only way to worship.

The things our people experienced from and by the white man is hard stuff for me to talk about. In fact, it's very painful for all three races who are born American and live in this country today to go back in time. But we must in order to benefit from the valuable lessons of our past. First of all, when the Europeans came to America, they soon began to kill off Indians by many methods. Some of those ways were not deliberately chosen by them. Nevertheless, they brought to this land many diseases foreign to Indians. History tells us that three million Indians died of foreign diseases in the first one hundred years. The Europeans came in the name of Christianity and it was genocide for us.

Let me share with you about the Carlisle Indian Mission School in Pennsylvania. In the name of Christianity the Europeans took, by force, Indian children from their families under the cover of darkness. They took them from all over this country, sanctioned by the United States Government. This school's stated purpose was to teach Indian children about Christianity, about God, so these children wouldn't grow up to be savages. One of the first things members of the faculty did to those children was to cut off their braids. In those days, Indians held their braids to be their badge of honor. To cut an Indian's braids was to shame him.

One can visit the site of the Carlisle Indian Mission School to this day and view the tombstones void of names of kids who didn't survive the trip there and of others of lost identity who died there.

Please don't get me wrong. I don't think Christianity is bad, but I do think some people are bad in the name of Christianity. When I read about true Christianity, it's beautiful the way it's supposed to be practiced, but some so-called Christians seem to have missed the beautiful meaning.

As I said earlier, the Europeans were determined that Indians must worship their way. That has continued to be the pattern through the past four hundred years until this present time. Take, for instance, the St. Paul Episcopalian Mission Church right here on Kenmore Road in Amherst County, Virginia. This church means so very much to the Monacans. The Episcopalians came here to help these helpless people and help they did in many wonderful ways. As to forms of worship, though, notice what has been done. The diocese provided a church building, a bishop, and a priest, and it was the diocese's funds in the beginning that kept the church going. But the order of worship has always been the Episcopalian way. To clarify my point, have the Episcopalians ever allowed us to have a sweat lodge on church grounds? No. Have they ever allowed us to bring our drums inside the church? No. Now do you see what I mean? The white man doesn't really want

Indians to be white men, but they do want Indians to act like white men, even in the customs by which men worship God.

One of the things about religion I question personally is this, why do most Christians say they don't believe in artificial insemination of the seed of man into woman? They say they don't believe God intended it to be so. All I want to say on that subject is I'm so glad God did not condemn artificial insemination when the Virgin Mary was inseminated by the Holy Ghost of God, and Jesus the Prophet was thus conceived.

I still cannot believe in Jesus as the Son of God who has been since before time began or that, together, they created this world and everything in it in six days. I believe Jesus was a prophet. However, I'll continue to read and listen. Surely if Jesus is the Savior, He will nudge me in the sweat lodge of my heart. Then—I shall see and know.

I'll speak of the violence, the raiding, the killing that Indians are known for in the long ago. We have to tell the whole story. There are two sides proven in recorded history. Yes, Indians of long ago did all those things. In those days, they had to. The Europeans came here and taught us evil ways we had not known. They taught us by their example to raid and rape and scalp. Anyone who has studied American history will know I speak truth. We had to embrace the evil ways of the Europeans in order to survive.

When the United States Government started forcing our people to go west, the government hit men gave out blankets and told the Indians they wanted them to be warm on the trails west. In reality those blankets had been gathered from the beds of white people, people who died from smallpox. Those blankets were infested with the killer germs. That was the first form of chemical warfare used by the United States Government. Indians died of smallpox by the thousands along the trails.

The Indians were a peaceful people before all the horrors began. They had a high regard for life, not just mankind's life, but all forms of life.

Prior to the Europeans' arrival, whenever an animal's life was taken, that animal's life was prayed over. The Indian hunter would sit down, offer tobacco, and pray to the Creator, "Thank you for this animal's life, sacrificed to feed and clothe my family."

Even when trees were cut down to build shelters, they gave thanks for the life of that tree. Whenever possible, dead, fallen wood was used for fire building in order not to sacrifice a living tree.

The Europeans came and started killing animals for sport. The buffalo herds were soon dissipated and the white-tailed deer became almost extinct. This waste of life broke the hearts of Indians.

The words some white people use when referring to an Indian woman are often insulting. I realize that white people using the derogatory terms are possibly not aware in this new millennium of what the actual meaning of some words are. For instance, I don't want anyone calling my wife, K. Lynn, by the word squaw. The least offensive way I know to tell you what the word squaw means is to tell you the word in French slang meant vagina. Long ago when the French traders came down out of the mountains for a night on the town and when they were well on their way to being drunk, they would begin to call out, "I want to buy a squaw for the night." In other words meaning, "I want to buy a vagina for the night."

The word squaw is an Algonquian term which originally meant wife, but then the French traders took away respect of the word by using it insultingly as a bought woman for a roll in the hay.

Also in Tutelo language the word for wife was never "squaw." In Tutelo the word is Mihani, meaning she is married to him. Mihani is pronounced almost like saying, me honey. The "n" is the short sound. Phonetically it is pronounced ME-hawn-A.

I realize Indian dialect sounds perhaps like a foreign language. For instance, the road not far from our mission center on Kenmore Road bears a Lakotah name, Matohe (ma-toe-EE), and it means bear. In Tutelo it's Munti. Again the "n" is a nasal sound, Mu-ahn-TI, meaning bear. To say Bear Mountain, you would say, Munti shukME hawn TIE. The word shuk is pronounced sug and sug meaning a mountain, whereas sug sug means more than one mountain. Asel (ah sell) means, many mountains. Indian dialects are difficult to understand in this day and time.

There are particular numbers that have meaning to the Monacans. Consider the number four. Four is a significant number because there are four cycles in life consisting of infancy, youth, adulthood, and old age. There are four seasons consisting of spring, summer, autumn, and winter. There are four fundamental directions consisting of north, south, east, and west. Also, there are four quarters of the moon: new moon, quarter moon, half moon, and full moon. To illustrate further, there are twenty-eight rocks used in a sweat lodge. They consist of seven sets of four. There are many more, but these examples are enough to point out why number four is an important number.

The number seven is very special. There is God, the Creator, who created the earth, sky, sun, moon, vegetation, and living beings. He did all this in six days and rested on the seventh day. Seven is very special.

The number two is special because it gives a sense of balance. There are mother and father, brother and sister, husband and wife; there is you and me. The number two seems endless, but it affords balance to so many things.

Now, consider the number three. Three means communication with God.

Right now you and I are sitting here discussing many things, and we might assume there are two of us; but that's not the literal truth. The Creator is always present. He listens and he is involved with us, so actually, there are three of us present. When one of us performs a spiritual ceremony, that one holds the pipe in his hand. The tobacco-filled pipe sends up the uttered prayers on the rising smoke. Therefore, there is one of us being the bearer of a plea or pleas, and there is the Creator receiving the plea and these three form a triangle in a ceremonial communication.

The numbers we've discussed are considered to be perfect numbers. Now, let us consider the imperfect numbers. In my humble opinion, to deal with imperfect numbers is sometimes beneficial. It helps remind us we are imperfect human beings, never perfect. If you have two outside doors and both are shut tight, set one door ajar. When I am making jewelry, I sometimes add an extra bead on the string to throw it off balance a tad.

It's also good to allow the spirits we sense around us to work for us. They appreciate the opportunity to help us out. At the evening meal, don't completely empty your plate of food, leave an offering for the spirits. My spirits that I offer food have four legs and wagging tails and they look an awful lot like dogs. Now this isn't as far-fetched as it may seem. As I feed my dogs their special treat, it reminds me of God's word in Ecclesiastes 9:4, "For to him that is joined to all living there is hope: for a living dog is better than a dead lion" [King James Version].

Drums are very important to Indians of all nations. The drums are made from animals' skins or hides. Those two words are used interchangeably. Skin is the protective covering for human beings, but I'm sure you're familiar with the slang term sometimes used by a parent to a child to warn of an imminent spanking by saying, "I'll tan your hide."

The small animals' coverings are called skins. The large animals' coverings are called hides or pelts. Skins, hides, or pelts mean the covering from which rooted hair grows.

The head of a drum is made from rawhide. Instead of curing the hide and therefore making it soft and pliable as one would do if the hide was to be made into clothing, the treatment is different. For the purpose of making a drum one strips the hide from the animal and immediately submerges it in water. The hide is left soaking until it swells and its pores release the hair. This is similar to pouring hot water on a dead chicken, so that the chicken's feathers can be plucked out in gobs. A hide takes a lot more soaking, though, but once the skin/hide is free of hair, it's ready to stretch over the drum's frame and tie down securely. When the skin/hide dries out thoroughly, you've got your drum. A long time ago, the Indians would have tanned the hide by using the brains of the slain animal. The brains have known chemicals so that when the brains are smashed and smeared onto the hide, the brain chemicals are absorbed into the hide and the hide becomes brain tanned and enriched. All forms of life are by the Creator and therefore are to be treated with respect; and so if at all possible, all parts of a slain animal were put to use so as not to have wasted any part of that life. When the drums are uncovered and brought out to be played upon, we offer up a sheaf of tobacco. We join hands and pray, asking God's blessings upon the drums and the drummers. The music is the heartbeat of the drum.

Once upon a time Indians had no blankets. That was before the government claimed to help us out with their offering of blankets. The Indians' bedding as well as their covering and clothing were made of animals' hides.

The practice of a sheaf of tobacco as an offering to God is very often misunderstood by the white man. Tobacco is a sacred plant to Indians. It is used as a sign of honor and respect. Long ago the Indian leaders would gather in council meetings and smoke a shared pipe and pray. It was believed the prayers wafted up to God borne on the smoke. Smoke always goes up and we always think of praying to God who is up above the blue sky.

John Son Eagle and Sharon are members of the Mattaponi Tribe. They sort of adopted me and have helped me greatly in my research efforts. John has taught me a lot, especially about the meaning and purpose of the sweat lodges.

Originally, the framework for a sweat lodge was red willow trees or wild cherry trees. The framework is like the ribs of a person, like your mother's ribs shielding you when you were yet unborn. The wood stripping, the ribs of the sweat lodge, was covered with the skins of animals (again, like your mother's ribs are covered with skin). But times change. Nowadays it would be wasteful, unnecessary, and cruel to kill animals for their hides and brains to build a sweat lodge. There are plenty of other materials easily available such as blankets, quilts, or tarps in this day and time.

The framework of the sweat lodge rises from the ground and at the top the protruding sticks form a star shape. The smoke from the heated rocks rises and spirals out at the star, again wafting our prayers up to God, the Creator.

The sweat lodge is the oldest church known in this new world of America. Remnants of sweats have been found by archaeologists. Our sweats are built in a dome shape. They represent a woman's womb. A woman's womb is the most sacred place anyone has ever lived in. Any of us, when in our mothers' wombs, knew nothing of bad, evil, or meanness of any kind. A woman's womb represents the Mother Earth. When we enter the sweat lodge and the door is closed, it is as though we return to the womb. There we can pray for God's healing—physically, mentally, and spiritually. When we enter into our sweat lodge church we don't get all dressed up in suits and ties and name-brand shoes. In fact, once upon a time, our ancestors stripped down to what God gave us to be born in and the women worshiped in a lodge separate from the men. Nowadays the men wear shorts, and the women wear shorts and tops, and we can worship together. Some people still voice objection to men and women being in the same sweat lodge with what they consider scant clothing. Listen, it's very dark inside the sweat. A man sure can't stare at a woman or vice versa. It's also very hot and uncomfortable, and besides, we're busy praying. It is not a conducive atmosphere for a man or a woman to entertain sexual thoughts. There are six or seven hot, sweating, repenting souls jammed together into a smoky, steamy, smoke-filled tent. Are they thinking sex? No way!

Remember the sweat lodge is likened unto going back into your mother's womb. If God can put twins, triplets, quads, quints, or sextuplets into one womb for nine months, I know six or seven adults can handle four hours of togetherness in a sweat lodge. To use a pun, "It's no sweat!"

Sweats are always entered into for cleansing. Long ago, women during their menstrual period weren't allowed to take part in sweats. The menstrual period was called their "moon time." This wasn't because they were considered bad or unclean, since that's what the sweats are all about anyway. No. It was because during the menstrual cycle women were believed to be powerful beings. During this "moon time" the woman's body is in the process of ridding itself of what was the egg of a possible life. Now, that possible life, which was not impregnated to make it so, is leaving her womb, ebbing away through the flow of blood. Traditionally, women withdrew and stayed alone during this "moon time" of revolution.

Another important thing to know is, we must get down on our knees to enter a sweat lodge. We are entering a sacred place and we need to bow low. The rocks, heated to red hot outside the lodge, are brought in and water is poured over them in the centered pit causing steam to rise and there is the sound of bubbling water such as a babe hears in his mother's womb. The extreme heat has a purpose. When we enter the lodge, we are unclean. We take so many chemicals into our systems through food and drink. We also take in chemicals through the very air we breathe, which has become so polluted over time. And we also take into the lodge the influences the world has had upon us. When our bodies become so hot from the heat of those steamy rocks, then the sweat begins to pour off our bodies and it's salty tasting on our lips and it stings our eyes. Then we realize how polluted our bodies have become and with that realization one becomes aware of how polluted one's heart and mind have become, also. As we sweat the chemicals and toxins from our physical systems and pray, we sweat out and cleanse our inner selves.

This is different from becoming a born-again Christian, Baptist, Catholic, Episcopalian, or whatever you plant your hopes on. This is cleansing that enables one to turn oneself around from all the undesirable things one has allowed to enter one's life. This is renewal.

While inside the sweat lodge everyone is honor bound. You can talk out everything to the Creator. Your companions will pray with you and for you to the Creator and the buck stops there. Not a single word that was uttered will leave that lodge.

When you emerge from the sweat lodge (which is like unto the mother's womb), you come out head first, just as you were born as a babe.

Now, we come to the subject of being called anything but Indian. The state of Virginia didn't have a listing for Indian under race, since Indians weren't recognized as a race of people there. Their way of solving the problem was unorthodox to say the least. The government decided to list Indians as those of "color." It didn't mean colored as in Negro. It meant not black, but of "color." Then, since that proved very confusing, they came up with terminology such as Free Color. Free Color meant Indians were never slaves as Negroes were at that time. Our government wasn't set up until the Declaration of Independence was drawn up by Congressman Thomas Jefferson and adopted July 04, 1776. Those Indians who had been there in recorded history for over a hundred years prior to the signing—no provision was made to document them as Indians in their own right. Not one of those thousands and thousands of people were listed as Indians. That vague term of "color" became their fate.

The two reservations Mattaponi and Pamunkey in King William County, Virginia, are the two oldest reservations in the United States. It is the only land in the United States that has never been bought or sold since 1658.

Dr. W. A. Plecker was put into office in 1912 as the first registrar of the state Bureau of Vital Statistics in Virginia. That's when things got really messy. To Plecker's bigoted, judgmental mind, Indians did not exist under any heading as a separate race. There were only two races recognized by Plecker, white and Negro. Dr. Plecker, in his own venom, outdid himself. He inadvertently left us Monacan Indians a legacy of exactly who we are. In his passion to make us Negro or mixed, he spent much of his time in Amherst and Rockbridge Counties. In these counties he meticulously wrote down every surname of every family declaring themselves to be Indian and he recorded them as Issue, Mixed, or Negro. Old Plecker did our research for us. When the state of Virginia finally recognized us officially as Monacan Indians of Virginia in 1989, the Virginia Legislature used Dr. Plecker's records of family surnames. The state of Virginia has now agreed to correct our (messed-up-by-Plecker) birth certificates and to reinstate us as Indian. We are the eighth tribe in Virginia to be so recognized.

Dr. Plecker was killed when struck by a truck in 1947.

I know the Creator has a sense of justice and I've always liked to believe he has a sense of humor, too. I like to imagine that in the case of Dr. Plecker the Creator said to himself, "This man, Plecker, is busy making a fool of himself by writing down these Indians' surnames. I'll allow him full rein as he gloats and records every surname of these people he so hates. When his work is done and all these people finally get down to business to reclaim their heritage, they will have Plecker's documented records to tie themselves back to. The fool, Plecker, will be their blessing in disguise and he will be dead to boot!"

We have earned and been granted our Virginia state recognition and we are now working on our federal government recognition and one of their requirements is, "You have to prove your family line."

We can take Plecker's hate/hit list which he meant to be a killer list and in spite of his dark intentions, we can say, "Here is our legal proof of who we actually are. We are Monacan Indian."

May Dr. Walter A. Plecker's black soul rest.

5
Lucian Branham

The Patriarch in 1997

My name is Lucian Branham. I was born May 24, 1910. I'm eighty-seven years old now in 1997. My grandparents were George (Buggy) Branham and Mildred (Mallie) Roberts Branham. My parents were Walter Branham and Delia Terry Branham. My mother grew up on the Blue Ridge near Buena Vista, Virginia. Oh, Alta Terry was my other grandmother on my mother's side.

A lot of my people left Amherst County, Virginia, when I was a small child. They moved away to other states, to Maryland, New Jersey, Tennessee, and Pennsylvania. They wanted my parents to move, too, since we children weren't allowed to attend the public schools in Amherst County, because we were not white and refused to be black and so were not welcome in either group. We are Indian. The Episcopalian school which the diocese had mercifully set up for us was down on Kenmore Road at the foot of Bear Mountain. I had to walk fifteen miles to the St. Pauls Mission School. That meant thirty miles per day. That's a long way for a seven-year-old boy to walk five days a week.

I was only allowed to attend school four days. On the fifth morning, my dad said to me, "Son, this ain't going to work. Thirty miles is too much. School is over for you."

I've always had a good mind and a good memory. I feel like my mind was wasted by not having a chance to obtain an education. Why, children of today know more at age four than I knew at age fourteen. There is still cause for concern, though. Although there is every opportunity for a comprehensive education these days, children's minds aren't always put to good use and at what cost. Many children are spending far too much time watching the wrong kind of programs on television. It nearly kills me that parents don't take time anymore to teach their children by having conversations with them. Parents have no right to fault their child for any kind of trouble they get involved in. Children are home alone with no interaction except with what they see and hear on television. All children know about life these days is what they see enacted on the tube.

My daddy didn't have any schooling, as folks used to call it. He worked for ten cents per hour at High Peak Orchards. We lived in an old log house with two rooms downstairs and two rooms upstairs. There were eight of us children and our parents. After they lost three children in death, that still left seven people in that little house. The windows had glass, but the glass had been set permanently in the wooden frames according to the owner's wishes and therefore, couldn't be opened or closed. In the hot summertime we usually slept outdoors on quilts placed on the grass. People could sleep outdoors in those days without fear.

We children did the best we could to help our daddy. We worked most days in the tobacco fields, the corn fields, and the orchards. When we worked, we, too, were paid ten cents per hour. With no education, we had no choice of jobs paying a living wage. We were as poor as church mice, but we didn't go hungry. We raised our vegetables and there was an abundance of wild-growing edible plants. When we killed hogs in the autumn, we had smoked hams in the smokehouse, fatback meat, and sausage. We had our own milk cows. There was a springhouse to keep the milk and butter cold and whatever else that needed to be kept cold.

Our medical needs were taken care of by our own people. There were three white doctors in the area, one in Pleasant Hill, one in Monroe, and one in Amherst. Hardly anyone had cars in those days, so getting to those doctors was almost impossible. Two of the Indian women were midwives. We usually called them midwomen. After all, that term makes more sense than midwives, huh? Not all women are wives, but any woman can learn to practice medicine if she so desires. These two women didn't go to medical school to learn their trade like the doctors had done, but they were just as trustworthy. Whenever one of those doctors did come to minister to one of us, they always called one of the midwives to act as nurse and to carry on treatment during the days to follow until the person was back on their feet. Those two women would watch what the doctors did and make notes, and they could do it themselves the next time around. The women also knew a lot about herbs the doctors didn't know.

These two women wore big white aprons with two very large pockets. Whenever one of us became ill, one or the other or sometimes both of those women would come and check the patient; then they would go out into the woods and come back with those big pockets filled with different kinds of barks and roots.

Sometimes, we children tried to sneak along behind them and spy out what kinds of stuff they gathered. They always spied us and shooed us away by flapping those big aprons at us.

Then the big day came when I was ten years old. Those two midwomen said to me one day, "Lucian, gather the children who are ten years old or older and we will take all of you into the woods and show you what kinds of herbs we gather."

We learned they used the bark from wild cherry trees and mahogany trees. They also gathered ginseng roots that day. All of us pronounced ginseng as "ginsang." For many, many years ginseng grew in abundance all over these mountains. We gathered it to sell as well as for medicinal purposes. It brought a real good price.

When we arrived back at the house on that particular day, the midwomen skinned the bark and then washed it in water. They placed it in a large pot and covered it with water. They then boiled it over the heat on the wood-fired stove and made from it a hot tea. They washed the ginseng and put it in another pot filled with water and made yet a different tea. These teas had a bittersweet taste.

Sometimes, in spite of all any of the doctors or midwomen could do to heal illnesses, somebody died. When a person died, it took a couple of men one day to build a casket from poplar wood. While the casket was being built by the men, some of the women would come together to sew a cotton tick and fill it with feathers or straw. Then they would shroud the body in strips of cloth and the men would lay the body in the casket and place the filled tick on top of the body so the casket lid would not be right in his or her face. Two split-bottomed chairs were carried to an outbuilding, such as a shed or barn and the chairs would be positioned facing each other. Then the casket was placed on the supporting chairs, and the lid was put in place and nailed securely. You see, there wasn't any method to embalm a body, so it didn't take long for a strong odor to seep forth, especially in the summertime or in a heated building.

The relatives and friends would gather in the grieving family's home for the two days of the wake. They would sing hymns and say prayers. Everybody brought food already prepared so there would be no cooking during the two days and nights of the wake. Cooking would have been a sign of disrespect.

My dad owned two white horses that were called into service on the burial day. The casket was placed on the wagon and the two horses pulled the wagon up a steep mountain road to the cemetery. The preacher always rode horseback right behind the wagon/hearse. Anybody else that owned a horse rode their horses behind the preacher. Some families owned wagons with seats along each side and those wagons could seat eight people, so the elderly people rode in the wagons. The young people always walked.

My dad was proud of his two white horses and glad to use them to be of service. He didn't have much else as far as worldly goods go. The old tenant house we lived in was just before falling down. When my dad asked the owner about providing badly needed repairs, the owner replied, "No. We'll be glad when you people are gone from our property and hopefully from Amherst County. Maybe when this house finishes falling down about your ears you'll do just that."

What the owner really meant was that by this time most of my older siblings had grown up and left home. My dad was getting old and bent with arthritis. My mama was old and weak. The landowner had used up our family and so he was ready to cast off my aging parents like so much chaff.

The prejudice against Indians was hard for me to deal with, especially the name calling. The white kids taunted us by calling us names like Isshy, Nigger, Mixie, and anything else they could think of except by our proper names. I firmly believe everybody has a God-given right to be called by their Christian names and/or their surnames. I finally decided enough was more than enough and I started fighting whenever anyone called me a name I didn't like. I had no problem winning fights. I was very tall and I was very muscular from years of hard work as a tenant farmer's son. Now, as a young teenager whenever anyone called me a name I didn't like I would sail into him while shouting, "If I'm damned, then we'll both be damned!"

It really didn't take many fights until the word got around and the white kids became convinced. I then became known and addressed as Lucian or Lucian Branham.

You asked me about foods. As I've said before, we were poor, but we never were hungry. Sunday was special for meals. Following church service we feasted on chicken and dumplings, vegetables, and desserts. On Saturday, our main dish was potatoes. We didn't tire of potatoes because Mama was a good cook who knew how to cook potatoes many different ways. We ate corn bread three times a day. For breakfast we ate salty mackerel. That's fish soaked in salty brine in a wooden barrel. When breakfast is being prepared, the portion of fish needed for the meal is taken from the barrel and rinsed in clear water several times, then rolled in flour or cornmeal and fried in bacon drippings. We were also served one egg each for breakfast. We also sometimes had a slice of fatback, ham, or a cake of sausage. Now about those eggs, there wasn't any profit in marketing eggs. The store keepers would only pay Mama one penny for one dozen eggs. Of course, the store owners sold the eggs at retail for a few cents more, which was only fair. Our mama, being the practical lady that she was, figured since she could only profit one penny per dozen eggs, she could realize a better profit by feeding us one egg per day.

In my teens, some of my young friends began to pester me about moving to Buena Vista, Virginia, with them. I wasn't really interested in moving anywhere because the girl I had been dating for the past two years was right here in Amherst. I might have known my situation would soon begin to change, but my friends had already gone. My girlfriend's parents decided to move their family to

New Jersey. My girl began to plead with me, "Please, Lucian, please move with us. If you will move, too, then I won't mind at all living in New Jersey."

I said, "No, but I will ask your parents for your hand in marriage and then you can stay here."

The next day, I asked Ollie's mother, Callie Johns, for Ollie's hand in marriage. Her mother said, "No, Lucian, Ollie is too young for marriage."

The next day, I asked her dad, Charlie Johns, the same thing and he said, "Lucian, you'll have to ask her mother."

I went back down to Ollie's house on Saturday and received permission from her mother to take Ollie to Lynchburg with me just for the day. I promised to bring Ollie back by night. I took Ollie shopping in Lynchburg and I told the store clerk to fit Ollie with new clothes from the skin out and from the top of her head to her feet.

I brought Ollie back to her home that night and her mother took one look at the new clothes and began to cry and she said, "Ollie's not old enough to get married." Ollie was sixteen years old and I felt like she must feel like a woman. I was seventeen years old and I knew for sure I felt like a man.

Ollie's daddy decided to make up his own mind and he said to me, "Lucian, I'm willing for you to marry my daughter."

I said, "Sir, thank you, but I don't feel like she and I can live happily together with only one of her parents consenting. We'll wait until she is seventeen and I am eighteen. By then maybe her mother can give us her blessing."

The following Saturday they moved from Smoky Hollow, which is down near Sweet Briar. They moved to Baltimore, Maryland, with the idea of maybe moving on to New Jersey sometime in the future.

Ollie was looking back and crying as I waved goodbye and I was calling out, "I wish you all good luck and don't turn your heads and look back. Keep your vision steady ahead. My eyes will be looking steady and right here at Amherst County because here is where I'm going to stay."

Ollie kept on writing letters even though I'd told her to forget about me. The last letter I received from her she wrote, "Oh, dear Lucian, I'll steal away and find my way back to you."

I wrote back and said to her, "Ollie, don't even think about coming back. I know the trouble your mother would stir up. Besides, I've found me another girl. It's best you find you another man."

I really wasn't lonesome. There were girls on every corner flirting with me. Besides, work took up most of my time.

When I was twenty-five years old, I met a beautiful lady who was twenty-three years old. Her name was Cora Hamilton. She was the daughter of Mr. and

Mrs. Will Hamilton. They were Indian, also. We stepped out together for only a few weeks and then I asked Mrs. Hamilton for her daughter in marriage and her blessing. Mrs. Hamilton smiled at me and said, "Yes, my daughter is old enough to get married."

The following Saturday, Cora and I went to the Amherst Courthouse and got our license and were married. She and I were together for a wonderful fifty-six years until she died. She was the grandest lady I've ever known.

I was on the road a lot during our marriage. I drove trucks loaded with apples or peaches, driving the loads to Baltimore, to Washington, and to Pennsylvania. I would drive all night without taking any breaks, trying to get back home as soon as possible to make sure my family was all right.

There was an old woman living down the road a short distance from us. She began to flag me down whenever she would see me driving a loaded truck past her house. She would say, "Lucian, now don't you try killing yourself to get back home. I'll go up to your house tonight and I'll stay until you get back. Your family will be all right." A man could never ask for a better neighbor than that little old lady.

One of the questions you asked during this interview was, did I ever live in the log house that is still standing on the hill beside the packing shed at Morris Orchards.

No. I never did live there. Ned Branham was the first man to live in that house and there were several others after him. That log house is a hundred years old at least without a doubt.

You also asked about the music and songs we enjoyed in our youth. That sure was a long time ago. Now that I'm in my eighties, the words to songs don't stick in my memory very well. There was one song that was popular from generation to generation and it was a ballad with verses galore. I used to sing that song at every Saturday night dance for years and years and years. I'm trying to remember some of the verses, but at this moment only one verse comes to mind. It goes something like this

> Yonder stands little Maggie
> With her dram glass in her hand.
> She will drink down her troubles,
> Then she'll court another man.
> Poor little Maggie,
> She's laying down to sleep
> With her dram glass in her hand,
> She will try to count her sheep.

A Note from the Interviewer

After reciting the poetry, Lucian looked at me and smiled his broad smile. He said, "I think you and I will end our interview with that verse from Little Maggie. After all, what more can I say?"

Lucian Branham, at age eighty-nine, died, or as we Monacans say, walked, on Wednesday, August 04, 1999. Lucian's life counted with man and with God.

6
William E. Sandidge, Clerk of Court

I am William E. Sandidge. I was born in 1904 and I'm now ninety-three years old in this year of our Lord, 1997. I was clerk of court in Amherst County as were my father before me and his father before him. I am the namesake of both my father and grandfather.

The Indians have been in Amherst County for probably a thousand years. As far back as anyone can remember the tribe was located about 4 ½ miles southwest of Amherst. They traveled back and forth, to and from the north. They had footpaths that went from Baltimore into Florida. Members from other tribes from the north used to come through here. Those were usually hunting parties. The tribe residing here was situated on about ten square miles of land. Way back then they did some farming, but they fed their families mostly by hunting and fishing.

There was another trail that was traveled often in this area. It led from where the mission center is now down to the James River. There were no dams in the river back then and migratory fish would swim up the James. When the fish were running good there was a lot of fishing going on. The Indians smoked and dried the fish they caught. The county was full of wild turkeys, squirrels, and rabbits. Those afforded a good meat supply. There were wild plants, wild fruits, and nuts for a balanced diet. They also raised a lot of corn crops.

Between 1910 and 1915, some of the Indians moved from Amherst County to Baltimore, and to West Virginia. Others, wanting to stay closer to home, moved to Lynchburg, Virginia, in order to find work paying a living wage.

I knew Dr. W. A. Plecker personally. He was definitely a segregationist, no question about it. He was rabid on the subject of races and his idea of a perfect race. I didn't agree with him, but he had gotten laws passed giving him the authority to classify Indians as Negroes. I was clerk of court in Amherst County. I was told by him in no uncertain terms I must write mixed or colored on any and all forms concerning Indians. Most Indians from here went to Baltimore or

West Virginia to get married because any place other than here and Rockbridge County in Virginia would write down Indians as white, since none of Virginia recognized Indians as Indians.

Plecker's laws had barred Indians from the white schools here in Amherst where he had so much control via frequent visits to this courthouse. Praise God, the Episcopalian diocese came in and took over. They built a church and a two-room schoolhouse so that the tribe's children could be educated in the best way they could provide. In fact, one of my cousins, a very fine lady who lived about a mile out of Amherst, became a teacher at the Indian school. She taught school there about twenty-five years. She and a co-teacher were paid by the Amherst County School Board. I don't know about the legality of using county funds to pay teacher's wages to teach at a Christian School when the Indian students weren't allowed to attend the public schools. I just know it was done that way.

The census takers were also told they couldn't write Indian on census forms. They must write mixed or colored.

Dr. Plecker used to send us lists of names of people whom he said weren't pure white. When we had our yearly meeting of the clerks for the state of Virginia he would stand before us. I can still see him in my mind's eye standing before us and proclaiming, "If anyone of you disobey these laws having to do with so-called Indians I will see to it you are prosecuted to the fullest."

That man was mean and rough. There was a time when the Episcopalian minister and the bishop out of Roanoke came to see me. They wanted to know why I was refusing certain people proper marriage licenses and proper birth certificates. I explained to them it was because of Virginia state laws. "I have to obey the law," I told them. They replied, "Can't you disobey such laws when these laws are wrong?"

I told them if I disregarded those laws, then before the sun went down, Dr. Plecker would have me locked up in the Amherst County jail. Dr. Plecker has stood in my office and shook his finger in my face on quite a few occasions and said, "If I can ever catch you listing these mixed people as Indian or white, I'll personally see to it you are prosecuted by law and you will go to prison."

I knew according to the law, he could do it. I wish I had tried harder to fight him, but I was young, I had a family to support, and I didn't want to go to prison.

Dr. Plecker concentrated on Rockbridge County, Nelson County, and Amherst County, with the most emphasis on Amherst. Dr. Plecker estimated there were about fifteen hundred people here in the tribe which he refused to acknowledge as a tribe. There were also two other tribes which he picked on. One tribe was on the Mattaponi River and the other was on the Pamunkey River. Both of these tribes were in King William County.

The police here would tell me privately they had less trouble to contend with concerning the Indian tribe than they did with the other two races of white and black. The tribe really was a good people. Their life centered around the Episcopal church.

I circumvented Plecker's law whenever I could (even though I knew I was stealthily breaking the law) because I knew these people were Indian just as they claimed to be. They did believe in those days and I also believed they were Cherokee. They had been taught down through generations that this was so. Through more scientific research in later years they have definitely established a Monacan heritage and have been so recognized by the state of Virginia as Monacans.

As I said earlier in this interview, Dr. Plecker was rabid of mind and determined to banish this tribe of Indians into the African American race. He would drive up here from Richmond without advance notice and spend several days inspecting the files in my office. He would also stand outside the courthouse where men had a habit of gathering on the courthouse square to trade news with each other. He would keep glancing at the paper list in his hand of surnames of Indians he had put together. We called it his "hit list." He would command I stand beside him and he would point to first one and then another of the copper-skinned people and he would inform me, "This one to our left is a mixed breed. The three over there are mixed. That light-skinned man, he's white. The one with the red hair is white, too. See that really dark man, he's colored. That one over there looks white, but he's colored."

What Plecker didn't realize was that he had pointed to cousins and in some instances to brothers, fathers, and sons. Believe it or not, he had designated those people as three different races.

Sometimes I could get marriage licenses by him. Other times he would catch the records in Richmond. He would turn the documents over and write his untruths on the back of those papers. He would do the same with birth certificates. It was a sad time.

There was actually no problem in recognizing Indians from black people. The hair of the Indians was long and straight. The hair of the blacks was short and very curly. Also, the black people's skin was really black in those days from working in the fields. The wind and sun tended to blacken their naturally dark skin, whereas the Indians' skin was the color of copper and somehow stayed that way when exposed to sun and wind. Therefore, whenever one saw individuals from those two races standing near each other it was easy to tell the difference.

To my knowledge everybody in Amherst County now in the new millennium accept the Indians as equal. There was only one Dr. W. A. Plecker with his biased laws and the authority to enforce those cruel laws. Dr. Plecker will answer to a higher court, Lord, yes.

If it hadn't been for Dr. Plecker laying his blight of hate upon this region, this area would have been known as a good area in those days. People from Jamestown and Williamsburg settled this area. They migrated here because, in those days, one could find fertile land for raising tobacco crops and that was like finding a gold mine. This was tobacco land long before it graduated to apple and peach orchards. There is even a long range of mountains named Tobacco Row Mountains.

Besides the main crops the landowners raised, people raised or made everything they needed. Materials that couldn't be woven at home were purchased for clothing; also, sugar and salt. Even lighting they provided for themselves by making candles. Kerosene wasn't available here until in the neighborhood of the year 1850.

When the Southern Railway was built through this area, then kerosene was shipped in by rail and it came in wooden barrels. It was a rare barrel that didn't leak a little, so most of the merchants placed the barrels outside the stores. They had at first tried placing the barrels inside, but everything would end up smelling and tasting like kerosene. I remember one time when the barrels first started arriving and were placed inside, Mama bought a hunk of block cheese. As soon as we began biting into that cheese we knew the kerosene taste was bad indeed. The cheese didn't make us ill though. Foodstuff that had to be purchased was hard to come by and that's why we felt the need to eat the unappetizing cheese.

We were taught as kids not to be wasteful. I well remember when I was ten or twelve years old being well aware of the cost of some goods and of the wisdom of making do. Kerosene cost ten cents per gallon. The first gasoline was brought into our county about that time, too, and it sold for fifteen cents per gallon. Coffee was eight to ten cents per pound. The coffee beans had to be ground at home. Every household owned a hand-turned coffee grinder. One kind of coffee came in to the stores in the form of green coffee beans. It was a little cheaper than the brown coffee beans, because the brown beans meant those beans had been pre-roasted. The green beans had to be brought home and put in shallow pans and slow roasted in the oven of the wood-fired cook stoves. Oh boy, did those beans ever smell mouth-watering good as they roasted. The first pre-ground coffee to come on the market carried the brand name of Arbuckle Coffee and that was somewhere between 1910 and 1915. This preground coffee sold for fifteen cents per pound. My mama kept right on buying the beans and grinding it at home. She said coffee that was preground and packed in those little brown paper bags had lost all its flavor by the time it arrived in the stores and she wanted no part of weak coffee.

I am now ninety-three years old in this year of our Lord, 1997. I still drive my own car. I'm a member of a dance group based in Lynchburg and we're known as The Ageless Wonders. We formed our group about thirty-five years ago. Our group is made up of thirty-eight members. We have seven dance routines we

5. Hicks Country Store, in 2006, is one of the stores Monacan Indians walked to for supplies that couldn't be handmade, harvested, or gathered from the wild.

perform each show. We've toured nearly all over the world. When we tour in the states we have an old Trailways bus we travel on. Of course, when we tour in Hawaii or the Caribbean Islands, we don't travel by Trailways. [This was said with a still boyish laugh.] There are also two religious routines we perform in church fellowship halls and church sanctuaries. When we're on tour we put on three shows per day. We do a morning, afternoon, and a night performance and each show lasts two hours. Is it any wonder we call ourselves The Ageless Wonders?

I am no longer a clerk of the court, but I still have a job and an office. I'm located in the Shrader Building on Main Street in Amherst, Virginia. Shrader J. Thompson and Associates are good friends of mine and they see to it I stay busy and I'm grateful to them for their wisdom. They don't need me, but I need them. I'm licensed by the Court of Virginia to perform civil ceremonies and I'm ordained by the church to perform religious ceremonies. I marry those who come to me who have no church affiliation and who don't want a Christian ceremony. Then there are those who want a Christian ceremony without all the expense and trimmings of a church wedding. I also marry those who have been previously divorced and are trying to make a new life, but whom most all denominational ministers refuse to accept as proper candidates for marriage.

I am an accountant, too, and I do quite a bit of estate work. I still use my trusty, manually operated Royal typewriter that I started out with in 1940 when I became clerk of court. This typewriter is now fifty-seven years old and there's not a day goes by, except when I'm on tour that I don't type on this little Royal and it still does its job just fine.

It's just common sense to stay busy. Anybody ought to know if exercise is good for the physical body, then it has got to be good for the mind, also. I've observed the truth of this firsthand. All the boys I grew up with and continued to know as men, when they reached age sixty-five, each in turn said they had worked all their adult lives and they weren't going to hit a lick of work anymore. So, they sat themselves in front of their television sets and watched lots of mind-stupefying stuff and there's not a single one of those old friends still alive; most of them died within five years of their respective retirements. Even in my own family, becoming inactive in retirement had the same results. There were five of us boys of which I was the oldest. My youngest brother died first, then next to the youngest, then the next to that one, and then the next, in that order. There is only me, the firstborn, and the only one to keep on being very active, still alive. Everybody says it's very unusual to die in the exact reverse order of which you were born.

Until last year I wore the same prescription glasses I had worn since I was sixty-five years old. Then last year I began to have a little trouble reading fine print, so I decided it must be time for a new prescription because I still read a lot even now.

I realize most of the Monacan Indians in this area must hate me and I don't fault them in their feelings toward me. I do wish there was some way they could know I did try to help whenever I could sneak the proper paperwork past Dr. Plecker's vigilant eyes. I did stop short of that and wrote in what he wanted me to write whenever he was checking closely behind me. As I said earlier, I didn't want to be imprisoned as he kept reminding me I would be if I did not do exactly as instructed. I have wished so many times that I had been older and stronger of courage. It seemed so impossible to stand out against such a powerful man: the cruel inventor and keeper of Virginia's Racial Integrity Laws, crass laws to be exact.

A Note from the Interviewer

At this point in the interview, I interrupted Mr. Sandidge's recollection of those long ago years to show him copies of my grandfather Edmund Branham's marriage licenses, which recorded Edmund's first marriage to Bettie Ann Johns, and then after her death, his marriage to Elena Nora Willis, who would later become my grandmother.

6. Monacans Edmund and Elena Willis Branham, who were born, grew up, and married in Amherst County, Virginia. This photograph was taken in Big Island, Virginia, in the late 1940s.

Upon reviewing those documents, Mr. Sandidge had this to say, "Look at the dates and the names of the two different clerks of court who filled out these marriage licenses. In 1890, when Edmund married Bettie Ann Johns, Mr. Ellis was clerk of court. In the space provided to write in the race, Mr. Ellis wrote in 'col,' meaning Colored as the race for both of these people. Surely Mr. Ellis knew that Mr. Branham and Miss Johns were both Indians, not colored, but he also knew Indians were disallowed as a race in Virginia. He followed Dr. Plecker's rules. I doubt very much if Mr. Branham or Miss Johns could read well enough to realize what race Mr. Ellis had written in on the license. They were at a disadvantage at reading documents since they were prohibited from attending regular schools in order to be educated.

"At any rate, when the widower Branham married Miss Willis in 1896, my grandfather, William E. Sandidge I, had become clerk of court and he wrote in Edmund and Elena's race as white, which was correct since they weren't allowed to be Indian.

"Then, when their daughter, Dora, married Frank Clark in 1909, my father, William E. Sandidge II, had become clerk of court. He signed their license, listing their race as white, which was correct since Virginia law forbade them to be Indian.

"By the time I, William E. Sandidge III became clerk of court, Dr. Walter A. Plecker had become birth registrar in Richmond, Virginia, and as I've stated repeatedly, a more radical man than Dr. Plecker I have never known.

"He came to Amherst Courthouse very often, checking our records against his sadistic hit list of surnames, which he had decided were part and parcel of the colored race.

"Here is a copy of Plecker's hit list which the Monacans refer to, and rightly so, as Plecker's hit/hate list."

Names of Mixed Families in Rockbridge and Amherst Counties:

Rockbridge	Amherst
Clark	Branham
Pultz	Johns
*Floyd	Adcocks (Adcox)
*Hartless	*Tyree
*Tyree	Clark
Sorrell	Suthard (Southerds)
Mayse (Mays)	Beverley (Beverly)
*Wood	*Duff
Southerds (Suthard)	*Hicks
*Painter	Roberts
Johns	*Lawless
	Knuckles
	Willis
	*Cash
	Terry
	*Floyd
	*Wood
	Redcross

This list was prepared in a conference of the State Registrar of Vital Statistics with a number of county officials and leading citizens of Amherst County in order to secure uniformity of classification as to race.

*Some families bearing this name are white.

A Note from the Interviewer

Several months after this interview in 1997, Mr. W. E. Sandidge, at age ninety-three, suffered a stroke that affected his speech. I am so grateful that I met with him before the stroke and for his willingness to recall those yesteryears. I am grateful, also, for his sincere wishes that it could have been different back then for the Monacan Indians of Virginia.

7
Dena Branham

I am Dena Branham. I live up the road about a mile and a way off in the woods. I'm not as young as I used to be but, no, I don't get scared alone in the deep woods. I'm not really alone. The wild turkeys walk right up to my door and wait to be fed. I've never killed a wild turkey myself, so they know I'll protect them. Wild turkey meat is too tough and too strong flavored for my taste buds. They're sure enough pretty birds, though, strutting around on foot.

I might invite you to visit me at my house sometime, I might just do that. I could show you quilts my mama made a long time ago. Our people had to make just about everything we needed in those days. About all we bought at the store was sugar, soda, baking powder, aspirins, and coal oil. Lots of times, we just did without some of that stuff because store items had to be bought with money and money was scarcer than hen's teeth. Leastways, that's what my papa always said.

We worked hard from sunup to sundown raising our own oat products, vegetables, tobacco, and even our own meat. Now, take these young people today, they don't want to work. Young people don't want to get dirty or sweaty or tired, not from working, that is. I don't know if you know it or not, but I know it.

I didn't bother to ask many questions when I was growing up so I know very little about our Monacan history. I wish now I had asked questions of my elders, but I thought I was so smart in the things that interested me when I was a little girl, surely there couldn't be anything else worth knowing. One important thing I knew was something Mama told me in a loud whisper. She told me where babies came from. Every time a new baby was born Mama would carry it in from the shed in her apron and she said she found the new baby outside. Several years passed by and several more babies were born before I learned not to believe everything my mama told me.

Mama also told us Santa Claus brought oranges, apples, and nuts on Christmas Eve night and filled our stockings after we were fast asleep. I had learned not to trust Mama when she whispered secrets to me, so one Christmas Eve night I managed to stay awake and peep out when I heard a noise in the front room. I saw Santa Claus. He was two people! He looked just like my papa and mama.

Early on Christmas morning, my mama came to my bed and whispered to me to come and see what old Santa had left for me and for my younger brothers and sisters. I pushed back those heavy quilts and I looked my Mama in the eye and I said, "Mama, I saw Santa last night."

Mama smiled at me and she said, "I'm sure you did. Old Santa was all dressed up in a red suit, Santa was."

"Mama," I said, "I'm a big girl now and I saw what I saw. I saw old Santa last night and both of them were dressed in blue-striped cotton nightshirts."

Mama had to be many other people to us. She was our doctor and our drug-store. She made her own medicines from nature's supplies. I especially remember the horehound tea she made from horehound roots and barks. It sure did help heal our sore throats, caused by colds. I remember, also, that Mama would mix baking soda and crushed aspirin with a drop or two of water to make a paste and wrap it in a tiny bit of cloth and place it on an aching tooth one or the other of us were experiencing. It sure did help.

Did we ever do anything for fun? Oh, Lordy, yes and amen. Let me tell you about our square dances. The dances were held in people's homes and there was plenty of mountain music and good food. We'd dance and eat and dance and eat and keep on keeping on for two or three days without a break. We knew how to put on a shindig in those days. Young people today, what they call having a dance don't amount to much. They don't know much about cooking tasty vittles, either.

I might let you see my pictures of those times one of these days. Maybe I will. I could show you some pictures of some fine-looking men from back then. God knows the men back then were much finer looking men than the men are these days. Those men looked dandy. I feel sorry for the girls of today, because there just ain't no dandy men anymore.

A Note from the Interviewer

Dena was eighty-five years old in the autumn of 1998 when I interviewed her at Parish Hall on Kenmore Road in Amherst County, Virginia. She had been one of the Monacans who had been barred from attending public school and, therefore, she couldn't read or write. It was obvious she was intelligent and a pity she hadn't been given a chance in life to achieve.

Dena had never married. Some people who have known Dena most of her life say, with a smile, that Dena always seemed to be too independent to have ever wanted to settle for a man and woman relationship, or could it be she had just enjoyed the looking, kind of like she enjoyed her wild turkeys and their beauty, but only just in her backyard.

Our interview ended at dusk and Dena left to walk home. Dena looked back and grinned her toothless grin and waved her hand in farewell as she began her four-mile walk to her weathered cabin in the deep woods.

Dena seemed to me to be as tough and enduring as the mountain itself. As I watched her turn to wave once more and then disappear around a curve in the road, it seemed kind of like she did become as though one with her beloved Bear Mountain.

8
Jo Ann Staubitz

My name is Jo Ann Johns Taylor Staubitz. My father's name was Scott Johns and my mother's name was Virginia Johns Branham. I have an identical twin sister whose name is Jean. Jean was raised by our biological parents and I was raised by foster parents: Chief Harry Branham and his wife, Edith.

Jean and I grew up knowing we were twins. We attended church and school together at St. Pauls Mission.

In the interview, you asked about housing for the Indians. Most of our people worked in the orchards for the white people and we lived in tenant houses. A few of our people rented or owned their own homes. The size of those homes varied from four rooms up to seven or eight rooms.

We lived at the old Coleman Place and that house had seven rooms. The younger girls, older girls, and the boys all shared separate bedrooms. Daddy and Mama had their own room. There were also boarders from time to time.

Hereafter in this interview when I speak of Daddy and Mama, I mean my foster parents, Harry and Edith. Harry and Edith had twelve children of their own and yet they found room for one more little girl, me. Sometimes there were visitors in our home for a few days or someone in need of a temporary place to stay. Daddy could never turn anyone away from his door. He always said, "If there is room in your heart for someone, then there is room in your home." Those big bedrooms got awfully crowded at times in Daddy's house. To this day I can't turn a relative away. I always hear Daddy say, "There is always room for one more."

There was always room for Christmas, too. I remember the big Christmas trees with gifts of homemade dolls and homemade clothes waiting for us on Christmas morning beneath the big tree. There were also fruits and nuts. Oh, how well I remember those Christmas dinners of chicken and dumplings and hot biscuits dripping with homemade butter topped off with peach pies and apple puffs. I remember those foods in particular because they were my favorite dishes.

7. Monacan Jo Ann Staubitz, at the time of her interview, in Herbert Hicks's golf workshop, Madison Heights, Virginia.

I remember also our excitement on Christmas Eve night when we would gather at St. Pauls Church and there would be a gift baggy for each and every child.

Just about everything we had was homemade. My mama and grandmama made all of our clothes from the skin out. The younger children always wore the hand-me-downs of the older kids. After the older kids learned how to knit and crochet, how to embroider and quilt, and how to make baskets, they in turn taught us these skills.

We were poor, but we were never cold or hungry, because we were always wrapped in love.

Originally, there was a two-room mission school located behind St. Pauls Church and the Episcopalians sent in mission schoolteachers. Eventually, the Episcopalians built a new building. I was one of the first students privileged to attend the added eighth grade. Many before me had to stop off with the seventh grade because of lack of space and teachers. In the past our books had been furnished by the diocese, but now, in the eighth grade we must buy our books. We made more baskets of split oak, honeysuckle, pine needles, and grape vines. We then sold those baskets for money with which to purchase our books. At that time, we had four schoolteachers. They were Miss Hicks, Miss Smith, Miss Orphen, and Mrs. Whitehead. One teacher taught the first three grades. The other two teachers taught two grades each, and the remaining teacher taught the new eighth grade.

Since we were not allowed to attend the public schools in Amherst County because they would not accept Indians, there was no opportunity for us to go on to high school. There were many of us who could have made more contributions to society. We could have fulfilled our hopes and dreams had we been afforded a higher education. It still makes my heart ache to remember the feeling of helplessness and failure in my young life. Granted, a few people who are naturally talented can overcome the barriers of a lack of formal education and become whoever they desire to be, but most of us aren't that fortunate, so we must acquire an education to use as a foundation, as a springboard.

It breaks my heart anew when I see kids today, white kids, black kids, brown kids cutting classes just to wander the streets and shopping malls. They think they're being so smart when actually they're being young fools.

If only I could reach out and tell them, "Please listen, you have the opportunity for an education. You can learn to be anything you want to be. Don't blow your chance. What will it take to make you understand how it was for the Indians to be denied that opportunity? If only I could explain to you how a few school board members could, in essence, say to us, 'No we will not allow you to learn to read a book, to learn a foreign language, or to become a doctor or a teacher. You will not acquire the skills necessary to earn a decent living. You won't even be allowed to become a learned Indian chief. Why? Because in Amherst County Dr. Plecker says you don't exist. You are visible but Indians or issues just don't exist.'

"Yes, young people, you're cutting classes and you think it's cool. There was a time when Indians had to beg for their God-given right to an education. Please get off the streets and don't walk—run, run as fast as you can to your classes. Classes lead to knowledge. Knowledge leads to ability, confidence, and power. So don't walk—run, better yet dance—dance to the rhythm of the drums!"

My grandmother used to beg of me, "Jo Ann, when you grow up and finish at the mission school, leave Amherst County and never look back. Marry a man far away from this county so your children can be educated properly."

Now, as to how Bear Mountain got its name, I don't really know. I do know there used to be lots of bears on this mountain. This mountain was well inhabited by black bears and, in far lesser number, by brown bears. That order has become reversed in recent years. Why, I don't know.

When we used to walk to the mission school out Kenmore Road, it was not at all unusual to see black bears coming out of the dense woods and crossing the road. They paid no attention to us nor we to them. They just ambled on about their own business and we just laughed and talked, grumbled and skipped, and minded our own business of going on to the schoolhouse.

I don't remember much about home medicinal remedies. I know there were all kinds of teas brewed from various roots, barks, and leaves. I remember ginseng roots, horehound barks, and mint leaves in particular. I do remember the remedy for cracks between the toes which came about from going barefoot a lot. There was good old stinky turpentine sprinkled on a small piece of cloth which was placed between the toes over the raw crack and tied in place with another strip of cloth that came up around the ankle to secure the bandage.

There were always home remedies to cure any and all ills. For instance, whenever we misbehaved, we had to go to the orchard to gather our own medicine in the shape of a switch cut from a peach tree. Then one of our parents administered its healing influence with several sharp licks across our backsides.

I don't recall much about music when I was growing up. Most of us couldn't afford radios in our homes. We played hand-held instruments and sang and made our own music. Whenever we did have opportunities to listen to radios, our favorite music was gospel and country. A few favorites come to mind from the 1940s. There was Kitty Wells singing "Whose Shoulder Will You Cry On." There was Lester Flatt and Earle Scruggs singing "Sweet to Be Remembered." And there was one-of-a-kind Hank Williams singing "I Saw the Light."

I guess its past time to put the past behind us, so let's bring ourselves back into the present. This February of 1997, I am fifty-six years old. I am continuing my education. I went back before this and earned my GED. Then I went to nursing school and earned my nurse's assistant license. Now, I'm studying commercial art at Central Virginia College. I guess I'll be taking classes about something until the day I die. There are so many subjects I want to know more about. The desire to learn lives on in me.

A Note from the Interviewer

I shall never forget the gay sound of Jo Ann's laughter as she talked about the love and security of a large family and of being there for one another. I shall never forget the pain in her eyes and the sounds of sobs forcing their way from a constricted throat as she dealt anew with the hurtful memories of a child whose mind was pleading to learn, yet the door to that world had been slammed shut in her face. The rejection embodied in her memory of her people being forbidden to enter the doors of public schoolhouses had left scars on this woman's heart. As I listened to her memories, I, too, was brought to tears and we cried together in what would hopefully be tears of healing.

As we put an effort into bringing back our smiles, Jo Ann slipped a beautiful western ring from her finger and said to me, "Slip this ring on your finger to see if it fits." I slipped the lovely ring on my little finger and she said, "It fits. Now it's yours." The ring is made up of a silver base and on the base is a curving, silver leaf and there, nestled beside the leaf, is a gemstone of blue turquoise and an elongated stone of red coral. It has become my favorite ring. In the photograph of Jo Ann in this book, look closely at the little finger of her left hand and you can see this beautiful ring.

Jo Ann has learned something very valuable from her people and from life itself. It's something some people never learn even though they may have earned several diplomas and degrees. She has learned the value of being wrapped in love and of wrapping others in love. Jo Ann is a warm, loving, giving person who gives from her heart. I shall never forget her words at the beginning of this interview when she said, "One is never really cold or hungry when one is wrapped in the love of a caring family."

9
Lee Branham

I am Lee Branham. I was married to Virginia Johns and we had five children.

I grew up on High Peak Mountain. My folks were sharecroppers. We lived in a house that was considered a part of our wages. The house was on land belonging to the owner of the apple orchard. My father and mother and we kids all worked in the orchard. The owner gave us all the apples we could use for ourselves, so my mother canned and cooked apples in every shape and form apples could be cooked. Those apples were our pay for picking and packing the orchard's harvest of apples for the owner's livelihood. We could also raise other crops in his fields so we raised corn and wheat, vegetables and tobacco. At harvest time the owner got half of every crop we harvested as his pay for our use of his fields. Some landowners in Amherst County would settle for a lesser percent of yield, but not this man.

The white race had taken our land from us and then would not allow us to work jobs for monetary pay, but we were still the ones who worked the land. The white man took the strength of our best years in hard labor, working for him for his benefit.

I thank my God they couldn't take Him from us. No siree, we didn't have to share God with the landowners, because God refuses to be divided up into any kind of percentages for any man. He's always there a hundred percent for all of us who ask it of Him.

A Note from the Interviewer

I was glad I talked with Lee in the summer of 1998. Lee Branham died in December 1998 after suffering terribly with cancer. He was eighty-six years old. He

8. This windowless log cabin, over one hundred years old and now vacant for many years, still stands at one of the orchards in Amherst County. Many years ago it was the home of Monacan Ned Branham and his family, who worked in the orchard.

lived in a mobile home beside the Monacan Memorial Cemetery and kept an eye out for visitors to the cemetery. He welcomed visitors to sightsee in the cemetery and he was willing to answer their questions. He asked only for their courtesy when visiting on sacred ground.

10

Annie Johns Branham

I am Annie Johns Branham. My grandmother was Kate Johns. My mother was Edith Johns and she married Harry Branham, my father. My late husband was Albert Mays Branham and we have three children. My husband passed away in 1973.

I've always lived in Amherst County, Virginia. I attended St. Pauls Mission School, which was set up by the Episcopalian diocese for Monacan Indian children. I attended eight years. The grades stopped off with the seventh grade, but I longed so to have the opportunity to continue my education. I just hated to have to quit, so I attended the seventh grade for an extra year. There were schools for white students and schools for what was then known as schools for the colored, but we weren't welcome in either system. The law of Virginia would have allowed us to attend the schools for the colored, but they let us know they didn't want the white's rejects and we knew we were supposed to be listed as white since Virginia didn't recognize Indians.

I nearly cried my eyes out for weeks after my second year in the seventh grade. All my hopes for a higher education were over because of Old Plecker. That was the only name I ever heard Dr. Walter A. Plecker addressed as by my people when I was growing up. He was not the kind of person any of us would ever have anything nice to say about because he was not a nice person to us. He hated us with a blind hatred because he had set himself up to be the ruler of a world made up of a few destructive people of his (thank God) limited kind. He was not by any means representative of all white people. For many years he had the state of Virginia and Amherst County, in particular, in his hip pocket. He was a powerful, cold, cruel man. Old Plecker would come to Amherst County Courthouse and spend days examining the birth registration records, searching for Monacan surnames. Then he would mark through the entry of race:

Indian, and write in: Negro, colored, mixed, or issue; apparently whichever race definition took his fancy on a given day. He would also, when back in Richmond, the capital of Virginia, pull birth records and write on the back of any that had made it there with the correct race of Indian, such names as I've mentioned.

My grandmother, Kate Johns, delivered me as well as many other Indian babies. She was the midwife for the whole Indian community. She always registered us as Indian, and some of those certificates managed to escape Old Plecker's searches. Those records that survived, and even the ones he attempted to change on the back, have helped us obtain state recognition as a Monacan Indian Nation.

My grandson, Joshua Tolitol, had learned when he was in play school and then in kindergarten that being Indian in Amherst County was still a touchy subject with some people. He put up a protective shield by saying when anyone asked him if he was Indian, "No, I am not Indian. I am cowboy."

As far as Joshua was concerned, he thought everyone loved cowboys and he wanted to be accepted and loved. This went on for those two years, and then in 1997, he entered first grade. Doby Thompson, an Indian lady, visits the area public schools now that we're accepted and she reads and tells stories and sings to the children. All the children love her. She talked with Joshua one day after school had ended for the day. He came home just bubbling over with joy. He ran to me and threw his little arms around me and said, "Grandma! Guess what! An Indian lady came to my school today and she gave me a cassette tape with Indian stories and songs on it and she said I'm just like her because I'm Monacan Indian, too. All the kids at school just love her. She's neat. I'm glad I'm just like her. I'm Indian!"

I've had a stroke and sometimes it's hard for me to say what I want to say anymore, but what I'm trying to say is I'm so glad for Joshua. He can go on to high school and college or he can even be a cowboy if he so chooses. And he can be proud to be an American Indian.

Yes, times and people are changing. This world is changing as people travel around the world more and more and become acquainted with other cultures. Even Indians are changing in the things they do and in the things they are interested in. My grandmother, my mother, and really all the women I've known or know of were great quilt makers and basket weavers. They were never very interested in jewelry making or pottery. The young women of today are more interested in learning to make jewelry, or in oil or water painting and designing regalias for the powwows, or office type work. These occupations are somewhat easier on tender skin and manicured nails. These young women have entered

9. Split-oak basket and with patchwork quilt, both items made by Monacan Virginia Branham.

into a different work force than the farm and field and orchard toilers. All of the work of long ago was very hard on women's hands, causing cuts and pricks, calluses, tough skin, and broken nails. Their hands really took a beating. The young ladies of today smile and say, "Those lost arts had their own rewards, but now we're moving on."

11
Phyllis Branham Hicks

I'm Phyllis Branham Hicks. My maternal great-grandmother was Kate Johns. My paternal great-grandmother was Althea Terry. My maternal grandparents were Harry and Edith Branham. My paternal grandparents were Walter and Delia Branham. My parents are Annie Johns Branham and the late Albert Mays Branham. Mom and Daddy had four children: two boys and two girls. I need to clarify that last statement. I think when you interviewed Mom, she told you she has three children. She meant three living children. The second boy, Harry, was killed in the Vietnam War.

This is how crazy it used to get according to our legal records on being born in Amherst County. My brother, Harry, and I were born at home (I, in 1947). My great-grandmother, Kate Johns, delivered each of us, which was nothing for us to brag about as we were among over five hundred babies all told that midwife Kate delivered. In the space to list nationality on the birth registration form Kate wrote in "Indian" for Harry and I. The forms were processed in Richmond and somehow escaped Dr. Plecker's eagle eye and heavy hand. It gets even crazier. My older brother and my younger sister were both born in Lynchburg General Hospital in Lynchburg, Virginia. As per Dr. Walter Plecker's orders concerning Indians' births, in the space to list race on the birth registration forms, the hospital personnel wrote in the word colored. When my mother discovered at a later date what had been done, she engaged a lawyer and he won the case. So the Bureau of Vital Statistics had to change my brother's and sister's records to state Indian.

Our Monacan records are still a hodgepodge today because some of those older records are still in error with some brothers and sisters registered colored, black, Indian, or mixed. It gets really wild. Many Indians are also listed as white.

The governor of Virginia has issued a decree that any of us who need to have our records reissued to state correctly the race of Indian can send in the falsified records and the Bureau of Vital Statistics must do the research to correct our records free of charge. The trouble with that is it doesn't help with births that were registered in Richmond before 1916 because no birth certificates were issued before that date. It also does nothing to rectify marriage records and also lots of census records that are in error.

The causes of the race mix-ups are a comedy of errors since 1790 when census records began. The skimpy education of some census takers, the bias of others, and the confusion caused by some government bureaucrats' vague rules concerning the filling out of official forms and the further breakdown caused by the Race Integrity Act of 1924, are all factors that contributed to the state of confusion.

I may be incorrect on this statement, but I think I'm accurate. I've been told the official forms on which to register people's births, marriages, and deaths no longer contain a space on which a person's race must be listed. If true, this method is going to cause a different kind of problem.

Even today, whenever I'm in Parish Hall, or across the lawn in St. Pauls Church, or across the little wooden bridge in the tiny log schoolhouse, I feel like I'm standing on sacred ground. I believe God sent the Episcopalian diocese to help us so many years ago when so many others in Virginia wanted to force us from their midst. Many of us could not have gotten any education at all had it not been that the Episcopalian diocese provided this little separate schoolhouse and teachers for us. They cared when no one else cared.

I say this, not in bitterness, but simply to point out that even among Christians there are some inbred forms of reasoning, one form being that we must be taught by the white man's standards. Religious services were conducted in the mode of the white man's forms of worship. We had to sing the white man's hymns to the white man's music. We prayed the white man's prayers, et cetera. We were never allowed to use the Indians' drums. We couldn't utter chants. Sweat lodges were never allowed on church grounds. In short, there was never an Indian form of worship service observed.

I understand that this form of blindness is beginning to disappear in the 1990s. Missionaries serving in other countries now understand that it's harmful to attempt to take away the native forms of worship completely. After all, one wants to help people know God, but it's wrong to attempt to make Americans of people from other countries against their will. It's also wrong to force Indians to be carbon copies in all ways of the white man. We Indians are of America, but we have a few ways that were traditional of our people before the white man came to America and we'd like to sing and dance and pray our way at times in honor of our forefathers.

Some authors and students have stated in books, theses, and in newspaper articles that we Monacans kept to ourselves and even at times tried to hide ourselves from other people. That's true, but we were given no other choice until 1963. Before that date, back in 1954, the Supreme Court ruled that all people, regardless of color, had equal rights to an education, yet attitudes and circumstances began to change very, very slowly. Of course, there have always been some nice exceptions to any rule of thumb. I remember one boy in particular who didn't harbor a biased attitude. I was among the first five Monacans to be allowed to enter the public high school. I well remember those first two days of riding the school bus. On the morning and evening of both days, we Monacans had to ride standing in the aisle because no one would allow any of us to share a seat with any of them. Neither would anyone free up a seat by sharing a seat with any of their friends. I remember going home and crying in my mother's arms.

I shall never forget the third day. A boy invited me to share a seat with him and after that third day he always made sure I had a seat beside him. That boy will always stand tall and manly in my memory.

I remember going home and telling my mother that some of the students were calling me insulting names like issue and issy.

My mother said, "Don't retaliate by calling them ugly names. Don't put yourself down on that level. We are poor, but we have nothing to be ashamed of. Be proud of who you are and always be the best that you can be."

I remember times when I had to put rubber bands around my socks to hold them in place because the socks were so worn the elastic had grown weak. I remember coats my grandmother made for me out of scraps of materials left over from sewing garments for the white folks. I remember the dresses she made for me were out of the floral sacks our flour and cornmeal were packed in at the mill where they ground our wheat and corn. How often when I've heard Dolly Parton sing of her coat of many colors have I remembered and cried because in those young years I had been ashamed of my clothing. I was all grown up before I realized my parents had cared for me with unrecognized toil and sweat, resourcefulness, and priceless love and care.

Yes, our small homes were crowded with people and only basic foodstuffs were served on our homemade tables. Our mamas and grannies, papas and granddads all worked equally hard for the advantage of the white folks to eke out a bare living for themselves through the heat of summers and the cold of Virginia winters. But along with the hard living there was always music and laughter and prayers in our homes. There was always the assuredness of being there for each other in the bad times as well as the good times. I was all grown up before I realized I had been a rich little girl.

During those growing-up years square dances were the most popular forms of entertainment for social gatherings. I can remember well when the dances were held at our house. Mama would direct us, and with her and Papa's help, we would empty a bedroom completely of furniture. That bare floor would be used for dancing. Every family attending would bring at least one dish of prepared food. The word would pass quickly up and down those mountain roads and everybody came. The party sometimes went on for a couple of days, especially at harvest time and then everybody would move on to another house to continue the celebration in thanksgiving for the food that had been laid in store for the cold winter months.

While the grown-ups were feasting and dancing and telling tall tales, we younger children were just as busy playing the typical children's games and the older children were playing baseball. In fact, we were all having a ball.

I remember doing homework by lamplight and again thinking of the town girls with their electric lights shining so brightly upon their papers and printed matter. This was the case for several of my school years. I'll never forget when Papa finally managed to have our house hooked up with electricity. My mama and papa worked until seven P.M. five days per week, and it was dark when they arrived home. My brother and I were so excited that first evening, so when it grew dusky dark, we turned on every light in that house upstairs and downstairs and the porch light, too. We ran to meet our parents and we were chorusing, "Mama, Papa, see all the lights!"

My mama said, "Yes, children, I do see all the lights. I also know there's going to be a light bill we can't pay if you continue to turn the house into a beacon of light. I also want to know, have you children had those lights burning all day?"

I remember when my papa had to go to town each Saturday to buy a block of ice for our ice box. Even this was a step up from the springhouses of my parents' day. We had wood-burning stoves, too. But after Papa had the electricity hooked up, he bought a television set. My brother and I thought we were really in high cotton now.

It was my job when I arrived home from school to begin cooking supper in order that most of the supper would be ready when my parents arrived after dark. I was in my early teens and that television set almost became the death of me. I would start the foods cooking on the stove and then I'd go into the living room and turn on the television and watch *American Bandstand*. I'd become so engrossed in dancing rock and roll along with the images on the screen, the beans and corn and "tators" always ended up scorched and, more often than not, burned.

My mama finally said, "You've got to leave that rock and roll stuff alone so we can have something for supper other than what we scrape off the bottom of these charred pots."

On Saturdays, our day was always spent at Parish Hall. We teenagers were all

members of the church choir. A few of us could sing, the rest made the prover-
bial joyful noise. Toward the end of the day, we'd have a cookout of hamburgers
and hotdogs.

Papa John Haraughty always saw to it that we did have a social life during
those difficult years.

During that period of time we were not allowed to attend the public high
school. Therefore, by not having the opportunity for high school prior to 1963,
I was sixteen years old when I began my freshman year. Things didn't improve
much during my sophomore year and so I didn't return for what would have
been my junior year. I am an affectionate type of person. My heart reaches out
to people regardless of race or color. I could not deal with the animosity without
cause among young people in those days of transition.

I took courses and earned my GED after I married Roy Hicks. I went on to
earn my CBC and I took some courses in accounting.

In an earlier discussion prior to this interview, you asked me why I made the
statement that I don't hold newspaper reporters in very high esteem. Let me
elaborate on that statement somewhat. I have grown very reluctant to talk to
newspaper reporters. You will find this to be true with most of my people. They
came in here and convinced us they were working with us and gathering information to find ways to help us out of the deep rut that had been our portion for
many, many years. They claimed their articles would aid us in obtaining better
jobs and so forth. The missionary ladies at St. Pauls Mission believed the newspaper people, too. So, with their blessing, we did talk of our needs and hopes and
hurts. Well, when the newspaper reporters had garnered the information they said
they needed, they wrote their articles and twisted and turned in print that which
they said we had said and ended up doing us harm.

The newspaper people in this Piedmont area may be quite different in this
present time than those of my youth. I surely hope so. It's just that once you have
been given solid reason to be suspicious of a person or a group of people, it's hard
to learn to trust again unless proof has come to pass.

Our people of past generations grew to hate even the name of Dr. Walter A.
Plecker, but perhaps the man would deserve his day in court, not in order to excuse what he did to Indians—what he did was inexcusable. But does he deserve
all the blame for trying to force Indians to be registered and known as colored?
I have given this matter a lot of thought and I have questions. Questions like,
how could one man even as state registrar of Vital Statistics have full authority to
force clerks of courts and hospital personnel in several chosen areas to falsify records and list Indian births as colored? How could he possibly have been the sole
authority to falsify our records in Richmond and write his lies on the backs of
our birth certificates? How could he force his clerks at the Bureau of Vital Statis-

tics to use his hit/hate list and bring those names to his personal attention? How could one lone man have that kind of power over census takers? How could one lone man set himself up to be the sole god and judge of all the Indians of Virginia?

Dr. Walter A. Plecker was a powerful man, but it doesn't make sense that he could have been all powerful for thirty-four years as registrar and the legacy of his genocide to have effects for many years into the future even into this very day in 1997. No, this pitiful lichen of a man had to have been backed by Virginia's Legislature and by the acquiescence of Virginia's governors during those years.

I know we have conferred with officials from the Mattaponi and the Mattaponi [pronounced differently from the former] and the Pamunkey tribes. And we have learned that these people have been subjected to the same discrimination by Dr. Plecker as we Monacans have endured. From contact with these three tribes, I'm sure it stands to reason the other remaining tribes in Virginia have also been subjected to the same treatment during Plecker's time.

It is also beyond my understanding how the Europeans could have accepted the help, the food, the know-how of survival in this (for the Europeans) strange land; then they turned on the Indian Samaritans and wrested everything from them. They even attempted to wrest our very heritage from us. Greed is a very real disease. It can eat the very heart right out of man as it did to those Europeans.

The material things of life can last a man's lifetime and then they are gone, no longer of any benefit at all to that particular person. It is the qualities such as love and of being there for one another, which are often not clearly seen with the naked eye, but these are the things of the spirit that will go with a person into eternity.

I do believe there is an eternal heaven and an eternal hell. I do believe there is Satan, the Destroyer, and there is God, the Creator, the Eternal Great Father. I want to share with you two experiences in particular when God has walked with my family in a special way. I speak to you of this with tears of thanksgiving wetting my face. There were many tears back at those times, too; tears of sadness and good tears of healing. I shall never forget.

My husband, Roy, and I were living in Maryland at that time. My brother, Harry, was serving in the army in Vietnam. Roy and I were called home when my brother was killed in the line of duty.

The afternoon we returned to my parents' house after the memorial service, I sat with my mama in the living room. I was experiencing a really tough time. I was seriously questioning God. I kept asking in my heart and mind, "Why, God, why did this have to be? Why should my brother die so young in a war he did not cause?"

"My mama and daddy have never hurt anybody. Why should they have to hurt so now?"

On and on my heart cried out in turmoil. Finally, I knew I could not cope alone. I must seek my mama's wisdom and strength. I laid my weary head in her lap and asked of her, "Mama, how can you accept that God did what was best when he took your son, my brother?"

Mama answered, "Phyllis, your brother is all right."

"Mama, you can't know that. I mean, I know he's all right, but Harry was still so young. It's just not fair."

I need to pause here and fill in some background to clarify the time and place. Mama and Daddy lived in a house on the grounds of Sweet Briar College. Mama worked in the restaurant and Daddy was a groundskeeper. On that fateful day, the messenger brought the ill news to Daddy first. Then my dad left work to go with the messenger to the house to break the dreadful news to Mama. Daddy knew Mama's shift at the restaurant had been the early shift and she would have left the restaurant for home.

Now, we will return to my conversation with Mama and she will answer my question with a startling revelation.

"Phyllis, when I arrived home that day, I was so tired I sat down here in the living room in this very chair. When Albert came with the messenger, I already knew."

"Mama, how could you have known?"

"Your late great-grandmother, Kate Johns, came to me. I didn't dream it. I was not asleep. I saw her clearly. She came as out of nowhere and she stood here by my chair. She told me Harry had died in battle, but he didn't want me to worry or grieve. She said he was with God and with her too, and Harry was just fine. And she said, 'Annie, girl, hold on to what I've told you.'"

I said, "Mama, are you sure this isn't just something you want to believe?"

"Phyllis, I swear to you, I saw Granny Kate in full figure and she told me my boy was just fine. It's very hard to have to give up my son, but I can cope because of God's message through Granny Kate and oh, how I thank Him for sending my mother to comfort me."

"Did she stay with you until Daddy came?"

"No, she only stayed long enough to tell me and just as instantly as she had come, she was gone. About five minutes after her visit Albert and the messenger came to tell me my boy had been killed. They were five minutes late."

As I said, I still had some doubts, not that Mama would lie to me, but could it have been real to her, or out of her imagination?

A few years went by and my dad became very ill. My dad and I had grown very close in the past two years. I had married Roy and moved with him to Maryland and had lived there for two years. I guess I became more adult during that period of time. Anyway, when Roy and I moved back and bought a house right next door to my parents, it seemed as though Daddy and I grew to know each other better, not just as father and child, but as friends and we really enjoyed doing things together and talking one on one with each other. So, when Daddy became very ill and was in ICU in the Lynchburg hospital, I became a basket case. I refused to believe he was seriously ill. Surely he would soon be well and home again.

My family and I stayed at the hospital around the clock to be near him. And then, on the eighteenth evening, Mama said, "We're all going home tonight. We can do no more for him with him being in a coma. We must get some rest. We will need our strength."

My older brother and my twelve-year-old sister, Pam, told Mama there was no way we were going home. Mama insisted we were. My brother went to his home and Pam and I went with Mama to her house. Upon our arrival Mama told me to take Daddy's truck and go to the church and ready the church for Sunday morning services. I was bone weary and I didn't want to be alone, but I knew she was going to insist I go, so I went.

I walked to the front of the sanctuary and sat down on the front pew. Weeping uncontrollably, I prayed to God about my daddy. "Oh, God," I sobbed, "I can't let my daddy go, I can't, I can't. Oh, God." As I continued to cry and pray, all of a sudden, it was as though I sensed someone had sat down beside me. I felt the weight of an arm placed around my shoulder. At that time it was as though with that touch I felt a sensation pass all through my body and as that happened, it felt as though a thousand-pound weight had lifted from my heart and the unbearable pain and hurt ceased. I found myself praying a different prayer. I was praying, "I'll understand, God, if you need to take my daddy home with You and heal him there."

I felt myself giving my daddy up. My daddy. One moment I had been crying out, "I can't," and the next minute I was saying with a trembling voice, "I hear what you're telling me, God, that he'll be better off with You. You've given me what I need to cope. I know You're doing what is best for Daddy."

I got up from the pew, cleaned the church and set everything in order for the morrow, and then I went home to Mama. I told her all that had happened. I said, "Mama, now I can believe and understand what you meant when you experienced Granny Kate coming to you from God, because tonight, God touched me. He gave me of His strength to ask His will, not mine."

Mama said gently, "I knew you needed time alone with God to realize God knows what's best and we do not. That's why I sent you to the church even though you were exhausted." She smiled at me with a soft look in her eyes. "You thought I didn't know, dear one."

About three o'clock that Sunday morning, someone called from the hospital to tell us Daddy had passed away.

I became heavily involved with the church. I wanted to give as I had been given to. I am now the church administrator. My life's work is with my people, to help my people find ways to help themselves. I don't have children of my own, but the children of my people are like my own. My heart's desire is that I can, that we can, make life for these children better than the life we knew. We teach them, "There is no longer anyone who says you cannot have an education, no one who says you cannot have a profession or own your own business. No one today denies you the right to openly be an Indian. You are equal. You have a future of promise, goals that are attainable. All you have to do is study and learn, work and achieve, reach out and catch hold to make your life count for something worthwhile."

When we were coming along, up until 1964, we were afraid to stand up and be counted. We were isolated from the mainstream in Amherst County, but God never gave up on us and praise to Him, life has never been all bad, all hurtful. We have been blessed with a spirit of survival against all odds. No longer do some people look at us askance. In 1989, the Virginia Legislature has officially declared, "You are the Monacan Indian Nation."

My mama hasn't had an easy life, but she would be the last to say that. Besides losing her youngest son in the Vietnam War, soon after, she lost her husband to death, leaving her with a twelve-year-old daughter to raise alone. Mama had already lost her parents and a brother, therefore, she had lost the under-girding love and understanding provided by her extended family.

Now, in these later years of her life, she has gone through open heart surgery and is recovering from a stroke. She is having to learn to speak all over again. She always has and still does pick herself up and look forward. She begins each new day with a prayer, a cup of coffee, and a lovely smile upon her face.

My mama, Annie, is a rock and I long to be like her. I hope to remember without resentment back over the years. Back before 1908 when the Episcopalian diocese built a church here on Bear Mountain for us, even a place to worship God or to hold a funeral service was denied us. There was so much discrimination. I can remember my grandparents telling of how whenever they tried to attend church at Bethany, the Smyrna Church, or other churches in Madison Heights they were always told to sit on back benches reserved for African Americans. Funerals for Indians or blacks had to be conducted at home or at the cemetery. There was no church in which to have our babies given the christening rites.

Also, in those years, discrimination was practiced in restaurants. Whenever any of our people had occasion to be in Lynchburg and needed a place to eat, they were made to go to the back and sit with the black folks who were also restricted to the back of any restaurant. Only the white folks were privileged to take the middle and front sections. Blacks and Indians were only deemed worthy of the front rows/lines during wars.

I've been told that a few people in Amherst used to make remarks such as, "Oh, those Indians have serious problems with drugs and alcohol, also divorces and children born out of wedlock."

I would be the first to admit we have those problems. Of course we do. Remarks such as those make me want to hold a meeting on the courthouse square and say, "If there is any man, woman, or child present who can inform me of a nation, race, or group of people who does not have these same problems, please kindly step forward and share that great news."

I can tell you with the same assuredness that I can tell you I opened my eyes this morning that I would be met with utter silence. As young people of today say, "Get a life." That means, be realistic, folks.

We have programs at Job Corps to help our people with serious problems. We have a psychiatrist on duty as well as counselors. We have job training. We have study classes. In other words, we have rehabilitation programs. Those efforts don't always bear fruit, but does anything always work 100 percent? For the ones these programs do help, that makes it all worthwhile.

Of course, we are a minority race, but is that any reason to term us less than another race? We are an enduring people. God created all mankind and scattered man over the earth. Since He designated us to be Indian, I find no fault with that. God's wisdom is without question.

The state of Virginia has finally acknowledged and is beginning to support with legislation its very first pioneering people, the Native Americans. This particular nation, the Monacan Indians, has centuries' old roots in Amherst County, Virginia.

We are buying back 110 acres of our original land on Bear Mountain. We hope to greet you here at our Homecoming Bazaar, always held the first Saturday in October. That's when the Virginia mountains are at their peak with autumn's glorious riot of breathtaking colors.

Since 1987, we have our own tribal council. We have our own Monacan drums. We are invited to speak at schools and universities to teach our culture, too. We have opened our museum in the renovated building where the second Monacan school was once housed at St. Pauls Mission Center. Our Homecoming Bazaar grows larger every year and last year, people coming to our powwow were from other states as well as local.

10. Monacan Memorial Stone, on Kenmore Road on Bear Mountain behind the former site of Crawfords Store. The stone commemorates the families of Monacans buried in this area dating to the 1800s.

As far as our research can determine the Monacans were never big on pottery or jewelry. Monacans were known for their basket weaving and homemade quilts. Our fear is that those who are still experienced in these crafts are dwindling. Those of us born in the past fifty years have become so involved in other interests, the elders are concerned that if we don't start taking time to be taught these crafts, they will become a lost art.

We have four ancestral cemeteries in Amherst County. The most ancient one is on top of Bear Mountain at Snead's Place. Chief Harry Branham and his son, Curtis, hauled the stone for Harry's father, George Branham, to the top of the mountain by horse and wagon. The only way now to find that cemetery is to locate that one stone. Before George's stone, our people couldn't afford grave stones and the graves were marked only by native rocks placed at the grave sites by loving hands and committing the site to memory. Of course, after many years the land became the property of white people. Eventually, the cemetery became unused and overgrown with briars and weeds. The rocks also shifted or were covered over through the years.

The second cemetery is down on Kenmore Road where Lee Branham's mobile home is situated behind what used to be Crawford's Store. That cemetery is being cleared of brush, a memorial stone is now in place, and the entrance road has been graveled. There is also a small cemetery at Bethany Church where some of the Tennessee Monacans are buried.

The fourth cemetery is on Father Judge Road and is named St. Pauls Cemetery. That's where my grandfather, Chief Harry Branham, is buried. It is with thanksgiving to God I can now stand at my grandfather's grave and say, "Chief, your dream has come to pass for us, and we can now lift our heads and proudly say, 'We are Monacan Indian.' Chief, the dream you worked so diligently toward has come true for us."

Thelma Louise Branham-Branham

I am Thelma Louise Branham-Branham. I'm the great-granddaughter of Richard Branham and Christine Wise. I'm the granddaughter of Ramsey Branham and Louise Terry. My other grandparents were John Branham and Ella Beverly. My parents were James Branham and Carsia Branham.

My grandfather Ramsey's siblings were James, Chester, Joe, and John; also William, Harry, George (Buggy), Abraham, and you, the interviewer's, grandfather Edmund. The girls were Mallie Ann and Lula. I think there was another girl named Rachel and two more besides. The elders think there were sixteen children in all.

I'm married to Harry Curtis Branham, youngest son of Harry Branham and Edith Johns. We have one daughter, Linda Branham Rose.

I have one sister living, Ella Branham Mays. My brothers are John, Joe, and James. Another brother is now deceased.

I have lived in Amherst County all my life, except for fourteen months in Maryland. Life wasn't always easy as a child, but this is my home. I was ten years old and my brother, John, was eleven years old when we began attending school at St. Pauls Mission School. Our parents wouldn't let us attend school before then because we had so far to walk.

We were more fortunate than some of our relatives though. Mr. Ell was employed by Home Beneficial Life Insurance Company as an agent. When he made his weekly stops at our house to collect the premiums due on our insurance policies, he would bring paperback books, including the reader *Dick and Jane*. He also brought along a spelling book and a numbers book. He would stay at our house a couple of hours, teaching us from those books. He would assign us homework and the following week he would check our work and help us make any corrections needed. Mr. Ell was very concerned about our need for an education. When John celebrated his eleventh birthday, Mr. Ell brought John a bicycle. John rode his

11. Thelma Louise Branham at the back of the school-on-a-rock, St. Pauls Mission school. The two-room school dates to 1908 and was in use until 1963. The Monacans have received a government grant to restore the school as a historical site.

bicycle the long way to St. Pauls School. The teachers tested him for grade level and found him capable of third-grade work, thanks to Mr. Ell's home teaching.

The following year when I was ten years old, John would double me on his bike to school. Near the end of that school year, John's bike became worn-out and our teacher agreed to let us ride with her. That was helpful, but we still had to walk five miles to an intersecting point where we would meet up with her.

I only made it to the fifth grade. My mother became very ill and I quit school to help out at home where I was sorely needed. Miss Garland, my teacher, entreated me to stay in school and failing that, she beseeched me to return to school at the earliest possible opportunity.

I don't really know why I didn't return to school after my mother recovered. Was it lack of effort or interest on my part? Was it discouragement because I had gotten so far behind in my studies as a result of my long absence from classes? I'm not really sure. I do know one thing of a surety. Miss Garland was a wonderfully dedicated teacher who tried to instill in all of us pride in our Indian heritage and the courage to stand up for our rights as Americans. Her words to me personally still ring in my ears, "Believe in yourself, Louise. Never fail to believe in yourself."

John finished the seventh grade, which was as far as he could go at St. Pauls Mission. It was many years later before the eighth grade was added. John was an apt pupil, and he greatly desired to continue his education. John couldn't really comprehend why he was not allowed to attend the public schools the white people attended. None of us could comprehend the injustice of such rules. These were rules that seemed to apply only to Amherst County because any of our people could and did move to other counties and the Indian kids attended public schools with the white kids. No problem. That knowledge became the reason John left home at age seventeen. He moved to Maryland. He quickly found work, but it was a daytime job. He sought a nighttime job because he wanted to further his education and at that time there was no school available except in the daytime. While he was working at ironing out those problems, he met a girl, fell madly in love, and got married. Now his responsibility of making a living multiplied and at such a young age. There was never a way clear for him to return to school. He did go into business for himself at age twenty-one, first in oil and then later into drilling wells for water. John became a very successful businessman.

My oldest brother's story is the saddest concerning the lack of an education. He was thirteen years old when Mr. Ell came into our lives. Big Brother refused to study along with John and me at our kitchen table with Mr. Ell as our teacher. Instead, Big Brother would shrug and say, "I'm too old and too big for that book stuff. I'm a man now. I work with my dad and my grandpa, cutting pulpwood."

Big Brother was a good boy. He reminded me so much of Grandpa Ramsey. He was of a gentle nature, very quiet, very polite. He was never rude to Mr. Ell. Mr. Ell was wise enough to understand that Big Brother was embarrassed at the very thought of studying from a primer book when he was old enough to have been in the sixth or seventh grade of school.

I shall never forget the new coat made for me by my mama and my aunt Orrie when I entered school at age ten. I don't remember what kind of material the coat was cut from, but the color was a sooty gray and I thought it was the ugliest coat I had ever seen. I would burst into tears every morning when my mama insisted I wear the coat because she was afraid I would catch my death of cold walking five miles to catch my ride.

I shall also never forget the most beautiful Sunday-go-to-meeting dress anybody could wish for that my mama made for me. The dress had a sky-blue background with little red and yellow flowers scattered around on the blue. How I loved that pretty dress. I wished I could wear it to school, but of course, I couldn't, because it was for Sunday-go-to-meeting. Always, as soon as we arrived home from church at St. Pauls, we had to undress and don our old, everyday clothing. I used to wish I was a rich white kid because they probably got to wear their Sunday's best all day.

I need to backtrack to tell you the origin of my beautiful blue dress. When our wheat was harvested and taken to the mill to be ground into flour, the resulting flour was then packed into floral printed cotton sacks at the mill. When Mama used the flour and emptied a sack, she saved it until she had enough to make our dresses, shirts, bedding, dish towels, and on and on. We were all very poor people because Indians were never hired for good-paying jobs. Those jobs were for white people only. We had to be a thrifty people out of necessity. Even our caps were made at home. The only things my people couldn't grow or make seemed to be shoes and sugar.

My mama was also a wonderful cook. I used to follow her around in the kitchen as a five-year-old, standing on tiptoe to peek into pots and mixing bowls and asking questions. When I was only seven years old, Mama began to have really severe headaches, often disabling her for periods of time. Then the all-but-constant headaches would cease and she would be free of the agonizing pain for periods of time. It seemed as though every time she became pregnant the headaches would attack her and she would be very ill until she either miscarried or the baby was born. By the time I was twelve years old, I often felt like I was the mother taking care of my dad and the other children and my frail mama, too. Poor Mama, she tried desperately to care for her family. It was not to be. When I was twenty-one years old, Mama began having blackout spells along with the headaches. We would send for the doctor over in Amherst, but by the time he would arrive she would be past the blackout stage, but not able to remember many things. Then she became ill with pneumonia and was in the Lynchburg Hospital for two weeks. Then the doctor said, "She is over the pneumonia, but I want to send her to the Charlottesville Hospital to see if they can find the cause of her headaches."

We didn't have any means of transportation to take Mama there, but my dad's employer, Bill Hodges, of High Peak Orchards, came to the hospital and took Mama to Charlottesville in his station wagon. The doctors there soon discovered Mama had had a brain tumor for many years and now it had become cancerous. One week later Mama went into a coma. She never regained consciousness, but she lived three more months at the hospital. Then on September 03, 1957, she was transferred to Staunton State Care Facility in Staunton, Virginia, and there she died on September 04, 1957. Monacan Indians don't usually say the person died, instead they say, "He or she walked." Therefore, I would say, "Mama walked."

Evidently, all those pregnancies and miscarriages had caused even more pressure on the tumor and in turn had caused those severe headaches through the years. Poor Mama had tried so hard to be there for us. Even when suffering she was a very sweet, loving person. I can never recall any instance in which she bad-mouthed anyone. She had always reminded me of Grandpa Ramsey, just as my

Big Brother had also. Grandpa Ramsey loved everyone. He loved life. These two elders left for us a kind and wonderful heritage.

My husband, Curtis, and I are very active in our local tribe. Getting everything ready for our annual Homecoming event and our annual powwow is time consuming, especially when we both work full-time jobs. A group of us are also putting together a Monacan cookbook. It's being funded by a Lynchburg Community Trust Grant. All proceeds from the cookbook sales will go to help fund the Monacan Food Bank for the needy.

Perhaps a good way to close this interview session is to share with you and your readers one of my favorite recipes. As you can see from the following measurements, this dish will feed an army. I don't think I'm going to include this one in our cookbook as it's such a long one. All you need to serve with it is a tossed salad, coffee and iced tea. You can rest assured no one will go away hungry, it's a gracious plenty.

Louise's Pizza Casserole
1 lb. wide egg noodles
1 lb. hot sausage
1 lb. hamburger
1 large onion, chopped
1 small green pepper, chopped
1 med. jar mushrooms, drained
1 (64 oz.) jar spaghetti sauce
2 (8 oz.) (2 cup size) packages Mozzarella cheese, shredded
1 large package pepperoni

Cook hamburger and sausage in heavy skillet over med. heat until crumbly and beginning to brown. Add the onion and green pepper. Cook until onions and green pepper are tender. Remove from heat and drain well. Cook noodles according to package directions. (Reserve pepperoni.) Have ready two (2 ½ qt. size) (Pam-sprayed) casserole dishes. Divide cooked noodles into the two casserole dishes. Pour the skillet mixture over noodles. Sprinkle Mozzarella cheese evenly over the mixture. Add mushrooms and spaghetti sauce. Top with pepperoni slices and bake in 325 degree oven for 15–20 minutes. Serve hot.

13
Eugene Branham

I'm Eugene Branham, but most people call me "Gene." I'm Lucian Branham's son. Lucian holds the title of being the oldest living Monacan in Amherst County now at eighty-seven years old in 1997.

Dad and I batch it and we have a good time. He does the gardening and I do the cooking and take care of the flower gardens. We share the household chores and we watch sports on television together. Dad's a big tease. He loves to pull tricks on me. I can discern his tricks, but sometimes I pretend he's got me fooled and does he enjoy thinking he's pulled one over on me. I don't mind. That's what keeps him so young at heart and his mind active with plots and puzzles.

I'm glad we own our own home now. Dad can sit on his front porch and watch his neighbors come and go when he's tired and needs to take a load off those big work boots he still likes to wear.

I remember how hard it was for my parents to eke out a scant living when my people were treated more like slaves.

Life's lessons haven't always been as easy as ABC for us in Amherst County. At one time it was more like XYZ. Sometimes we were called everything under the sun but Indian or child of God. As a child and early youth, there were times when I struck back with fists. It took some growing up to learn fighting wasn't the answer. I had to first learn to live my life and to be proud of who I am.

I recall the day I stopped at a local service station in the year 1989 and a man I knew walked up to me and said, "Hey, Gene, have you read this morning's newspaper?"

I answered, "Nope, there's no need to rush to read it that I know of. It's probably the same old bad news as written everyday. News reporters never seem to know any good news to print."

He answered, "True, but this morning it's a different story, especially for you.

It's an article about your people. The Virginia Legislature has finally recognized your people as Monacan Indians."

I said, "Gosh, are you kidding? My people have been around these parts since the 1700s and in Virginia before it was a state. Now the state legislature has finally recognized who we are. Thank God."

The man said, "Gene, I hope from here on life in this area will improve for your people."

"Thank you, sir. It means a lot that you've been there for me."

14
Herbert Hicks

I'm Herbert L. Hicks Jr. My paternal grandparents were Frank Hicks and Lizzie Johns Hicks, and my maternal grandparents were Ellis Branham and Hattie Johns Branham. My parents were Herbert L. Hicks and Amy Johns Hicks Faucett. My wife is Betty, daughter of the late chief Harry Branham and Hattie Branham. Betty and I have no children.

For centuries the title of chief was a title that was handed down from the former chief to one of his choosing. The last time this was to happen was when Chief Harry handed down the title to his grandson, Ronald Branham. Unfortunately, Ronnie began to have health problems and all the duties that go with being chief were too burdensome so Ronnie wanted to step aside. The acting committee decided to change the rules and to have a chief elected for the people, by the people. So Kenneth Branham became our first elected chief in 1995 and has been reelected by popular vote.

I was born in Amherst County on November 23, 1942. I left Amherst in 1961 and joined the Marine Corps. I served in the Marine Corps 22½ years. I then retired from the marines and became a PGA golf professional. I've worked as a pro for the past twelve years. That's why I came back to Amherst County. I've been involved in building a golf course here in a residential community.

I went to school at St. Pauls Mission through the seventh grade. The eighth grade wasn't added until years later. Our parents didn't talk about Dr. Plecker and his hatred of Indians in our presence, so we were not really aware of why the white people attended public school and we attended the mission school. I finally learned we could have gone to the school for blacks, but it was a substandard school. We refused to be black and we weren't allowed to be Indian or white. It's very difficult to be a non-people.

From the time the Europeans first came to America, they allowed greed to dominate them. They didn't want to share the land. They wanted all the land.

They firmly believed their customs were the only customs. It's human nature, really. I served in quite a few countries while I was in the marines and when we went into a country, we were supposed to be there as advisors. The more involved we became, however, and the longer we stayed, we would gradually begin to push our ways and our methods to the forefront. We would begin to promote our democratic government and our forms of worship.

I'm speaking of the American Caucasian way, of course. Then American government decided the best thing for Indians would be to put them all on reservations, which meant they crowded very large groups of people onto very small portions of rather worthless lands. The Indians were not allowed to attend government supported schools, and they were not hired for jobs in the mainstream of people. Thank God we Monacans were never forced onto a reservation. To take the right of land use from Indians is to break the hearts of Indians. Indians believe in nurturing the land, never taking more from the land than you are willing to give back to it. Take, for instance, these 118 acres we've bought back on Bear Mountain, land that once was ours until taken from us for taxes due, which our people couldn't pay on nearly slave wages. We are now told there is valuable timber on this acreage, and there are people wanting permission to come in and cut timber. Scalping acres of land of its trees has become a major concern with environmentalists all over America and justly so. Trees are very important to the land in many ways and also to our well-being. Wildlife in some forms is also dependent on forests.

You asked me about this fable of liquor being as fire water to Indians. Personally, I don't think so. I think some people have a low tolerance for alcohol, and I think that tendency can be handed down from a father or mother to an offspring, but not because of race. I've traveled much of this world and have been acquainted with people of many races. There are alcoholics among all races of people that I've encountered. I used to drink myself. When I drank, I didn't stop with one or two beers, no way. I drank twelve or thirteen. I quit drinking alcoholic beverages years ago. So, whether I choose to drink or choose not to drink has nothing to do with being Indian. Whether I can be a social drinker or a drunkard has nothing to do with being Indian. It's a matter of choice, a matter of strength of character or weakness of character, no matter what the race. You, the interviewer, mentioned there seemed to be a problem with alcoholism on reservations. That is caused by circumstances. It's all but impossible for a person to be productive in any vocation that is profitable and geared to raise their standard of living while confined to a reservation. Whenever people are not productive, they tend to lose their sense of self-worth, and in so doing, they may use alcohol as a means of escape from real life. Becoming blotto drunk only causes more problems, so the person gets drunk again to blot out those problems and yet again and again. It becomes a vicious cycle for any person of any race at any age.

You also asked about the games we played. I think Indian children played the ordinary games other American children played. Roy and I did have one game all our own, but that was just because we were Roy and I. This particular game sticks out in my memory because Roy and I invented it. It started with a baby carriage sent to our mother from her sister in Maryland. It was a big thing with black leather covering and rubber wheels. When it became dilapidated, my mother discarded it and Roy and I confiscated it. We took the body parts off that thing and left the frame, the rubber wheels and the hand brake on the side. We would take our newly invented race cart high up on the hill above the lake where we would take turns careening down the hill. We learned to be rather skillful applying the brake just before busting that lake wide open. As we skidded to a stop, we would raise our hands in a victory sign and let out a reboant yell. Sometimes we did crash into the lake, but we don't talk about those times.

Roy and I weren't much into games. We mostly fished in the lake, hunted squirrels and rabbits, or just sat and talked for our leisure pursuits. We had very little time for leisure anyway.

One of the most touching moments in my life didn't come about until 1989. Betty and I were living in North Carolina when we received the notice of our state recognition as a nation of Monacan Indians. Betty and I drove to Richmond, Virginia, to attend the ceremony. The state of Virginia gave official recognition that the Monacans are an entity. In essence, they said, "Yes, you are a people that have been here all the time. Yes, you are a tribe, a nation. Yes, you are a people in your own right."

That was the most heartfelt moment I have ever felt in my life. We were not the first tribe to receive state recognition. The state of Virginia had already recognized some tribes in the coastal area. At last, after centuries of denial, Virginia's Legislative Assembly decreed Virginia does have a tribe of Monacan Indians in western Virginia.

"Yes," I cried. The hot tears on my weathered face were not tears of weakness. They were tears of healing, of a man's pride, his joy and relief for the young Monacans of today and for those yet to be born.

Karenne Wood
and Diane Shields

I am Karenne Wood of Monacan descent. I live in Fredericksburg, Virginia. I commute back and forth to Madison Heights, Virginia. I work at our tribal office doing research and compiling records as we work toward obtaining our long-overdue federal recognition.

There have been some books written about the Indians of Virginia including the Monacan history, but those books haven't detailed all of the contacts that were made by the English explorers. What we are told by government officials is that we must go back to sustained contacts, which means more than just a few explorers' records. There were Monacans in this area around 1750 and we have to show historically and genealogically that our people were here at the time the white people came on the scene.

We're finding a lot of interesting material. We've gotten a lot of written reports by the early explorers who came here even before 1750. Then, beginning with the Lynchburg history, we've found reports by European settlers themselves that the Monacans were here at the time they, themselves, arrived. We are in the process of trying to trace the Branhams and the Johns back to that time with documented evidence.

One interesting discovery we've made that helps us prove we are who we say we are as a distinct race was found in some written materials from the 1920s to the 1940s. Those records state that during those years, whites, blacks, and Indians all worked in the orchards together. At noon there had to be separate tables set up for what was then called dinner time. There were three separate tables because the three separate races refused to eat together. Working together could be tolerated because that was a time of labor, but eating together was a time of socializing and that was a no, no.

Since Diane Shields and I are being interviewed together, there may seem to be breaks in the subjects being discussed. I'm going to comment on the Anglo-Saxon group and their ideology of a pure white race. There has never been such

12. *From left,* Bertie Branham, Judy Branham, Diane Shields, Hattie Belle Hamilton, and Karenne Wood, March 15, 1997. Taken during the Third Annual Governor's Conference, Washington, D.C., where these delegates appeared on behalf of Monacan recognition.

a race since Adam and Eve. Then Adam and Eve succumbed to Satan's wiles, and they had children and the children scattered and married and so it goes. The English mixed with the Moors and with people who filtered into the Mediterranean from Turkey and other surrounding lands. So much for a pure race.

Another important point that needs discussing is that in the beginning Indians had laws that they must marry within their own tribes in order to keep their race pure. Over a long period of time they discovered this was not sound reasoning. They were becoming so inbred they were actually weakening within their own race. They changed the laws so as to allow intermarrying with other tribes. Over a period of time they discovered that method didn't work either. In states like Virginia with only a few small tribes they were still running into the strong possibility of kin marrying kin. It was totally inevitable, as also the Anglo-Saxon group's idealistic, irrational dream of a pure white race.

There are eight Indian tribes in Virginia that have finally been granted state recognition. State recognition of a tribe is by proof a particular group of people has existed a minimum of two hundred years. We were able to establish that through our lineage records.

13. *From left,* Jean Branham, unknown, Jo Ann Staubitz. Displayed are baskets of oak strips, honeysuckle, and pine straw made by Jo Ann Staubitz.

Some Monacans used to find fault with those Monacans who moved away from Amherst, but now as some of our people are moving back into the area and others whose businesses keep them away do come back for the Homecoming Bazaars and the powwows, we shouldn't find fault either way. Those who have stayed here in spite of the prejudice and oppression because this was their home and their heritage, and those who went away, together these two groups have something to contribute to make a whole.

George Whitewolf came back and taught us how to organize powwows. He taught us that other tribes in other states were willing to advise and commiserate. George, along with Danny Gear, brought the drum and the music. Danny also brought a section of the Tutelo language, learned in Pennsylvania, that he was prepared to teach to us. Yes, those who went away brought back learned minds because they had the opportunity for higher education that had not been available here. They brought knowledge of a much larger world than these here had ever experienced. Those experiences helped the people here to regain their self-esteem, to reach out for their self-worth, and those here helped those who went away to learn endurance and to have faith in our Creator. Together. That's what it's all about, learning something about the old customs while living for today and preparing for and anticipating tomorrow.

I am Diane Johns Shields. I work at the Monacan Tribal Office as community service associate.

Karenne and I have been deeply involved in researching our heritage. According to our research findings my understanding of the Racial Integrity Act of 1924 is that only those people having one-sixteenth or less of Indian blood and no other bloods except Caucasian could be designated and recognized officially as white people. All other people not being officially white/Caucasian were to be recognized as colored.

The Anglo-Saxon group had this vainglorious vision of bringing into being an all-powerful, totally pure, white race. This totally pure white race would evolve and then they would erase all other quite inferior (to-their-way-of-thinking) people. These pure-blooded people would be invincible and inhabit all the earth. This theory was so utterly preposterous. To my understanding, Dr. W. A. Plecker was very instrumental in helping get the Racial Integrity Act passed into law.

Dr. Plecker extolled the merits of a study conducted at Sweet Briar College in Amherst County. The study resulted in the publishing of a book titled *Mongrel Virginians,* written by Arthur Estabrook and Ivan McDougle (1926). Estabrook and McDougle called their study a scientific research study. It was not that at all. They stated in their treatise, the Monacan Tribes' origin was Cherokee, which is without fact. In his book, Dr. Peter Houck (1993) states that Estabrook and McDougle made this assertion despite the fact that Indian scholar James Mooney had previously written an extensive piece on the Siouan Tribe of the East. There are other erroneous statements in the Estabrook and McDougle book. It is not a treatise that is respected by other, more reliable researchers. These two writers closed their minds to the fact that Indians were not allowed to marry in Amherst County except as Negroes, which they were not. They weren't allowed jobs except in the fields and orchards for extremely low wages. A marriage bond was $150.00 at that time. It wasn't just the Indians, other poor people also could not afford a marriage bond. Therefore, some of them just lived as married without benefit of a legal marriage certificate. Yet Estabrook and McDougle write as though only the Monacan Indians were immoral if they failed to marry because of the cost of the marriage bond. One can easily determine the cold, closed mind sets of these two men.

A Note from the Interviewer

Ivan McDougle visited some of the Monacans in their small, dilapidated homes. But even seeing, he did not see. He viewed their overcrowded, unpainted homes. He looked at their deeply tanned skin, made much darker and roughened by sunup to sundown days and years in the orchards. He looked at their children, home on school days, and blinded his mind to their plight of not being allowed in public schools. Then he attempted to write about these people with the help of Estabrook from Carnegie Institute in Washington. In essence, both of these men were as from another world, a world of bias and pride, a cocooned, learned world of book knowledge. They were ignorant of life and poor people and circumstances outside their own quiet, comfortable, narrow circle.

When knowledge comes from an educated mind and wisdom and understanding come from a warm heart, therein is a person who is authentically learned. When knowledge comes from an educated mind and pride and prejudice come from a cold heart, leaving no room for wisdom and understanding, therein is a person who is an educated fool and their writings are but foolishness.

16
Sharon Bryant

I am Sharon Bryant and my father was Jesse James Bryant. My mother is Mary Frances Branham Bryant. My grandparents were Harry and Edith Johns Branham. My other grandmother was Kate Johns.

Grandpa Harry was the unofficial Monacan chief until he voluntarily gave it up when he became very aged. Harry's grandson, and my first cousin, Ronnie Branham, became our first officially elected chief by vote of our people in 1989. Then Ronnie resigned in, I believe it was 1996, and Kenneth Branham became our elected chief.

I helped organize a video of our people. Chief Kenneth Branham, Gary Verril, head of the Focal Life program, Rob Vaughn, the director of Virginia Life Foundation, along with Professor Helen Rountree from Norfolk, Virginia, and also J. David Smith, professor and author, have been an invaluable help and support group with their guidance and encouragement in the making of the video documentary *Reclaiming Our Heritage.* They also helped us receive some grants for the project.

I believed it was my duty to read every written word I could find about the Monacan Indians while working on the video. I gathered materials and I sat in a motel room in Charlottesville, Virginia, day after day while reading, *Mongrel Virginians* by Arthur Estabrook and Ivan McDougle. I read *The Travels of John Smith.* I read also *Indian Island* by Dr. Peter Houck and I read *Backward Virginians,* a thesis written by Bertha Pfister Wailes. I read every article I could find in the University of Virginia Library. *Indian Island* and J. David Smith's research were by far the most helpful.

Dr. Jeff L. Hantman, the Monacan historian, is a professor of Anthropology and Archaeology at UVA. He teaches about Monacan history and culture. He sometimes gets rather emotional when he talks of the abuse by Europeans of the

Monacans and about us being a denied and forgotten race. He sometimes speaks of Chief Amorolek and how, so long ago, John Smith asked Amorolek why Amorolek's people were shooting arrows at John Smith and his party when Smith and his party had come in peace. Amorolek answered John Smith, "We have heard that your people came from under this world to take our world from us."

Doing research among my own people was difficult. Many of my people didn't want to reminisce about that dark period of time in Amherst County, Virginia. The elders said, "Those years are best forgotten. Leave the past in the past."

There were younger people who asked, "Sharon, why did you interview mostly the Branhams?" I broke into laughter as I answered, "Most of the Johns and Hicks and Willis women seemed to have married Branham men, so now there are many more Branhams around these parts."

I well remember my grandmother, Kate Johns, telling me when I was a little girl, "You are Monacan Indian, but you must never tell anyone that."

Grandma would whisper that tidbit in my ear as though the wrong person might hear. Most of the Monacans reasoned thus and so. "If you don't look Indian, just don't talk about it, then white people can't hurt you with words or actions."

The Indians that left here to make a better life for their children elsewhere didn't even look back. For instance, George Branham (Whitewolf) grew up in Maryland. He told me his daddy always told George, "Don't go searching for your history in Amherst County. There is nothing there for you."

Many others who have returned searching for their roots since Dr. Houck published *Indian Island* will tell you they had not a damned clue that Indians were treated like non-people in Amherst County because of Dr. W. A. Plecker and his poisonous pen and tongue.

It's difficult to understand how a community of Monacan Indians could have been made to feel guilty, to feel ashamed of their birth origins, as though anyone has control over whether they are born Indian, Caucasian, African American, Jew, or Gentile.

I was only seven years old the first time I remember running into the prejudice of white people against Indians, not that I understood then that it was born of learned prejudice. I was walking on my way to school when a little white girl passed by, looked back at me, and called me "issue."

I wasn't sure what that word meant, but I knew from the tone of her voice and her facial expression she hadn't meant it as a compliment. I hauled off and hit her right across her mouth.

After we were finally allowed to attend public schools in Amherst County, I knew that sometimes in small groups of white children, the word "issue" was sometimes whispered, but they dispersed if they spied me approaching. The word had spread that I would fight about that word.

What happened at the high school in Amherst in the year 1963 was really a hoot. The public schools now had to accept students from races other than Caucasian. There wasn't any major trouble in elementary schools, but the high school students turned volatile over this desegregation issue. They fought—the black and the whites; they blackened each others' eyes and threw each other in the campus trash cans; they screamed insults at one another. Then it would become really strange when the dismissal bell rang. According to my relatives who attended high school, the whites would line up on one side of the hallway and the blacks would line up on the opposite side of the hallway. Then the Indians would walk down the center of the hall undisputed except for calls from both sides to come over to their side. That in itself was a riot! Both sides reasoned if they could persuade the Indians to side with one or the other, then that side could win any battle because Indians were known for their strength. The strategy didn't work for either side. Indians had had to fight their battles alone for generations upon generations because of race. They wanted no part of rejecting any race. In today's lingo, they had been there, they had not done that, but they had had that done to them and they longed for the American flag to fly in true meaning of freedom for all Americans.

A school counselor once told me I laughed too much, that being Indian I laughed as a way of hiding pain. I answered her, "Mrs. Smith, my people have been oppressed and called everything others could think up except Indian. For hundreds of years we were denied an education to equip us for decent jobs with living wages or careers. My people have never been allowed the privilege of hiding pain. Lots of people have gone the extra mile to make sure our pain was public. In our own humble dwellings, though, where white people shy away from visiting us, my people are loving, sharing, giving people. There you will hear more laughter than you would on a canned comedy reel, the difference being our laughter is for real and free. My people believe crying brings on headaches and puffy eyes, but laughter feeds the soul.

"I think God laughs a little with us. He doesn't want us to take ourselves too seriously, nor this world either. He does want us to seek His ways. In so doing, we'll find some joy in this world too. God's world isn't bad, but we'll find a percentage of bad people in His good world. So you see, Mrs. Smith, when I laugh, and often I do laugh, I'm not hiding pain. I'm finding joy."

I've traveled to at least half our states in America and I've been out of the country to Jamaica, but when I return to these Blue Ridge Mountains and arrive on Bear Mountain, I know I have arrived home. I believe Bear Mountain itself is a sixty-mile radius, a very small mountain. I was born here. Despite anything that has happened to me or my people, this is my home, my roots.

To go back to my youth, there was one white girl who dared to be friends with me openly. Her parents, too, were polite to me. I was allowed to spend the night at their home on weekends, although she couldn't come home with me. That could have been because of the overcrowded conditions in my home. We were very poor. We lived in a three-room house. The kitchen and so-called living room were on the ground floor and there was one large bedroom upstairs. All of us slept upstairs. There were eight of us. My grandpa and youngest brother slept in one double-sized bed. My mama and oldest sister slept in the other double bed. My sister, near my age, and I shared one single bed. My big brother slept in one single bed and my grandma slept in the last single bed. We had a routine worked out. The females donned their long gowns first, then we filed out and back downstairs while the males went upstairs and donned their sleepwear. Then they let out an all-clear yell and we females filed back upstairs. We repeated this same order in reverse in the early mornings. The men filed out and waited downstairs until the females dressed and descended, then the males went back up and got dressed. The reason for the reversal of female-male, male-female was because the womenfolk had to have breakfast cooked and ready by the time the men descended and washed their hands and faces and combed their hair.

I never knew that all people didn't share beds with others until I was in high school and spent the night with my white friend.

Our grandma Edy ran our household like she was a military sergeant. She worked very hard from sunup to sundown, cleaning, cooking, and canning. She also worked in the fields shoulder to shoulder alongside the men. Yet she found time to raise a houseful of youngsters of all ages. Mama helped, but Grandma Edy ruled the roost.

Grandma Edy said children were to be seen but not heard. Of course, that was the way most mountain folks believed. We were never allowed to discuss the things of this world we wondered about. We were never allowed to voice our opinions about any grown-ups' way of thinking.

If we attempted to cross those boundaries we were told to, "Get on with your chores. Fill the water buckets. Chop that wood. Feed the hogs. Work will solve all your problems."

Grandma Edy also taught us to mind our manners. She said we weren't to be angry with anyone, not even with each other. If we began to fuss and shout at one another she put a quick stop to it. Poof! Out came the razor strop. The matter of who was right or wrong didn't enter into it.

The problem with that reasoning was that it never provided us with any outlet for our anger or frustrations. That meant we had to devise our own solution, which we did. We waited until we got a chance to sneak out behind the barn and there we slugged it out with one another. Grandma Edy tried to teach us, too, to always treat others with respect and kindness. She said that in so doing, others would always reciprocate. In a pig's eye! I went out to the public schools and into the larger world of Amherst County, which had been profoundly affected by Dr. W. A. Plecker's hate of Indians. I found that what Grandma Edy had taught us was darned sure not true in this larger world. This bigger world outside our tiny Indian community provided us by the Episcopalian diocese was a world more like "Go out behind the barn and slug it out and don't pull your punches because these ain't your brothers and sisters."

I still have to pray for God's mercy, hoping He will do for me what I haven't been able to do for myself and take away my anger against Dr. W. A. Plecker (Old Plecker). He's dead now and I still despise him. I even think the manner of his death was rather fitting. He was holding his head arrogantly high as he was in the habit of doing. He stepped out into oncoming traffic as though asserting he had the right of way. He was run over like a dog, struck down by a bus that was too close to stop.

I really do try not to hate Plecker because no one deserves to be hated the way he hated Indians. I feel sure I'm not even capable of the kind of hate Dr. W. A. Plecker had for all people who were not white. In our small community, the Episcopalian ministry and our parents had tried to create the kind of life for our youth we were barred from otherwise. Our spiritual and social life centered around St. Pauls Church and its Parish Hall.

Every Saturday the rector, John Haraughty, would drive that ancient yellow school bus the Episcopalian diocese had purchased from the school district when the school district had replaced it with a new bus. He would drive it up and down the narrow (mostly dirt), curvy roads and pick up all the Monacan youth.

On the way back to Parish Hall, Papa John as we called him, would zig and zag that old bus around those hairpin curves with a bunch of crazy teenagers singing at the top of their lungs, playing instruments, walking in the bus aisles, and jumping from seat to seat, and he did it in all kinds of weather like there was no tomorrow. Papa John wanted us to have that one day a week, just having fun with all worries and cares laid aside.

None of us knew the first thing about learned music or singing, having no opportunity to take music or singing lessons, but we could bang on instruments and sing real loud from the hymn book and call it choir practice.

While we were enjoying ourselves singing at the top of our lungs, Papa John was busy in the kitchen cooking a pot of chili beans. Around five o'clock in the evening, we would eat to our fill and then we'd help Papa John clean up the dining hall and kitchen. We would shove the tables and chairs to one side of the room to clear the floor for dancing. He would let us turn the lights down low (our parents would have freaked out). There was no need for worry, though. Papa John and his wife, Katherine, kept a sharp eye on us.

Papa John also wanted us to have an opportunity to learn to swim. He arranged with the Catholic school authorities that we could swim in their pool. Where the Job Corps is now on Father Judge Road, there used to be a seminary for Catholic boys. The Catholic priests thought having us girls come over once a week to swim could be a good training tool to help toughen up these boys in resisting the tempting charms of pretty girls, since these boys would be entering a life of celibacy. We couldn't resist teasing these boys and sometimes a few of them would sneak away from the school grounds to walk us home. It was a good time for all of us. They were good Christian boys. We loved all of them, the boys and the priests. The priests walked around all the time in those long black robes with the high white collars. I remember one priest in particular. He was Father Joseph and he was as old as dirt. He smiled all the time and he always had a joke to tell us. I don't remember the exact jokes, but this one is along the same gist of those he told us.

The parents of a drifting son made and kept an appointment with a soothsayer. They told him of their worry that their only son was nearing the close of his first year of college, but they said the son didn't seem to have a handle on what he wanted to study so as to prepare himself for a profession. The soothsayer sat with his fingers intertwined as he listened to these two intensely focused people, in dead-end professions as law clerks in a law firm for three aged attorneys.

The soothsayer said, "This may take several experiments, but we'll begin with an experiment that may give us a clue as to your son's interest. I want you to go home and on a table in his room, I want you to place a bottle of wine, a hundred-dollar bill, and a Catholic Bible. Then I want you to hide in his closet with the door slightly ajar and watch to see how he reacts, what draws his interest when he enters his room and sees the objects."

The son soon came home. He entered his room swinging a golf club and whistling a gay tune. He stopped quickly when he spied the objects on the table. He picked up the wine bottle, uncorked it, took a sniff, then a swig. He then recapped the bottle and tucked it under his arm. Next, he picked up the hundred-dollar bill, held it up to the light, folded it, and shoved it deep into his pant pocket. He looked at the Bible, opened it, and seemed to read a few words. He closed it and, tucking it under his other arm, resumed whistling a gay tune and left the room.

The boy's parents ran from his room, down the stairs, out the back door, went to their car, and sped back to the soothsayer's office demanding an audience with him at once. They told him of their son's reaction to the experiment. The mother sobbed, the dad cursed, and they both blamed the soothsayer. He looked at them and grinned as he said, "This experiment was a smashing success. You now know what your son's profession will be."

They looked at him in amazement and said, "This experiment told us nothing. He drank some of the wine, glanced at a passage in the Bible, pocketed the money, and left the room whistling a catchy tune."

The soothsayer grinned as he answered, "Your son is going to be a politician."

Ah yes, we enjoyed our time spent at the Catholic school that summer. The priests were interested in learning more about our people and ways, too, so it was a learning time for them as well as for us. One question asked by several priests is this: "Are there medicine men in your tribe?"

I've never known any medicine men. My great-grandmother, Kate Johns, was a midwife and she delivered over five hundred babies in her time. She also doctored us with homemade remedies and wild-growing herbs, greens, and berries. For a spring tonic, she pried our mouths open and promptly shoveled in a big spoonful of a mixture of castor oil and turpentine. I couldn't make myself swallow that concoction and I would run outside and spit it out. I always got a spanking, too, but the spanking was easier to bear than the spring tonic was to swallow.

There was also the famous poultice made with flour and mustard and wrapped in a square of flannel cloth and slapped on many an Indian's chest to cure a chest cold.

Then there was the inevitable pokeweed used for purgative purposes. I'll not live long enough to forget that concoction. Our mothers boiled the poke just a touch. Then the water was squeezed out and the poke was mixed with eggs and onions and fried in side meat drippings in an iron skillet. Now my great-granny, Kate Johns, made sure we ate a good-sized helping of that spring tonic. She called it cleaning out our systems and damned if it didn't do just that.

Granny Kate also made a tea using the roots of wild blackberry vines.

There used to be an abundance of ginseng growing wild on the mountains. Ginseng sells for a high price today. Customers will pay as much as one hundred dollars for one pound of fresh ginseng. We Monacans don't gather it to sell. We gather it for our use. It's not really used for medicinal purposes, but it is a good health food.

Let's talk about some really good eating. I can feel the stirrings of hunger pangs just thinking about wild mushrooms. These mushrooms grow on the north side of fallen poplar trees. They look like toad stools. They are very white and firm to the touch. To prepare the mushrooms, first wash them in cool water, then slice them. Dip the slices in an egg batter and fry in side meat drippings. Ahh, they are good and tasty.

Then there is another kind of mushroom that grows up in a day's time following a rain. The orchards are a good place to search for this type of mushroom. They look like chicken legs. Some people refer to these mushrooms as dry-land fish. They're considered a delicacy when dipped and fried.

Something else we never tire of is preserves made of wild strawberries. They are popular with visitors, too. Curtis and Louise Branham have made these preserves their specialty. Curtis practically stands on his head by the hour gathering the tiny red berries. Then Louise spends many hours making the preserves from her own special recipe. She cans them in pint jars and these beautiful preserves sell out quickly at the Homecoming Bazaar the first Saturday of every October.

In the late summer months, we also gather chinquapins. We jokingly call the nuts "hickory chicks." The nuts are encased in a porcupine-like shell. The shells are prickly and painful to one's fingers until one acquires a skill in opening the shells. The nuts are worth the effort.

When we receive much of our nourishment from the nature foods God has provided, it behooves us to learn what is edible for human beings and what is not. One can easily be poisoned if one isn't knowledgeable. We remember that it was our Indian ancestors who taught the first settlers who came from foreign lands what was edible and safe for food and what was not.

Speaking of wild things, some of my people had some rather wild superstitions in years past. I'll share a few with you.

There was a Pentecostal preacher on the traveling circuit that came to this area from time to time. He told my people they must never use scissors on Sunday. The preacher never explained why. My people took it for granted that since he was a man of the cloth, he must know a good reason for the admonition.

My people also believed one must never enter anyone's home by one door and exit by a different door; the reasoning being that if one exited by a door other than the door entered, that person would never return.

And never set a rocking chair into motion when no one is seated in the rocker. That is an omen that someone will soon die.

I remember another fabrication that wasn't a superstition, but just as mythical. Vernon Branham wore a wooden box on his left foot. The adults told us kids Vernon's foot box was full of worms that could get on us if we misbehaved. All of us kids were scared out of our skulls and we would run like wild rabbits whenever we saw Vernon stumping along toward us. Vernon lived to be one hundred years old, so he had time to scare many, many kids. As for me and my friends, we were grown up before we found out the truth about the scary box. Vernon's left foot was a clubfoot and shoes wouldn't fit on the misshapened foot. In those days there were no doctors in Amherst County who had any knowledge about ordering special shoes and our people couldn't have afforded to buy such a shoe anyway.

There was also my great uncle Nick Johns, my grandma Edy's brother. Uncle Nick had a gift called the third sight. He told me he could read a person's palm. He told my grandma Edy in confidence that what he really did was to look intensely into a person's eyes and it was as though he could see forever. When I was a child Uncle Nick fascinated me. I'd pester him unmercifully to read my fortune. One day he grew so aggravated with my pestering, he grabbed hold of my hand. Then he spit tobacco juice onto my palm. He stared at my palm for what seemed like a mighty long time. Then he said, "You will write songs, but you'll need help from someone else." I was ecstatic. It is odd that since I grew up I do write lyrics and sing. But Shane Branham puts my lyrics to music and plays guitar when I sing.

Uncle Nick looked into my brother Jeff's eyes one day and my mother said tears formed in Uncle Nick's eyes. He turned away from Jeff and walked outside. That night he told my mother that he could see Jeff's future when he had looked into Jeff's eyes. He said Jeff would have a hard row to hoe in the future and that most of Jeff's troubles and trials Jeff would bring upon himself because of his hard-headed ways.

I love my brother Jeff, but Uncle Nick proved to be correct. By the time Jeff became a teenager, he became a redneck from hell. He stays in trouble he brings upon himself by rebelling against man-made laws and rules. He insists on being his own man, right or wrong.

There was once a mountain woman among our ancestors named Cal Hicks. She claimed to have spellbinding power. She became known as the Conjure Lady. When I met her, she was already as old as the biblical Melchizedek. He was known as ageless. Cal Hicks had the power to remove warts and did so for a fee. As a kid I used to pray God would give me warts so she could perform her magic on me. God never saw fit to so indulge me. I've never had a wart in my whole life.

The grownups were most impressed with Cal's mystical powers to save a troubled woman's marriage. Cal would whisper to the young woman that to change the wandering husband's habits she must make a conjure ball and hide it in a safe place. If the young woman said she didn't know how to make a conjure ball, Cal would whisper the secret recipe in her ear. She whispered, "Take a clipping of his hair and a clipping of his toenails. Roll those two items together to form a tight ball. Then take this conjure ball and hide it under the front steps and keep the hiding a deep, dark secret from everyone. As long as that conjure ball is hidden, your man will never wander from home."

The young woman would ask, "Why will some of his hair and toenails keep him from following his roving eye over the hill to some filly's cabin?"

Cal Hicks said, "Because as long as some of his hair and toenails are buried on this spot and he can't find them, he can't leave. He is rooted to this spot, head and toes."

That's the magic of the conjure ball in case anyone hasn't guessed it. The word is "rooted."

Brenda Branham Garrison

My name is Brenda Branham Garrison. My late father was Jessie James Bryant. My mother is Mary Frances Branham Bryant. My grandparents were Harry Branham and Edith Johns Branham. My great-grandmother was Kate Johns. She broke her hip when I was eight or nine years old and she didn't live long after that.

My husband is Ben Garrison. He is not Monacan Indian. I have three step-children and two step-grandchildren.

I'm a registered nurse. I now work in Lynchburg, Virginia, at Central General Training Center. I've worked there eighteen years. I attended school at the St. Pauls Mission School in the first grade. Our little mission school didn't have school buses. I lived with my parents on Kenmore Road, which is the road the mission is on. It's a long, long road and I lived at the further end from the mission, so, of course, the distance was too great for a first grader to walk to the mission school.

My schoolteacher, Mrs. Davis, felt sorry for my plight and as she drove in from Amherst, she would stop at my house and let me ride with her to the mission. Then she would drop me off at my house on her way home. I shall never forget her kindness and concern.

Attending school at St. Pauls Mission really isn't a fond memory for me. That little two-room schoolhouse housed seven grade levels. Mrs. Davis taught first, second, third, and fourth grades simultaneously in one room, while at the same time the other teacher, Mrs. Paul Orphen, taught fifth, sixth, and seventh grades in the other room. It made for a very confusing learning experience.

By the time I entered the second grade in the autumn of 1963, the Racial Integrity Law had been declared unconstitutional. In fact, the Racial Integrity Act had been declared unconstitutional in 1954, but it had taken until this year of

1963 for the public schools in Amherst County as well as some other counties, for the public schools to conform to lawful desegregation.

To my surprise, when I entered second grade in the public school, I discovered Mrs. Davis had somehow managed to teach me well in that crowded, noisy room housing four grade levels, because I could easily work on the level the other public school students at this previously all-white school enjoyed. Again, I had much to thank Mrs. Davis for.

The school bus driver was very obstinate, refusing to obey the court mandate to pick up the Indian children along with the white kids. For the next two years our parents pooled the cost of having a taxi cab take us to and from school. The following year, that bus driver lost his job and another man was hired in his place. The next four weeks, this new driver picked us up and brought us home. Then the weirdest thing happened. After we were seated on the school bus one afternoon, the bus driver got up from his seat and said, "Beginning in the morning, I will not stop the bus to pick up any issues."

We thought he must be kidding, but sure enough, the next morning he passed by all the Indian students. Our parents had to call a taxi to get us to school.

That afternoon by mutual agreement, we all boarded the bus. When the driver started yelling for us to get off the bus, we started yelling right back, "This is our bus, too, and we will stay on this bus until you decide to take us home. In the morning our parents will be standing with us along the road and in the road if necessary until you decide to pick us up."

The white children started yelling, too. "Let them ride, let them ride."

I remember two other occasions when the name calling ruined my day. One of those instances was on Students' Day at the county fair. My cousin and I were riding the merry-go-round when a few boys, also riding, started yelling: "Get off you issues, issues; mixed, whatever you are, get off."

The name calling by those boys turned what had been a fun day into a miserable day.

The other occasion that sticks in the recess of my memory was during a recess at school. We were playing, running, jumping, and dodging one another up and down the steps and across the walkway, playing chase me and catch me if you can. All of a sudden as I was racing along the walkway, a boy grabbed me by the arm and said, "I got you, issue."

This particular boy was from a prominent family in Amherst and he was quite handsome. Those thoughts flitted through my mind as I looked up at him and burst into tears. The boy quickly let go of my arm and I made a dash inside to the restroom. I bathed my tear-drenched face in cleansing water. I was quiet and composed when I entered my classroom. I didn't report the incident to my teacher. I hid the hurt in my heart.

From that day forward until we graduated from high school, that boy went out of his way to be polite to me. I guess that was his way of saying he was sorry. He went away to college after high school and he must have settled away from Amherst because I never saw him again.

You know, I pondered those incidents in my heart that following summer and gave up on reaching a conclusion. On each of these three incidents, it was a boy that seemed so biased. Were girls more tolerant of differences in people or were they less brazen in those days in voicing their opinions? Some questions have no easy answers. Oh, I knew there was a lot of prejudice among both men and women against Indians in Amherst County, but it seemed to be less in degree than in former periods of time. I know I had learned to forgive some prejudiced people in the area for being white and I hoped those who were prejudiced against us would learn to forgive us for being Indian.

I realize I have wandered away from my childhood years during this interview, but there's nothing wrong in retracing my steps, so let's step back in time, so to speak.

There seemed to be a tacit agreement among our elders that to talk about being Indian was a taboo subject. We were expected to talk, dress, and act like white folks in a predominantly white world. We lost our Siouan language because of it and are now trying to learn it anew. I'm really glad it's different now. We are free to research the ancient ways of dress and worship, of crafts and manner of living in the olden days. We can openly teach our heritage as a true part of American history. We now have the right to be proud of who we are alongside all other races. We can say, "Yes, we are Indian, we reside in Amherst County. This is our home."

Time spent at school gradually became enjoyable and that first year in public school, I soon began to have friends among the white children. In high school I had some really neat friends. In particular, there was Laura, Jane, and Lloyd—white kids from Amherst. We exchanged school pictures, Christmas gifts, and talked on the phone and all that stuff teenagers do.

During those growing-up years my mother worked in a shoe factory: Craddock Terry. She left each workday at 5:00 A.M. and returned at 7:00 P.M. We lived with our grandparents, Harry and Edith Branham, and they helped raise us kids.

I think you have interviewed others about our activities and so forth, so I'll just mention a few that were especially meaningful to me. Sunday dinner was special to me. Fried chicken on Sunday was a given. Vegetables were fresh from the garden in summertime. Vegetables were canned in mason jars in summer to eat in wintertime. Fresh fruits or canned fruits were also plentiful. The staple food in winter was generally a huge pot of homemade vegetable soup or chili beans and cornbread. We ate lots of macaroni year 'round. Most people prepare macaroni with cheese. We would have had to buy the cheese at Crawford's Store, which we couldn't afford. But we had lots of fresh, churned butter, so my mother and grandmother cooked macaroni with lots of butter. To this day I still love buttery macaroni. We never had dessert on weekdays. That was a special treat for Sunday. The cake was always a yellow cake served with strawberry jell-o.

Before and after Sunday's midday meal, there was playtime for the menfolk and us children. That playtime took some ingenuity on the children's part. We couldn't play in the front yard because tables had been set up there. We couldn't play in the left side yard because all the men gathered there to play horseshoes and the Indian card game, 100 Pedro [see interviewer's note at the end of this chapter]. That left us with the right side yard which had a shallow creek running parallel with the narrow yard on this side. On the far side of the creek there was a one-acre potato field. We loved to play ball after the potato crop was harvested, so we set up the craziest ball field one could ever imagine. The batter's portion of the field was in the side yard and the outfield was across the creek in the potato field. Did you ever try tagging a runner out before he ran into the creek?

During those many years when we were banished from the activities of the white folks, St. Pauls Mission Church tried very hard to be there for us with many activities. The ladies got together for spaghetti suppers and quilting and Papa John and Katherine chaperoned dances for the youth in Parish Hall. Once in a while, Papa John would pick us up in that old yellow school bus and take us to the drive-in theater. I remember seeing the movie *The Bible* and also *The Sound of Music*.

All of us sang in the youth choir whether we could sing or not.

Despite the long, weary hours of slaving in jobs for menial wages and quilting, canning, basket weaving, sewing, and striving to care for their families; these weary bodies and hurting souls of the Monacan Indians found their way to St. Pauls Mission Church for succor and joy.

While I was still in high school I knew I wanted to become a nurse so I studied and strove for good grades, especially in chemistry.

Our priest, Papa John, knew of my longing. He also knew my parents couldn't afford to send me to nursing school. Papa John continued to encourage me by saying, "Where there's a will, there will be a way."

During my senior year of high school, Papa John made arrangements for me to take some tests at Virginia Baptist Hospital in Lynchburg, Virginia.

The test day dawned—would you believe that was the day Papa John's car broke down? I was trying not to cry when I heard that big old yellow school bus come roaring up to my house with Papa John at the wheel. He motioned for me to climb aboard because he was determined to get me to Lynchburg for those tests. I laughed and cried at the same time.

Oh, I was so embarrassed when we pulled into the parking lot at the hospital. He sat in that old bus and studied his Sunday sermon while I took the tests and filled out all the necessary papers. When I finished, I went out and climbed back into that faithful old bus. Papa John handed me a wrapped sandwich, a cookie, and a thermos of hot tea. He had a similar package that Katherine had packed for us.

My folks and Papa John and Katherine rejoiced with me when I received notice I had passed all the tests and was accepted for the fall term.

Nursing school was really tough subject-wise, but I found that here I was among fellow students who wanted to learn how to help others, physically and emotionally; being of Indian heritage as I was, was no big deal to anyone. There was only one other girl from Amherst taking the same courses as I. We had known each other in high school. She was a Harris and though we had never been close friends, she had never taken part in the name calling. The other students were from other towns and cities and a few were from out of state. They all knew I was in a minority because my scholarships were for minorities. We were all working toward a common goal and we became friends as well as classmates.

Following graduation I was employed as a registered nurse at the Baptist Hospital for two years, then I applied for and got a position at Lynchburg Central General Training School and I've been there these last eighteen years. I thoroughly enjoy my work and fellowship with my coworkers. A nurse needs to be a people person, and I am definitely that kind of person.

I think I've learned some valuable insights along life's way. My grandparents and my parents had been put upon and put down because of Dr. W. A. Plecker's biased laws to treat Indians as a non-people. He boxed them into a miserable existence. Some of the elders, even today, because of their bad experiences, tend to say, "Don't talk about being Indian. You will only be hurt."

Their memories hindered them from realizing times and people's attitudes were changing. Dr. Plecker, with his maniacal desire for a pure race of in-his-dreams people, was now dead.

Now, in this progressive age with all people, not just Indians and black people, but all races and nationalities becoming better educated and more world traveled, there is a big difference. It broadens our horizons. The Caucasians, the African Americans, the Native Americans, all of us have learned we are all in this world as people God created. We can all learn from one another. Each race has something of worth to contribute to our American culture.

A Note from the Interviewer

Kenneth Branham explained the game of 100 Pedro as follows:

Required are four players, or two sets of partners. A bidder must bid 40 points on a hand and a team must have 100 points to win. The bidder chooses a suit as the trump. If the player seated at the left of the dealer is dealt a king, he/she must bid whether or not he/she has a winning hand. If the player to the left of the dealer is not dealt a king, they can pass and someone else can bid. Whoever wins a bid must lead with a king on the first play in the suit the bidder calls trump. On the next round, the bidder can lead with whatever card he/she chooses, trump or not. If another player plays a stronger counting card, that player will win the lead on the following play.

Points are: king trump is 25 points; number nine is 9 points; joker is 2 points. The joker is wild and counts in any suit chosen as trump. The ace, ten, jack, and two count 1 point each in trump. The five counts as 5 points and can be played as a trump card in both red suits (hearts or diamonds) if either are trump; and can also be played as a trump card in the black suits (spades or clubs) if one of those are called trump. The queen, one, three, four, six, seven, and eight have no point value. The called trump in those noncounting cards can sometimes save a bidder's bacon as a trump card to play when it is wise to delay playing a counting card. The first set of partners to reach 100 points wins the game.

Hattie Belle Branham Hamilton

I am Hattie Belle, the daughter of Harry Branham and Edith Johns Branham. Edith's mother was Kate Johns, and Harry's parents were Richard and Christine Wise Branham. I lived with my parents until I was eighteen years old when I married Willie Bay Hamilton.

My father had moved to Father Judge Road when I was six months old. He rented a house from Judge and Beverly Ambler and worked for the judge.

Jim Higginbottom owned adjoining land and Willie Johns owned land behind Ambler's.

My father worked hard for a living. He was in charge of hiring other Indian men to cut pulpwood and drivers to drive teams of horses to haul the pulpwood. My father also drove a team of horses and they delivered pulpwood to the Faulkener Mill and to the Monroe Wood Yard.

My dad also planted and raised crops for the judge, with my dad receiving a small percentage of the harvest. The crops were corn, wheat, and tobacco. Our share of the wheat and corn was ground into flour and cornmeal.

Judge Ambler sold a portion of land on Father Judge Road to the Monacan Indian Nation for our newest ancestral cemetery. St. Pauls cemetery is not far from the Job Corps.

I attended the St. Pauls Mission School until I was fifteen years old. The mission school cut off with the eighth grade, so I went through the eighth grade twice because I didn't want my education to end. I longed for the right to attain a higher education. I couldn't really understand why we Indian students were not allowed to attend Virginia's state-supported schools, especially in Amherst County.

Our teachers at the Indian mission school were Caucasians from Amherst County. I remember some of my teachers. Miss Lewis, the daughter of Dr. Thomas

14. The late chief Harry Branham's home on Father Judge Road. It is believed that the house is over one hundred years old.

Lewis, was my teacher in the first grade. I remember a Mrs. Martin, but not which grades she taught. Dr. Sandidge's wife was my eighth-grade teacher. I remember my dad talking about a Mrs. Prior and Miss Lucy Bloxton and how well thought of they were in their dedication to helping relieve our plight.

We children didn't learn much about our Indian heritage when we were growing up. We learned next to nothing about our Indian heritage or Indian customs. We children sometimes discussed and wondered why people acted as though being Indian was a bad thing.

When I grew up and married Willie Hamilton, I ran into another obstacle. I went to a doctor in Amherst for my blood test. The blood test results were labeled "issue" by the doctor. I informed the doctor I would not accept the test as labeled. The doctor refused to change the label, so I threw the paper in his face and walked out of his office. I then went to a doctor in Lynchburg. That doctor labeled this second test "white." Willie and I married in Lynchburg as Caucasian.

You, the interviewer, have asked me to tell you my opinion as to what kind of person Dr. Walter A. Plecker was. As you know, he was Virginia's registrar of vital statistics from 1912 to 1946. The Racial Integrity Act stated that one could not be white unless they possessed only one-sixteenth or less Indian blood. Dr. Plecker firmly supported the Racial Integrity Act and he was determined the world needed to be rid of Indians and African Americans in order to bring about what he termed a pure English Caucasian race.

You also asked if we referred to Dr. Plecker as "old Plecker." You mentioned that some of our people had referred to him using that term. I'm not going to tell you the adjective some of us used in referring to him. We knew a word that fitted him much better than "old Plecker."

I know God doesn't want us to hate anyone and I try not to, but I can't help but hope, "—— Plecker" is where he deserves to be. He certainly worked hard enough to deserve that place. There's an old saying that every dog has his day. There must have been some reason "—— Plecker" had his day. There is also an old saying that it takes all kinds to make a world. "—— Plecker" and his ilk was a kind better left unsaid.

After many, many years of misery for my people, the state of Virginia has at long last recognized Indians in their own right. I am proud of being a Monacan Indian. My people are a strong, visionary, enduring people. Who could ask for more?

Bertie Duff Branham

I am Bertie D. Branham. My father was Eddie Branham and my mother was Dessie Johns Duff Branham. I have three sisters and two brothers.

I'm married to Preston Branham and we have seven children, Percy, Wilburn, Regina, Janet, Michael, Annie, and William, in that order.

Preston and I have one grandson, Curtis.

I attended St. Pauls Mission School and I don't think I ever questioned why. I think I took that for granted since my siblings, cousins, and friends attended St. Pauls, too, as had our parents before us. The thing I did question was why the big yellow school bus with lots of white kids riding on it, passed us by as we walked along the same road to our school. We always had to step aside into the ditches alongside the road as the big yellow school bus roared past us. So, one day I decided to ask my mama why. She always knew the answers to my questions.

"Mama, why do the white kids ride on a school bus and we walk to St. Pauls School?"

Mama answered, "Because the school bus is traveling in the wrong direction."

Somehow, I knew that was the only answer that would be forthcoming.

We lived way over on High Peak Mountain. Some black families lived out that way, too. They walked the same dirt road we walked out to the main road, where at the forks of the road, a big yellow school bus picked up the black kids, but we weren't allowed to ride on that bus either. We had to walk on miles and miles to St. Pauls Mission School. For those of us who were very young with short legs, the mission school seemed a distance away like on the other side of forever, especially on cold, snowy days.

On the walk along the dirt road, the black kids wouldn't walk alongside us just as the white kids would not. They walked in front of us or behind us, but never with us; nor would they play with us. Both black and white races preferred to pretend we didn't exist. We were grown before we understood those children in those days were only practicing what their elders had taught them was the proper way to treat a non-race such as we Monacan Indians were thought to be in Amherst County. We Monacans had our own set of rules as to the order in which we made our way to school. The older kids walked either in front or behind us younger kids. They had stuff they wanted to talk about that had to do with their age and interests and they certainly didn't want big-eared, younger kids overhearing their conversations. We didn't really care. We were busy hopping and skipping, playing chase, and chattering about things we thought interesting. We knew there was no need to be afraid they would let us get too far ahead or too far behind. The older kids accepted the responsibility given them by our parents to make sure we little ones were cared for.

We never had much time for fun and games, so what little time we had was precious to us. We had to rise very early each morning to help with chores. The boys busied themselves filling the wood boxes with firewood and we girls helped to clean up the kitchen after breakfast. Then we walked up to fifteen miles to the mission school and home afterwards to help with evening chores. Later, we did our homework by lamplight and then went early to bed.

We never had any complaints about any of our schoolteachers. They were all white women. At first, the Episcopalian diocese furnished the teachers for the mission school. Then later on there were two teachers from Sweet Briar College. Then, in the 1920s, Amherst County decided to send county-supported teachers to our mission school.

Later on, in 1954, by an act of Congress, the Warren Court passed the law that all schools must become integrated. But that law was not obeyed in Amherst County until 1963–64.

Sundays were always kept for the Lord by all three races in Amherst County, but even on the Lord's Day, prejudice was still in effect. We Indians still had to walk fifteen miles to St. Pauls Mission Church for worship services. There were churches for white people and churches for black people in shorter walking distance, but we weren't welcome in those churches.

We children were kept in the dark about grown-up happenings and one of those in particular was childbirth. Generally, the midwives helped the women during childbirth, but my mama insisted on birthing a child all alone. I'll never forget when she birthed her last baby in 1954. She had boiled some instruments. She made up her bed afresh and laid out some clothing. Then she walked across the fields a distance to Crawford's Store to purchase some items and when she returned, she told me to take my siblings down near the sawmill and gather greens for supper. I did as I was told and off we went to gather wild-growing greens.

My brother Wesley and I were old enough to sense something was out of the ordinary, so we rushed the other kids along and finished our chore in record time.
We raced back up through the fields and as we neared our back door, we halted
as Wesley came to a stop while holding a finger to his lips in a shushing motion.
Then Wesley said, "I hear a baby crying."

We raced into the house and followed the sound of a newborn's crying into
Mama's bedroom. There in the middle of the bed was the infant who would later
be named Dorothy. Mama wasn't in the bed or the bedroom. We found her in
the kitchen beginning preparations for our supper. We still weren't sure how the
baby came to be in the middle of Mama's bed.

Life in those days was what people of today would call rugged. But, to us at
that time, it was a normal way of life. Our coats were sewn from durable materials and served many youngsters before retiring to the rag box. The women
wove most of the materials they used for clothing. I can still remember my grandmother, Lottie Roberts Johns, sitting at the spinning wheel by the hour. We kids
usually wore hand-me-downs. We were a community of people who shared with
one another in order to survive. The women had a very hard life. They worked
in the fields each morning except Mondays, right alongside the men. On Monday and each afternoon, they washed clothes, worked in their vegetable gardens, did basket weaving, spinning, quilting, canning, cleaning house, sewing,
preparing meals, baking breads, and all else that comes with being a wife and
mother.

Saturday night was for fun and frolic but only during harvest season. Sometimes, harvest wasn't much to be joyous about. All crops raised had to be divided
with the landowners and much depended on which landowner a family worked
for. Some landowners asked for a fifty-fifty split, but those landowners were
few. Other hard-nosed landowners demanded eighty-twenty and some even demanded a ninety-ten split. For many families of sharecropping Monacans, that
meant no luxury items such as sugar could be bought. We drank an awful lot of
bitter tea and desserts were rare.

My mother, grandmother, and my future mother-in-law were all basket weavers. They used split oak and honeysuckle vines and wove baskets of every size
and shape. They also made corn-shuck dolls. If you come across any baskets made
by those ladies back in the 1920s, 1930s, and 1940s, you will discover you can tell
a basket made by women of today from a basket made in yesteryear. When my
people finished a basket, they always heated a rod and burned holes spaced around
the top rim of the basket. Then, they used thin strips as ties and bound the basket's top rim securely which rendered any basket very durable. In these modern
times, basket weaving is practically a lost art.

15. Honeysuckle baskets woven by Jo Ann Staubitz on display at the Monacan Museum.

In this interview, you have asked me if Monacan Indians are, or used to be, a superstitious race. I kind of lean toward answering, "yes." Most of our people will declare they are not at all superstitious. But there are a few favorite, shall we say, customs that used to be prevalent among our ancestors.

For instance, there was a man named Lincoln Johns. He was best known by the nickname Link. Well, Link could predict how many snows would fall each winter by keeping a written list of every foggy morning that occurred in August of each year. The total of foggy mornings in August determines the number of snows that winter. We children were in awe of him.

Then there was our uncle Sam Campbell. He used to bring us chestnut wood down from the mountain after my father died. Sam tried to help us out that way. The reason I'm telling you this is because some of our people believed one could receive spiritual visions from some departed soul whenever a kinsman was in dire need of help. A case in point is the story of Sam Campbell. Uncle Sam had walked down from Peter's Hollow to Mr. Broden's house one very cold morning. He hitched a ride with Mr. Broden to the city of Amherst to buy himself a new pair of boots. In the meantime, Mama had gone to Link's house to pick up some canned goods and Sam had told her he would meet her there at four o'clock P.M. to help her carry the canned goods back to her house. At five o'clock P.M. Mama began to worry because it wasn't like Uncle Sam to be late. Besides, it had begun to snow heavily early in the afternoon and the snow on the ground was now very deep. Mama decided she needed to check on Sam, so she left Link's house and walked to Mr. Massey's house and asked him if he had seen Sam. Mr. Massey said he had not, so she walked on to Mr. Broden's house. Mr. Broden answered her knock on the door, and in answer to her inquiry, he said, yes, Sam had bought a pair of boots in Amherst. He had ridden back with Mr. Broden as far as Mr. Broden's house and then had begun his walk up the mountain assuring Mr. Broden he would be fine. By the time Mama had arrived at Mr. Broden's house, it was dark on a snowy night in the mountains.

The following morning, all the Indian kids skipped school and joined the adults in the search for Sam. At one point, some of the kids reported they thought they heard someone calling but the voice grew faint and they couldn't follow the sound. At dusk the search was called off to begin again at dawn. The morning of the second day, they found Sam. He had fallen in the slippery snow, wearing his new boots with slippery soles, and he couldn't get up (Sam was in his late seventies in that year of 1957). Sam had lain there until he froze to death. Mama said the rest of that winter after Sam's death, she would hear him at night walking across the front porch and opening the door. He would walk across the room to the King heater and she would hear him open the door of the wood heater, then close it and walk back out. Then the sound of his footsteps would cease. Mama told us kids that Sam was just checking to make sure we had heat on the cold, snowy nights since he could no longer supply us with the chestnut wood for the widow and her children. Then, after that first year, Mama said she no longer heard Sam making that racket on cold nights of coming in to check on the fire to make sure we had heat. Mama said, "Sam's convinced now that we have learned to take care of our needs, so Sam will never again visit us on cold nights."

Yes, we had medicinal remedies or home remedies our parents used as handed down from one generation to the next. One of the remedies we kids dreaded was the one our mamas believed we needed each spring to clean out our systems and ward off stomach worms. Our mamas went out into the woods and gathered rosin from pine trees. They rolled the resin into tiny balls. One must be very careful to keep the balls small as too much rosin (turpentine) could make one's back grow weak. We were thankful for that belief because at least that kept the hated balls small. They would stand guard over us to make sure we ate that rosin ball. Ugh!

The remedy for colds or influenza was a tea made from horehound bark boiled in water. The tea really helped relieve the discomfort of colds and flu.

Then there was the cure for sties on the eyelids that only Mrs. Johns could cure. She always kept several black cats at her house. That way if one wandered off or died, she still had some black cats on hand. When any of us developed a sty we would be taken to Mrs. Johns's house. Mrs. Johns would hold the tail of a black cat in her hand and stroke it across our eye in the form of the letter, X. Supposedly, that healed the eyelid.

Diane Shields said her dad had a cure for bee stings. He would remove a leaf of tobacco from a cigar, wet the leaf in water, and place the damp leaf over the welt left by the bee's sting. Then he would wrap a strip of cotton cloth around or over the tobacco leaf and the tobacco leaf drew out the poison and relieved the inflammation left from the bee's sting.

During the spring and summer months, our parents' feet were often red with blisters from the long hours of toiling in the corn and tobacco fields. At nighttime they would fill a pan with steaming hot water and mix table salt into it to make a foot bath. The hot, salty bath worked wonders on their paining feet.

We also had homemade teas that we drank for pleasure much as we drink Coca Colas or Pepsi in this day and time. We made catnip tea made from catnip leaves, and mint tea made from the leaves also. We had sassafras tea made from the root bark.

Speaking of teas reminds me of the harvest time gatherings in the autumns. All the men would gather at a fellowman's barn and shuck corn all day on a Saturday. Their wives would gather in the fellowman's house and set up tables to be laden with foodstuff they had brought with them and the last-minute cooking they would all take part in during the day. They also filled canning jars and crocks with catnip, mint, and sassafras teas and made large pots of coffee.

When darkness descended, the men would wash up at the shed and then come into the house to eat and drink their fill.

Then with many grunts and groans and teasing of one another about gorging themselves on the good food, they would dismantle the makeshift tables and stack them outside. Then the men would play their instruments and all present would sing and dance until daybreak.

The following Saturday, they would all gather at another fellowman's house and the routine was repeated in like manner each and every Saturday until harvest time was ended. Harvest time was a time of helping each other and rejoicing for each other in the plentiful years and just being there for each other in the lean years.

No matter how hard they had worked all day on each Saturday, and no matter that they had played instruments, danced, and sang until dawn, they all arrived at St. Pauls Episcopal Church in time for the morning service. Our people never forgot that God should be thanked for the harvest, and the fellowship of neighbors, food, and dance. One of our favorite praise songs has always been "What a Friend We Have in Jesus."

I really don't know how we would have survived without our faith in God.

God doesn't love only one color of any of His creation. One only has to look at nature, his creation also, and it is obvious God is a creator of endless colors.

A small group of Monacan Indians had attended the Amherst High School in 1963, although it was rather an uneasy situation. In 1964, the Virginia state government decreed that Caucasian, Indian, and African American would all attend the same state-supported schools. So, St. Pauls little mission school for Indians closed its doors forever as a school. The white people of Amherst County were in a state of shock. Even up to the time I was grown, married, and with children of my own, prejudice was still raising its ugly head from time to time. I remember two occurrences in particular when my two oldest daughters came home very upset. The first time concerned a white boy on the school bus. The white kids had been insisting that the Indians and blacks be seated in the back of the bus. This particular day my daughter, Sissy, decided she had rights, too. She took a seat near the front on the opposite row of seats across from a white boy who lived just down the road from us. The white boy leaned across the aisle and spat in Sissy's face.

Sissy got off the bus that afternoon with tears streaming down her face and she told me what had happened. I took Sissy by the hand and we walked down the road to the white boy's home. I told the boy's father what had occurred on the bus. The father just looked at me. He offered no apology and neither did his son, who was standing beside his father. I told the boy and his father it had better never happen again. I didn't tell him in exactly those words. The words I used had some backbone in them. The boy was never rude to Sissy again.

On the second occurrence, my two oldest daughters came home in tears. They said some kids had ganged up and started chanting, "Hue bangies, hue bangies, that's what you are. You're hue bangies."

I explained to my daughters, "What the children meant as an insult was actually complimentary. Hue bangies refers to aboriginal of hue, the first known inhabitants. Indians are the true natives of America. The white man came later as foreigners in search of a country."

The census takers had done their part in recording incorrect data concerning Monacans in Amherst County. The door-to-door census takers had their own preconceived opinions of the Monacan Nation. They never asked us what nationality we were. They would look at us, at the color of our skin, and write down their own opinion. Sometimes there would be three children in one household, brothers and sisters, and the census taker would list them as three different races. The only question the census takers ever asked of us was how many children there were in each household. The census was only taken once every ten years. Therefore, by the time they returned, there were usually one or more additional children. That seemed of no consequence to the census takers. If we told them there were three more children since the last census, they would list three additional children at ten years of age. They never let us read the forms. Not that the opportunity to read the forms would have helped in the early years, because many of our people could not read because of their lack of opportunity to get an education. But in later years when many of us could read, we still were not allowed to read their forms. Now we are having to go through tedious legislation procedures to get the ages of our children corrected, as well as their race. How could groups of supposedly educated, intelligent, trained people in the employ of the state Bureau of Vital Statistics in Richmond, Virginia, have engaged in such a careless method of record keeping? I have learned through experience that there are many educated people and there are also a smaller group of educated fools. Needless to say which group we were stuck with.

There are some employees at Lynchburg General Hospital still trying to obey Dr. W. A. Plecker's misguided rules. Just a few years ago in 1992, my daughter Sissy gave birth to her firstborn in this hospital. The next day, someone from the business office at General brought a form to Sissy's room for Sissy to sign to register her baby's birth. Someone in the business office at the hospital had already filled in the blanks by typewriting onto the blanks the information required. The girl stood beside Sissy's bed and offered her a fountain pen while informing Sissy that all Sissy had to do was add her signature to the previously filled-out form. Sissy was wise enough to insist she read the form before signing it. When Sissy read the filled-in block for listing race of child, she saw that the word Negro had been type-written in. Sissy handed the form and the fountain pen back to the waiting girl and said, "No, I will not sign this form. My son is Monacan Indian. He is not Negro."

The waiting girl shook her head and refused to accept the proffered document. Sissy ripped it to shreds and let the pieces fall to rest on the bed sheet.

The following day, the girl returned with another form already filled out. But this form had the word Indian typed in. Sissy signed the form.

It still worries us, wondering if the office clerk at Lynchburg General Hospital actually corrected the record to be filed in their coffers or if she merely changed the form brought to Sissy's room. Evidently the hospital was still using the lists Dr. Walter A. Plecker had sent to them ages ago with orders the hospital must abide by his lists. On those lists that became known by us as Plecker's hit/hate lists were the surnames of our people. Plecker repeatedly stated there were no Indians in Amherst County. There were only white people and Negro. Dr. Plecker's intense hatred of the Monacan Indians in Amherst County, in which he had much control, continued to inflict injustice on our people for many years after his death.

You questioned me as to what types of employment were open to us. Other than toiling in the fields and orchards of white landholders for meager pay there was not much open to us. It was all but unheard of for any of us to be accepted for clerical work or managerial positions. Those jobs were for white people only.

I well remember my first job for which I was paid wages. I was hired by the owner of Morris Orchards to carry drinking water out into the fields to the peach pickers. I worked eight hours per day and was paid fifty cents per day. That was in the year 1956. In 1957 I was promoted. I picked peaches and was paid $1.50 per eight-hour day. I continued working in the Morris Orchards for several years, but I never received a pay raise. I quit the peach-picking job to help my husband, Preston, cut and haul pulpwood. That was our job for the next ten years. In 1967 we were cutting, skinning, stacking, and hauling pulpwood for $3.00 per cord. That means the trees were cut down, skinned, sawed into five-foot lengths, and stacked onto the truck five foot, two inches high.

We hauled pine wood to the Sweet Briar sawmill and all other wood to the Monroe wood yard.

All that area where Father Judge Road and the Job Corps are now, all that area used to be dense forest. Preston and I cleared that entire acreage of trees.

Yes, the work was very hard and the pay was meager, but Preston and I were so thankful we could provide for ourselves and our children.

Cecil Hamilton Terry

I am Cecil Hamilton Terry, daughter of Charlie and Dana Hamilton.

I grew up, kind of, and married Stewart L. Terry. We had seven children. Our firstborn were a set of twins and they lived only a few hours. They were jaundiced. The other five children are grown now and have families and homes of their own.

As I sit here this day, talking to you, the interviewer, it is the year 1997 and I am seventy-seven years old. Trying to answer your questions while remembering back over a period of my lifetime, some of my memories may sound like I'm jumping around as I view my life in my looking glass of memory. To begin with, I've never understood why I, a female, was christened with the name, Cecil. I've never really questioned why, so we'll skip that one.

We lived in a tenant house on the James River until I was in my early teens and then we moved to Bedford County. We attended school in Elon, Virginia. We Indian kids went to night school and the white kids went to day school. The reason for that was not because of prejudice against Indians, but because our Monacan parents were tenant farmers and tenant farmers' kids had to help their parents in the orchards and fields of various crops. One task I remember vividly was chopping out rows and rows of growing corn in fields of such long rows one couldn't see from one end of a row to the other end. Sweat would run down our faces and bodies in salty rivers.

When my brother and I were still young, one of our chores was to row our boat across the James River to gather driftwood to stockpile for our winter heat and for Mama's cookstove year 'round. A loaded boat is difficult to row with oars at any age, but especially for two children.

We also hauled passengers across the river on Saturday mornings and back at dusk. The passengers were going to visit relatives on the other side of the James or to catch a train to Lynchburg for whatever reasons. Each passenger paid us fifteen cents round-trip fare. My brother and I thought we were making big money.

When I started dating Stewart Terry, I was only thirteen years old. Mama would not allow us to go anywhere alone. She always sent one of my sisters with us.

When I was fifteen years old and Stewart was twenty years old, we decided to put an end to the threesome dating. We decided to get married.

My daddy and mama gave us their blessing and accompanied us to Preacher Ray's house. Preacher Ray was unmarried and lived alone, without a house-keeper. When we arrived that afternoon, Preacher Ray was coming out of his barn, dressed in bib overalls. When we told him we wanted him to perform the marriage ceremony for us, he smiled and said he really ought to get dressed up in his black dress suit for such a happy occasion.

He took us inside his kitchen. We saw the table was laden with dirty dishes. He looked at the laden table and down at the dusty floor. He shrugged and said he'd decided against changing clothes. He picked up his Bible from a sideboard and standing on one side of the laden table he motioned for us to stand on the other side with my parents behind me, and in moments Stewart and I were pronounced married.

We walked back to my parents' house where some neighbors had gathered to wish Stewart and me a long life together. One of Mama's friends asked Mama, "What are you serving for their wedding supper?"

My mama replied, "We have a big fat duck on the pond and I'm going to cook that duck!"

Stewart and I lived with my parents for several years. When we finally moved out on our own, we moved to the Rutger place and lived there the next forty-five years. In fact, we lived there until recently in this year of 1997. We still didn't have running water or bathroom facilities and Stewart was still cutting our firewood.

In early spring, Stewart had a heart attack.

Our children put their heads together and decided that their daddy couldn't keep on with such hard work of keeping up our place and making our living. They agreed their mama's health wasn't so good either, so they banded together and bought us this lot and this nice manufactured home.

God is good. We are so thankful God blessed us with such wonderful children.

Stewart works a few hours each day puttering around in the yard. He has been an outdoor man all his life and it's hard for him to occupy himself indoors. He has found a sense of accomplishment in building us this nice brick patio. The children love to sit out here in lawn chairs and chat when they come by to visit with us. Really, I think they come by to check on us to make sure we're doing well.

In answer to your last question about going back to my growing up years, no, we never encountered prejudice in this neck of the woods because we were Indian. The white people on the James River area are a live-and-let-live kind of people. The people in this region are kind and friendly. I think the agony encountered in Amherst County for the Monacans was because Dr. Walter A. Plecker spread his brand of mind poisoning against aboriginals, the Indians as first inhabitants of America.

21

Ella Branham Mays

I am Ella Branham Mays. My great-grandparents were Richard Branham and Christine Wise Branham. My grandparents were John Branham and Ella Beverly Branham, also Ramsey Branham and Louisa Terry Branham. My parents were James Branham and Carsia Branham. Carsia was generally called "Cassie."

I have one sister, Louise (Branham) Branham, and I have three brothers, John, Joe, and James.

I was married to the late William Mays.

I have ten children, twenty-one grandchildren, and five great-grandchildren. I must have done something right in the children department.

My children are a mixed breed because I am Monacan Indian and my late husband was white.

I am so thankful my children and grandchildren and great-grands have not experienced prejudice against Indians or mixed breeds as I experienced it growing up Indian in Amherst County.

I was a very sensitive, loving child and being called "colored" and "issue" by some of the white kids made me unhappy. As a very young child I didn't even know what the terms meant. I only knew the words were uttered in unkind voices.

I attended St. Pauls Mission School. I remember Mrs. Garland and Miss Smith were two of my teachers. All of our teachers through the years at the mission school were white people, but one and all of them were dedicated, farsighted teachers. One and all of those teachers went the extra mile for us and sought to teach us beyond the required subject matter. They knew we would not have the opportunity of a high school education since the mission school offered courses only through the eighth grade and we were not allowed to enter the public white folks' schools. Thankfully, some of us were like unto absorbent sponges and became educated beyond our school attendance years.

I am so thankful that all children are given equal opportunity now to obtain an education. One of my granddaughters, Becky Snowden, has won a scholarship to the University of South Carolina in Columbia, South Carolina. She is studying law in preparation of becoming an attorney at law. She is in her sophomore year and doing great in this year of 1997.

I am thankful also to see the attitudes of Amherst County residents changing and becoming more receptive of people of all races. I believe world travel has helped a lot. Also, exchange students have helped with a broader view. Television has helped tremendously to educate people about different modes of life. Skin color should never be the criteria by which any person or race of people is judged. The demented way Dr. Walter A. Plecker, state registrar of vital statistics in Virginia, tried to force all people of Virginia to believe and act was wrong. Thank God Plecker's law is as dead now as Plecker himself.

I'm the type of person who believes in dwelling on the positive side of life, but there are always some few who prefer to see the downside of life. Some people wake up each morning expecting it to rain on their day. Some mornings I'll arrive at my job and start the ball rolling by saying, oh so cheerfully, "Good morning, coworkers! Isn't this a good morning?" Someone or another will always turn to glare at me and mumble, "What's so damn good about it?"

I usually smile at that person and say, "Well, you survived the rush hour traffic and arrived here to work your eight-hour shift. Isn't that something to be thankful for?"

That usually elicits another glare. It's great that our group has such a good working relationship and we can have fun chattering with each other in mock discord.

I'm jumping around in this interview but bear with me. One of the questions you asked was about our health care. I believe Sharon said she discussed health remedies in some detail, so I'll only mention a couple Sharon may not have recalled. If any of us got cut on anything, my granddaddy would gather wood soot from the fireplace chimney and mix the soot with sugar and barely moisten it to make a thin paste. Then he applied the paste gently over the cut and it kind of stuck into the raw wound. The wound soon healed. Some people used the white of an egg over a burn and that worked, too, to help promote healing and new skin. Our mothers also gathered wild myrrh and made a tea with it to be used as a tonic for kidney infections.

People didn't get sick as easily in those days as they do now in the 1900s.

We only had two doctors and one midwife in our county. Some areas didn't have any doctors. Some Indian nations had one medicine man. Now there are several doctors in each small county and lots of doctors in cities. There are multitudes of over-the-counter medicines, multitudes of manufactured medicines, and yet sick people crowd doctors' offices and drugstores every day. Think about it. Modern progress is killing us off. There are so many pollutants in our air and water. Also we sit at desks by the hour for eight hours or more per day with few breaks, at school and in the work force. Our glazed eyes stare at computer screens and television screens. Our heads are cocked sideways on our necks as we cradle telephone receivers on our hunched shoulders.

Even the foods we eat have been so polluted with insecticides, sprays, and crop-dusting powders and waxes to make food stuff look better than it is. Food was also prepared at home instead of today's factory preparations.

Oh, my Lord, this conversation brings back memories of my dear mother's cooking. Oh, the delicious smell of chicken and dumplings bubbling on the stove was enough to bring us children huddling close to the range.

Mama used to make bean dumplings, too. Anyone who has never eaten bean dumplings has missed a culinary blessing. The old-fashioned recipe of no measurements given is simple and I'll share it with you. Cook the pinto beans as you normally would. Drain beans and set aside. Slice several onions and set aside. Make the dough using your usual "by-feel" method or by your favorite recipe. Roll out the dough on a well-floured dough board. Cut rolled dough into oblong strips. Place a spoonful of beans on each dough strip and top with an onion slice. Bring other side of dough rectangle over filled side and pinch dough edge together to seal. Drop dumplings into a pot of boiling chicken broth, a few dumplings at a time. They will cook quickly. Remove cooked dumplings to a large bowl. Place filled bowl in center of table. Everyone use their boardinghouse reach. Fill your plates with dumplings and enjoy. Ahhh!

Mama used to make a tasty jelly, too, by combining apples and pears. I don't remember the measurements. I wish I did.

We children usually gathered in the kitchen to concoct our favorite munchies. We used black walnuts we had cracked out of their shells on Saturday. Mix the nuts with popped popcorn and coat with hot sorghum molasses. Roll the mixture into balls and let stand for about thirty minutes.

It seems I only remember my childhood in bits and pieces. I guess we were just normal children doing normal stuff among our own people and attending our own St. Pauls Mission School. My siblings will probably tell you that applied to all but me. They will tell you I was the most aggravating kid that ever walked in a pair of shoes. At family get-togethers they still remind me of the time they were teasing me and I became angry and punched my brother, the ring leader, in the nose and he fell flat on his back. The other three brothers and sister, Louise, ran to the house to tattle to Mama. Our parents forbade us to fight, so I knew I was in for a spanking. I didn't want to face the music (an expression of mountain people), so I ran away far up the hill and hid myself in tall weeds. From my

16. Preparing food for Homecoming Day in the upstairs kitchen in the Parish Hall of the Mission Center are (*from left*), Louise Branham, Peggy Branham, and Eleanor Branham; Hattie Belle Hamilton can be seen in the background.

safe haven, I watched as Mama and my siblings hunted for me at the barn, the chicken house, and in the cornfield. Then I heard Mama call out to the others, "She'll come home by dark."

By five o'clock suppertime, I was very hungry, having missed out on lunch. I went home. My mama was so glad to see me, she didn't spank me.

My three brothers live in other towns and states now and the fourth brother has "walked on" in death. These three living brothers and sister, Louise, always remind me at family get-togethers that I still have a spanking due me.

My sister, Louise, has a tale she tells on me, too. She generally glides over her guilty part, but I make sure it gets told, too. I am two years younger than Louise. I was the tomboy and Louise was the little lady. We two were sometimes sent to the tobacco fields to help our brothers sucker the tobacco leaves. That meant pulling off the tobacco picnicking worms and killing them (we didn't use insecticides on any crops). Louise was scared out of her skull of any and all worms. Louise would walk between her assigned rows of growing tobacco and pretend she didn't see any worms. As for me, I had a sadistic streak in me when it came to suckering those fat suckers. The grade quality of the tobacco determined the price it would bring at harvest time. That meant I would have to go behind Louise and sucker her rows for her. Sometimes I would give in to temptation and chase Louise with a fistful of worms from her rows. Louise could run like the wind itself in her haste to get to Mama as her safe base. She couldn't tell on me, though, because she knew I could then tell on her.

We've all grown up now and Louise and I are as close as two peas in a pod. We lost one sister, Claudine, at only three months of age. We lost another sister, Helen, to spinal meningitis at an early age. We lost one brother as he "walked on" in death. We don't see our three remaining brothers very often except on major holidays. So, Louise and I depend on each other as family and we enjoy doing things together.

Uh-oh, that reminds me I'd better bring this interview to a close. I'm past due to help Louise and some others label all those canned goods for the Homecoming Bazaar.

A Note from the Interviewer

I turned off the recorder as Ella, laughing gaily, ran down the hall to the large room where Louise, Hattie, Eleanor, Peggy, and Frances were already busy, talking and laughing, while labeling many, many jars of beautiful vegetables, fruits, jams, pickles, and their famed apple butter.

22

Betty Hamilton Branham

I am Betty H. Branham. My maternal grandparents were Rob and Rose Johns. My paternal grandparents were Reece and Alice Hamilton. My parents were Dudley Hamilton and Rose Johns Hamilton.

I'm married to Colonel Branham. Colonel is not really a colonel in the armed forces. He doesn't know why his parents so named him.

I'm fifty-seven years old this year of 1997 and Colonel and I have six grown children.

My daddy said the St. Pauls Mission School was too many miles from us and we were too young to walk that far to school. What little I learned, I taught myself. I'm thankful I can read well enough to read the letters my children write to me since they've moved away to other states. I so wish I could read well enough to read books and newspapers.

My dad rented land upon which he grew crops of corn and tobacco. We children worked in the fields.

As children, we didn't know much about the grown-up world. It was as though children and adults lived in two separate worlds. Our parents believed children's minds must never be burdened with adult concerns, needs, and hurts. Whenever relatives or friends came to visit, all we children were sent to a bedroom to play jack rocks or outdoors, weather permitting, to play yard games. So, in that avenue, too, our educational opportunities were shortchanged.

I can talk to you, the interviewer, as we sit here in my living room. I can share with you my memories of growing up at the foot of Bear Mountain here in Amherst County, Virginia; but when the book we're helping you to write about us, the Monacan Indians, is published, I will sit here in my living room and hold the book in my hands. I will look at the written pages. I will long to read the book and cannot. Once again I will be shut out of the adult world because Amherst

County refused to allow me to ride the school buses and attend the public schools and learn to read.

All I will be able to do is hold the book in my hands and look at the pictures of my people.

23
Lacie Johns Branham

I am Lacie Johns Branham. I am the daughter of Luther Johns and Cammie Branham Johns. My husband was the late Rufus Branham. I am the mother of Monacan chief Kenneth Branham. I also have three daughters, Marilyn, Carolyn Sue, and Edith. They are four wonderful children. I thank God for them. I thank God, too, they are of the 1940s generation with more opportunities than were afforded the Monacans of older generations.

My mom and dad never attended school. My mom had a good head on her shoulders, though. She had an uncle who helped her learn the basics.

The situation had not changed when I was born. We still were not allowed to attend the public schools of Amherst or ride on school buses. The Episcopalian Mission School for us Monacan Indians was away from where we lived.

I was nine years old when the landowner my dad worked for began to feel quite sorry for us because we were being denied an education. He was of Jewish descent and he understood what it was like to be the object of some peoples' prejudice. He had an old army truck sitting idle. He hired a driver to take us to and from the mission school in that old (rheumatoid) truck.

We were too young at the time to appreciate the need he met for us. It was years before we realized the debt of gratitude we owed that man for his empathy and generosity.

His name sounded like Autavitch. I have forgotten the correct spelling. He was a rich man, but he was despised and resented by the white people of Amherst County because he was a Jew, just as we were despised and resented because we were Indian.

Mr. Autavitch owned close to a thousand acres of land. He owned High Peak Orchards and Montrose Orchards, both on the range of Tobacco Row Mountains. His enterprises included the orchards, farmland, and timber stands. He employed a lot of Indians, my father among them and my mother also. My mother worked for Mrs. Autavitch, cooking and cleaning in their mansion on the hill on old Route 130.

Mama also worked in the orchards whenever not needed in the mansion. She took care of us, too. I don't know how women managed back then. Their workload was monumental.

Time marched on and Mr. Autavitch entered his twilight years. As he became more and more senile, he also became more erratic in buying more land, more equipment, more stock, until his expenditures far outweighed his income. Finally, he went from being a rich man to being financially broke.

He began borrowing from the bank, larger and larger sums. There came a day when the bank president called Mr. Autavitch into his office and told Mr. Autavitch, "There will be no more loans granted you. You have become a very bad risk."

Mr. Autavitch collapsed right there in the office and fell to the floor. He was taken to the hospital in Lynchburg and several days later from there to the Staunton Sanatorium. He remained there until he died.

Mr. Autavitch has been deceased a very long time, but many of us remember him as a very kind man who reached out to a beleaguered Monacan race.

Let's travel even further back in time.

My dad worked in the apple and peach orchards and for his labor he was paid eighty cents per nine- to ten-hour day.

We were allowed to plant a vegetable garden near our cabin and we could gather wild-growing edible plants. We had difficulty meeting other needs. Sugar was a much coveted item. Coal oil, with which to fuel our lamps, was a necessity. Also, we had more hours of darkness in the mountains than in the southern flatlands. Materials with which to make our clothing and bedding was another item which must be bought with money, and there was the need for shoes to wear in the cold, snowy winters. These needs couldn't be met by planting seeds in the ground or plucked from wild-growing plants. These needs had to be purchased at the country store and paid for with money. Before the song was ever written, we owed our souls to the company store [.80 X 7 = $5.60 per week wages].

I was the biggest girl in the fifth-grade class at the Episcopalian Mission School. Because of my height I was chosen to be the chief cook and bottle washer for the school. The building beside the log schoolhouse housed a basement kitchen. Each day, a huge pot of soup had to be made from scratch. A huge pot of cocoa had to be prepared for the students' and the teachers' lunch.

At twelve years of age, there were days when I resented being the cook while the other students were seated at their desks, getting an education. There were other days when I enjoyed the oohs and ahhs from the students and the smiles from the teachers as they all practically inhaled their bowls of soup and mugs of hot cocoa.

Cooking became my vocation. I prepare tasty and attractive dishes and/or hors d'oeuvres for small or large groups at a local restaurant. Still and all, as I sometimes look back, I still don't think it was really fair to take me from the classroom for the better part of the school day just because I could make good soup and was tall enough to reach the stove top.

Whenever I speak of it now, which is rarely, my children will chuckle and say, "Mom, just tell everyone you attended a private school of culinary arts as the one and only student."

My children are urging me to tell you, the interviewer, about a remembrance of my childhood which I recall as "the age of innocence" and my children term "the age of ignorance." Those were the days before television with its portrayal of rawness of everything under the sun and on the moon. My parents' generation thought it best that children were not told the facts of life at what they deemed a tender age. A tender age had no exact ending. That was to be determined by each individual set of parents.

We asked the age-old question of my parents, "Where do babies come from, do they just fall from the sky?" Our parents answered, "They are found under rocks."

We children would sometimes spend an hour or two turning over rocks in search of babies. We could not understand how our parents managed to turn over the right rocks and we never could.

When my children recall this tale on some occasions and shout with laughter, I remind them that the day is coming when their day will become the old days. Each passing generation always has some remembrances that are hilarious to the new generation, but time marches on, so don't laugh too hardily. It will come back to haunt you.

24
Cammie Branham Johns

[This interview with Cammie was researched from an interview Cammie had with Sharon Bryant and Kenneth Branham. The interview took place for the purpose of being included in the documentary, "Reclaiming Our Heritage." This documentary was sponsored by Virginia Life Foundation.]

I am Cammie Branham Johns. My paternal great-great-grandfather was Ed Branham from Scotland. My great-grandparents were Richard Branham and Christine Wise Branham. My paternal grandparents were George (Buggy) Branham and Willie Roberts Branham. My maternal grandparents were John and Altha Terry. My parents were Walter Branham and Delia Terry Branham. My siblings are Virgie, Carrie, Cassie, and Allie; Lucian and Edith.

I married Luther Johns in 1929. He was the son of Ellie Johns and Lilly Duff Johns.

In this interview I'm going back to when I was a very little girl to give you an idea of how it was to be a Monacan Indian in Amherst County in Virginia. I was only four years old when Dr. Walter Plecker was sworn in as the first state registrar of vital statistics in Virginia. Dr. Plecker was the man directly responsible for messing up the records of Indians. He hated Indians with a blinding passion. He ordered our clerk of court and the Lynchburg Hospital to register our births, marriages, and deaths as people of color, colored, or mixed. He pulled filed records in Richmond and wrote his bile on the back of those records. Some he missed and, therefore, some brothers and sisters ended up being recorded as of different races.

We were not allowed to eat with white people. We were sent to the back of restaurants. Churches were also of the same order. Once I remember a traveling preacher loudly proclaiming that one must beware of Indians sneaking out of bushes at night. I wanted to ask him how he recognized people as red, black, or white under the cover of darkness.

Our people stuck together. Whenever any one of us needed a helping hand, we banded together to help out. For instance, at corn-shucking time, the corn must be prepared to take to the mill to be ground into meal. The women would gather to cook huge pots of chicken and dumplings and side dishes of vegetables. The men folk seemed to work up huge appetites while shucking and shelling corn. Our parents and grandparents didn't have material gifts to give, but they gave abundantly of themselves. For instance, my grandfather Terry received a government pension check each month. The check amount was five dollars.

Once upon a time my ancestors owned a lot of land in Amherst County. Taxes on land increased and increased but Indians weren't allowed jobs that paid living wages. It became more and more difficult for my people to pay taxes due on their land. Gradually, our land was bought up by white men for the price of taxes due on the land. That meant the white buyers got value for very little investment.

Circumstances such as those caused my people to grow distrustful of the white man. I remember an instance in my teen years when I traveled with my father to Lynchburg. While my dad and the store owner gathered together the items on dad's list, the owner's son and I struck up a conversation. The young man was very nice and polite.

My dad and the store owner came back into the store after loading the supplies on my dad's wagon. Dad nodded to me that he was ready to go. The young man turned to my dad and asked him for permission to drive me home to my house in Amherst in his buggy, that is, if I was agreeable. I was agreeable, but my dad said, "Thank you, but no. She will return home with me."

My dad was leery of leaving his young daughter in a white man's care.

I'm an old lady now, but memories of youth linger on.

How well I remember my courtship with Luther Johns. That romance goes all the way back to childhood. We met at St. Pauls Episcopal Church. Luther's folks lived out on Father Judge Road. Luther's dad, Ellie, would bring his wife and kids to church by horse and wagon. It was a sight to see with that horde of children practically falling over the sides of the buckboard.

Luther would invite himself home with us after church service. He and I and my brothers and sisters would play games all afternoon. Luther and I both loved horses. Sometimes, we would ride double on Dad's old mare. We never tired of horseback riding.

I wanted to go on dates with Luther, but he was too young. My goodness, he was still wearing knee-high pants! I guess I was too young, too, but that's beside the point.

When Luther grew old enough to put on long pants and grew a beard, we started stepping out together. After several years of stepping out, we decided we had known each other long enough and were now old enough to get married. Once that was decided, we didn't waste time on an engagement.

When Luther and I married, my uncle Don stood up with us. He looked at the marriage certificate after the clerk of court pronounced Luther and I man and wife. Then Uncle Don asked the clerk of court, "In the space designating race, why did you write in 'Indian mix?'"

"Oh, it's of no matter," the clerk said.

Uncle Dan said, "On both sets of parents' certificates of marriage, it states their race as white. How do four white people give birth to two Indian mix?"

The clerk shrugged his shoulders and erased Indian mix and wrote in white.

That's the sort of thing that has happened to our official records time and time again.

Luther and I had saved up enough money to buy two horses. We thought this made us a very prosperous young couple. Luther named his horse Slicker, and I named my mare Daisy. Every Sunday afternoon we rode our horses along country roads and across pasturelands. Ah, such happy memories.

We lived in a cabin on Ed Dawson's farm. Life wasn't easy there. I worked in the tobacco and cornfields alongside Luther and other hired hands. Near harvest time, Mr. Dawson said if Luther and I would help him sell his corn, he would pay us a share of his profits. Luther and I sold corn with the persuasiveness and exuberance of youth. All the large corn crop was sold. Mr. Dawson didn't pay us one thin dime of his profits from the sale.

We continued living in the cabin and working for Dawson two more years as we searched for other employment.

We worked for ten cents per hour each. We were not paid our wages until the autumn when the crops were sold. So, with no money to pay for needed purchases in the summer months we had to have credit at the company store.

Mr. Dawson devised a written form in which he guaranteed the store owner full pay at the end of harvest in the autumn for purchases made by us in the summer months. Each time we made a purchase, we had to sign that form agreeing the amount due would be paid by us in the autumn. When autumn came, Mr. Dawson withheld from our summer wages enough to satisfy the amount due the store owner. That left very little cash to sustain our needs through the winter months.

At the end of those two years with Mr. Dawson, we went to work for Mr. Autavitch at the Montrose orchards. Mr. Autavitch was a very different man than Mr. Dawson.

Luther and I raised our five children while working for Mr. Autavitch. They grew up and married and had children of their own.

At long last, while our grandchildren were still of school age, the state of Virginia agreed to try and right the wrong they had imposed on American Indians and African Americans. It was a beginning.

How well I remember the year of 1963 when the Virginia Legislature passed the Nondiscriminatory Law.

There was one hitch. These Amherst County school administrators still wanted to refuse to accept Indians. They agreed reluctantly to accept the African Americans, whom white people referred to as colored at that time.

Florence Cowan and her assistant, Dorothy Groff, decided it was high time to fight back. They asked my daughter, Lacie, to bring her son, Kenneth, to the courthouse square to take a stand. They had made arrangements for the county school board members to meet them at the square.

Florence Cowan was the headmistress at St. Pauls Mission School and Dorothy Groff was her assistant. These two ladies chose twenty-some Monacan children of varying ages to take with them to the square.

Lacie's son, Kenneth, who was scheduled to enter fourth grade come autumn and the new school year, led the march across the square. They came to a stop before the assembled school board members of Amherst County schools. Misses Cowan and Groff wanted these board members to look at these Monacan Indian children. They wanted the school board members to know it would be beyond their power to prevent these children from entering the public schools of Amherst County. They would be exercising their equal rights to receive an equal education.

The bite of discrimination is like a rattlesnake. You never know when it will raise its ugly head. This wasn't the end of prejudice, but it was a start in the right direction.

Coy Martin bought Montrose Orchards from Mr. Autavitch. Luther and I retired and moved in with my ailing father at High Peak Orchards. My father, Walter Branham, was overseer of the orchards. We lived in a large house built of native woods and stones taken from the land. Oh, those beautiful orchards were right at our front door. Wafted on the breeze in the spring and summertime were the delicious smells of ripe fruit. Those waves of beautifully tinted, fragrant blossoms, nothing can compare to.

We often sent our grandchildren Kenneth, Marilyn, Carolyn Sue, and Edith to pick the large, tasty cherries. They always came back complaining that it took a long time to fill those big baskets (the baskets weren't all that big). From the looks of the red stains on their innocent-looking faces, lots of those cherries had not found their way into the baskets, no siree.

Luther "walked," as Monacans say of death, on January 31, 1984.

I moved to the Ridgecrest subdivision to be near my daughter, Lacie. I don't expect I'll ever move again until it's time to join Luther.

United Indians of Virginia presented an award to Cammie Johns on a day designated as Cammie Johns' Day.

Phyliss Hicks read these words from the plaque as she presented it to Cammie:

Award of honor March 24, 1908–1992 to Cammie Branham Johns

Through life's journey, your moccasins have tread softly on Mother Earth, lending support and comfort. Father Sky has smiled proudly as you nurtured, defended, shared and lived your life as one of the people.

Today, at age eighty-four, the United Indians of Virginia and your tribe honor and pay tribute to you, the elder woman of the Monacan Indian Tribe and offer prayers for your continued prosperity and to the Great Father.

Presented this day, October 10, 1992 by Raymonette Adams, Chairman, United Indians of Virginia

Let us pray

Priest: The Lord be with you.

Congregation: And with you.

Priest: Oh, God, how gracious you are to your children. You have walked with Cammie Johns all these years and your blessings and your gifts have been made known to her. Above all, she knows your love, that embraces and keeps her and sustains her, and makes her strong. For this we give thanks and may she know that you are always present to her with all the power of your life and spirit to empower hers, that she may know there is nothing in this life that can ever separate her from your love which you continually make known to us through Christ our Lord. Amen

25
William Carson Branham

I am William Carson Branham, son of Preston Branham and Bertie Duff Branham. My maternal grandparents were Eddie Branham and Dessie Johns Duff. My paternal granddaddy is Lee Branham.

I am fifteen years old this year of 1997.

I attend Amherst County public schools.

In answer to you, the interviewer's question, yes, I've heard a lot about Dr. Walter A. Plecker, but no, we don't study about him in school. I'm glad we don't, really. It would only serve to dredge up the agonies my ancestors endured because of his persecution of Indians who did not meet his craving for a pure white race.

I have learned enough from studying about the thirteen British colonies to know the Indians were the first Americans. They were here before the Britons arrived. The Indians were a peaceful and helpful people. They taught the British how to cope in this land and how to provide for their families. It's a pity life couldn't have gone on in peaceful ways, but the British soon began to do a number on the Indians. I think basically the British were afraid of the Indians because of their ruggedness and different dress. Whenever anyone or a group becomes afraid of something they don't understand, their instinct is to get rid of the object of their fears.

Therefore, the white man began to treat the Indians like they were the lowest creatures on earth. The Indians were determined not to be driven out. They had been willing to share. After all, this was their land first of all.

It has been a long, slow process, but gradually over a very long period of time, people have become much more tolerant of one another. It was very sad for my ancestors to have been treated like a non-people. Good can overcome evil. Together, the white people, the African Americans, and the Indians have made peace with one another.

I never have any problems in school or other activities.

The term "issue," once used by white people in reference to Indians and meant as an insult, has long fallen by the wayside. My friends call me Will, and I call them John or Rick or Mary, or whatever their Christian names may be.

Chief Kenneth Branham and I are invited to speak at colleges, high schools, and elementary schools. We are also invited to speak at libraries and Boy and Girl Scout meetings. We've even been invited to speak at rodeos. We inform about our history and we take along some of our dancers and drummers, sometimes. We usually dress in our regalia we ourselves have designed and made.

The costumes are very colorful. For the men's traditional dance, the costume consists of a bustle worn on the men's backs. There is also a breastplate, a shield, and leggings. The dancer also carries a stick and some bells or deer horns. This costume portrays an armor to protect one against an onslaught from an enemy.

For the grass dance, one wears a roach. Perhaps I should explain the roach. A roach is a headdress like you've seen in the movies. The roach reaches back over the center of one's head to the back of one's neck. It represents a rooster's comb. One also wears a short vest with strings of yarn swinging from the hem of the vest. There is also a leather apron with long yarn streamers that swing and sway far out as one dances. The grass dancers are the first ones sent into the circle in the summertime. In those early years there were no such things as scythes or lawn mowers to cut or mow the grasses. So these grass dancers danced in the tall grass until their swinging streamers slashed the blades of grass and their moccasined feet matted it upon the ground, readying the circle for performances more elite to follow.

The Fancy dance is very fast paced. The men wear two bustles. One bustle is worn on their backs and one on their necks. The women wear shawls around their shoulders. As they dance, they lift their arms and the shawls fan out to represent butterflies' wings. The footwork is very swift.

There is also the Sneak-up dance, the Round dance, the Two-step dance, and the Jingle dress dance. These are but a few of the dances, but I speak of these because these are the most popular dances.

At this time, we have four drummers. They are Danny Gear, Bill Shields, Johnny Johns, and me, Will Branham.

The songs never have a name. There are different drum beats for different dances. For instance, there is the honor beat. It is faster than the regular beat. Only one drummer drums the honor beat while all the other drummers maintain the regular beat. There are ways to make the sounds of different animals on the drums.

The drums are prayed over before each performance. No one should approach the drummers or the dancers during a performance. Just sit back and enjoy the drumbeats and the swirling array of the dancers' colorful costumes.

God painted this world a multiplicity of colors. God loves the harmony of colors. God painted mankind, too, by dipping his paint brush in several hues and blending some as an artist completes his canvas. God never meant his colors to cause discord. Individual colors should never matter. It is the rainbow itself that matters.

26

Heather and Holly Branham

My name is Heather Branham. I am thirteen years old this past March 8, 1997. I'm in the eighth grade. I have a seventeen-year-old brother, Shane. He is living in Nashville. He hopes to get a break into the country music field. He writes music and lyrics as well as plays the guitar.

My parents are Roger Branham and Peggy Johns Branham. My maternal grandparents were Lewis and Bertie Johns. My paternal grandmother is Hattie Belle Branham Hamilton.

I'll let Holly introduce herself to you and then we'll both talk.

I am Holly Branham, cousin to Heather. Our dads are brothers and they married sisters. My parents are Ronnie and Eleanor Johns Branham. I have one sister named Edith Lucille. We call her Lu. She is a nurse at a Lynchburg, Virginia, hospital.

Heather and I are only two weeks apart in age. Heather was born March 8, 1984, and I was born March 21, 1984.

Our moms have told us of the trauma they endured growing up in Amherst County, Virginia. They were not allowed to attend the county public schools. The white people had public schools. The black people had public schools. The Indians had no school except the two-room log schoolhouse provided by the Episcopalian diocese.

The white people insisted the Indians were black people. To the black people, the Indians were white people. The Indians themselves insisted they were Monacan Indians.

My sister, Lu, had a rough time the first few weeks in nursing school in Lynchburg. It was mostly some of the instructors who were reluctant to accept Lu into the program. Mostly, it was no big deal.

My fifth-grade teacher is really cool. A couple of times this year, she has invited me to dress in my regalia and demonstrate and also explain the meanings of various dance routines.

My teacher is really into teaching on a broad scope. She understands this world is complex. The people are complex. This world of people needs reading, writing, and arithmetic skills; but they need much more scope. She has inspired me to enter the teaching profession.

Heather, it's your turn. What do you want to talk to the interviewer about?

Thanks, Holly. George Whitewolf and Danny Gear have taught us a lot about organizing a powwow. It's a teaching event. It's also a lot of fun. Visitors come from far and wide. They learn to feel comfortable watching the dance performances. They learn the regalias, the painted faces and arms, and the loud beat of the drums are a performance. It is not a prelude to an attack.

Visitors love the baskets and quilts. They enjoy tasting samples of foods they aren't very familiar with.

Visitors are intrigued when we explain the meaning of our dances. Our dances are a form of storytelling. Each and every dance has a different story to tell.

My main dance involves my jingle dress. The dress is made with 365 metal cones sewed to the fabric. Each of the 365 cones presents a day of the year. The cones are shaped from empty snuff cans or tobacco can lids.

The story is that a man's daughter became seriously ill. The medicine men tried every Indian medicine known to them, all to no avail.

One dark night, the little girl's father tossed and turned upon his bed. Finally, he dozed off into a restless sleep. He dreamed. In the dream he saw a beautiful dress. The dress was covered with bright, shiny cones. The cones jingled against one another, making beautiful music as the dress swayed upon an ethereal form.

The man awoke. He told his wife of his dream. He asked her to please make such a dress and dance in it at the bedside of their dying daughter.

She made the dress that very day. As she danced beside her daughter's bed that night, the beautiful, musical dress, embellished with 365 jingling cones, swayed upon the mother's dancing form. The young girl heard the sounds of jingles. She sat up. She was healed.

Holly, it's your turn to share about your favorite dance.

Thanks, Heather. My favorite dance is not as heartfelt as yours.

My favorite dance is the General dance. For this dance, we invite the visitors to come forward and dance around the circle with us. Usually, it's the youth who will venture forward. Even some of them are hesitant. The bolder boys and girls will race into the circle. The shy ones enter gingerly. Others approach and then stop, just short of the circle. I think I like this dance so well because it is all inclusive.

Some of the smaller kids will sidle up to us and ask, "Are you a real Indian?"

17. Holly Branham in her regalia jingle-dress, adorned with
365 metal cones.

There are other kids who want us to know they are wise to us. They will reach
out to touch our regalias and say, "Your costume is beautiful, but you're not really
an Indian. Indians only exist in movies."

My grandpa and grandma Johns used to live with us in their declining years.
Grandpa Johns was a trip. He could be in the living room and Lu and I could be
in the kitchen, raiding the refrigerator; and he would yell, "You kids get away
from that refrigerator. You'll spoil your appetite for supper."

Grandpa could be on the porch or in his bedroom and Lu and I could be reaching for the candy dish. He would yell, "Kids, back away from that candy dish."

Lu and I were never able to figure out how Grandpa knew where we were and what we were doing.

We were very sad when Grandpa died. He died in his sleep while lying on the sofa one afternoon. Grandma found him. He was already cold. Grandma was suffering from Alzheimer's. She thought he was just asleep and she covered him with a blanket.

We took care of Grandma as long as we could. The Alzheimer's progressed more rapidly after we lost Grandpa. She no longer knew us when she passed away a few years later.

Our other grandma, Hattie Bell Hamilton, lives with us now. She stays busy. When she isn't quilting, she's baking desserts. She also cans the best crispy lime pickles in these hills. Grandma Hattie is getting old. Mama tries to get Grandma to rest. Grandma puts her hand on her hips and she says, "I'm not working. I'm exercising."

Yesterday, you, the interviewer, asked to meet with Heather and me today. We agreed. We hope we have been helpful. One final thought we wanted to leave with you. Travel is so easy now in the late 1900s. People from all over the globe travel and interact. They come and go by land, air, and sea. People of different cultures or races attend schools together. They work and they play together. They intermarry. The color of anyone's skin is no longer a big issue. That's a reality check.

It was very shameful when the legislature allowed Dr. Walter A. Plecker to crucify the eight Indian tribes of Virginia. That is bad history now. Plecker's plague is no more. Amherst County is now a pleasant place to live and interact.

27
The Minister

I am the minister. That doesn't tell you beans, does it? Allow me to start over. I graduated from St. Martin's Seminary in New York in 1965. I had majored in theology. I was assigned to work in the inner city of Baltimore, Maryland. I worked in that field for three years.

I continued studying and became a captain in the church army. This is an evangelistic arm of the Episcopal church. This organization assigns ministers to a base of operation. The army generally gives a minister three choices of places to serve.

I informed the officials I wanted to get away from the inner city. My children were very young and I wanted them out of the rat race of anything goes. I told the officials I had given this much thought and prayer.

The officials gave me two choices. They said I could visit St. Pauls in Amherst, Virginia, and a larger post in Florida. Then I could let them know my choice of these two places of service.

I informed the bishop I would like to visit St. Pauls Church first since it was close to Baltimore and maybe wouldn't be such a big change for my wife.

The bishop said, "I'll inform the rector at St. Pauls we'll be there this coming Sunday to spend the day with them."

Very early Sunday morning, my wife and children, the bishop, and I crammed into my sedan and headed for Amherst County and St. Pauls on Kenmore Road.

We attended the morning service, after which we were served a scrumptious picnic lunch on the front lawn of the church.

After lunch, I decided to walk around and look the place over. I ended up crossing the little bridge to the building housing the kitchen and beside it, the log schoolhouse for the children because the Indian children were forbidden to attend the county schools. Chief Harry Branham and Floyd Johns found me there.

18. St. Pauls Episcopal Church for the Monacans, at the foot of Bear Mountain in Amherst County, Virginia. The church was originally built in 1908 and burned in 1930. In 1931 it was rebuilt and remains in service today.

We talked. They told me they had been without a minister for about six months. They told of the needs of this small Monacan Indian community. As we talked, I made up my mind completely. I left the two men beside the little creek. I walked back to the front of the church where my wife was in conversation with the ladies. I motioned her aside and I said, "Honey, I want to pastor here."

Our children had gathered around us, and she and they looked kind of worried.

My wife looked around at the small cleared area. She looked at the hills and dales. She looked at the rows of mountains surrounding her. Then she said, "Dear, do you really want to work out here in the middle of nowhere?"

I answered, "Honey, this isn't what I'd call nowhere. It's just down the road a piece from Baltimore."

We had served at St. Pauls two years when three things of note came to my attention. I had established a few Sunday School classes, whereas before there had been none. The older ladies were teaching these new classes. They kept insisting to me that I needed to turn these classes over to the kids. The kids were getting some education at the two-room mission school here at St. Pauls, whereas the older ladies had none or almost none.

These ladies were teaching invaluable lessons from life's personal experiences. It took some persuasion on my part to convince the ladies to keep on teaching.

The other thing of note that came to my attention was a lesson I learned from Bowman Nuckles. Bowman taught a class of men. I decided to visit his class one Sunday morning. Bowman read to the men from the Bible, using the text I had preached from the Sunday before. Then Bowman discussed the passage with the men, explaining some of the things I had said the Sunday before.

I realized after sitting in on that class that without Bowman, I had been wasting some of my time. I needed to rid myself of my New York and Baltimore accent.

The third lesson I learned had been learned after only a few months into my first year at St. Pauls. I was very much into making plans for repairs to the schoolhouse and repainting Parish Hall. I was busy introducing new programs. I urged the congregation to make plans for future needs. In the vestry meetings, the men would listen. They would discuss issues, but they never voted on the matters being discussed. They would put off voting until a later meeting. This scenario took place over a period of months. Finally, I learned what the holdups on voting were. The men would gather out on the lawn and further discuss with Chief Harry Branham the issues at hand and seek his individual opinion on each issue.

I knew Harry as a quiet man, not readily speaking out in called meetings. Harry had very serious responsibilities as chief. The men believed it very important to consider Harry's opinions on any issue affecting the entire tribe. Harry, in turn, took his responsibilities very seriously. He felt a need of time to digest any issue fully before voicing his opinions. Harry wasn't really a quiet man. Harry was a thoughtful man.

I had to laugh at myself when I understood how things worked at Monacan headquarters. Such unified cooperation caused one to think the operation was running itself.

Toward the close of 1967, our second year at St. Pauls Parish, my wife told me she needed to share her burden with me.

"Whatever your burden is, it needs to be my burden also, Honey," I told her.

My wife hadn't been an Episcopalian until just after we first met. Now here she was away from the city and trying to learn the ways of mountain folks.

My wife said, "Dear, I want to be of service to the Lord and to these people, but I grow lonelier each day here at this parish. I need some vehicle with which to get more involved in things these women like to do. I need your help and advice."

I had heard that some of the large churches were having success with church bazaars. I suggested she call a meeting of the ladies and asked if they would help her plan and execute a bazaar to be held in early autumn.

The ladies agreed they would help her in this venture.

True to their word, they began right away working, working toward their goal. They met often at Parish Hall to work on quilts. Some ladies wove baskets of different materials and formed those into various shapes and sizes. Younger women made huge kettles of apple butter. They canned vegetables and made crispy lime pickles. The last-minute baking of rows and rows of cakes, cookies, and pies were enough to make one sinfully gluttonous.

We only had a small building on the far side of Falling Rock Creek for our Parish Hall at that time. We had no running water. Water had to be pumped from a well and carried in buckets. The cooking was done on a wood-burning stove.

I advertised the upcoming event in notices sent to many of the Episcopalian churches. I sent ads to the local newspaper and to the Lynchburg newspaper. I created fliers and the children placed those in store windows as the store owners allowed. I advertised the event as the Creekside Café.

The night before the big day, the ladies were up until late at night. They ironed the colorful tablecloths they had sewn for the many tables. The men were busy setting up the tables in a grassy area on the far side of the creek. That meant all the foodstuff had to be carried, single file, across the narrow bridge. The teenagers willingly pitched in to help carry box after box of food and canned goods. The men loaded themselves down with baskets and quilts.

I left the finishing touches to the others and went to the rectory to finish up some paperwork. When the office clock struck the hour for the bazaar to begin, I stepped to my open window. I saw people coming by the wagonloads and in automobiles and others walking up Kenmore Road. I heard a group of Monacan women saying, "Look at all the people. We didn't believe anyone would come."

People bought everything that had a price tag on it. We had sold out way before the four o'clock P.M. closing time. People lingered on, seeming to enjoy just visiting with one another and complimenting the Monacans and stating they hoped there would be a bazaar next year, too.

The next morning, Annie Branham came to church early. She wanted a moment to talk to me. She said, "Pastor, I want to apologize. Some of the Monacan women stayed away from the bazaar yesterday because they didn't believe anyone would come and they didn't want to distress you."

I patted Annie's hand and said to her, "Annie, bless you. The ladies priced everything too low. We could have sold twice as much stuff as we had to sell, but don't feel badly. We made $400.00 for church needs. That's a lot of money for this day and time."

The following year the ladies changed the name of the bazaar from Creekside Café to St. Pauls Bazaar and now it has been renamed again to the Monacan Homecoming.

The bazaar has grown over the years until people from many states attend. In fact, folks from afar plan their vacations to include the first Saturday in October, so they can attend the homecoming. We have to run shuttle carts to and from the parking lots. God is good.

When I had left Baltimore to minister at St. Pauls, I had bought six cheap guitars. I think I paid $174.00 or thereabouts for the lot. I bought the guitars because I had been told the Monacans were a musical people, but lacked instruments enough to go around.

At our first July Fourth picnic following my arrival, I gave away the first of those guitars. I gave it to a young boy named Danny. That young boy strode up in front of the crowd and he began to pick and sing. Others came forward as I held up the remaining five guitars. Pretty soon we had a guitar-picking, gospel-singing jamboree.

Following that Fourth of July celebration, 1968, my question to the diocese was, "What do you want our main goal to be?"

The answer was, "We want St. Pauls to become self-supporting."

When I first introduced the goal to the congregation, I especially remember Betty Johns's reaction. I told the Monacans it cost forty thousand dollars per year to operate this particular church. I added what turned out to be the shocker that this forty thousand dollars didn't include my salary.

Betty Johns fell off the bench in reaction.

These figures seemed like a totally impossible goal. These were very poor people working at menial jobs for menial wages. Most of it was back-breaking work, too.

Monacans are a never-give-in, never-give-up people. If this is what the diocese said they must do, then somehow they would do it. They began working late into the nights making more and more items to sell. A store in town agreed to stock and sell their baskets. In just a few short, backbreaking years, St. Pauls became self-supporting.

I understand you, the interviewer, have already talked to Peggy about her experience at the Lynchburg hospital. Otherwise, I wouldn't discuss it. These Monacans are a wonderful people. It's a pity they have had to suffer so many injustices.

Peggy's husband was working and couldn't get off work when Peggy was dismissed from the Lynchburg hospital. That is why I was asked to pick her up. I learned that her newborn baby couldn't be dismissed with her. He was having difficulty with congestion of his lungs.

Peggy was crying and I thought that was the reason for her sobs. I tried to reassure her he would be all right.

Peggy said, between sobs, "I know he is, but the clerk insisted I sign papers listing him as colored. I was still groggy from the sedation and she was insisting it was state law that Indians had to be listed as 'colored.' Oh, what can I do?"

I looked at Peggy's tear-swollen face. "I don't know, but I'll soon find out," I reassured her.

I took Peggy home and then I called the chaplain at the hospital. He said, "I'm sorry. I can't do anything about the papers Peggy signed. It is hospital policy because it is state law."

I called PCL, that's People's Civil Liberties. The home office for PCL is in Washington, D.C. They agreed to investigate the matter. The first man they sent was ineffectual. I called and talked to the PCL director. He said, "I'll come down myself and look into this matter."

He came. He went directly to the hospital in Lynchburg. Then he went to the State Department. Then he called me. He said "Father, the matter you contacted me about has been taken care of. The papers in dispute have been corrected and the Lynchburg hospital authorities have agreed that in the future they will abide by federal law in these matters, not state law."

The state sent an order to the hospitals, decreeing the mother of the baby could decide the baby's race. The hospitals were to abide by each mother's decision. The drawback to that ruling was that most Monacan women weren't aware of the ruling and the Lynchburg hospital's personnel were not always well informed of the ruling. That at times resulted in some records still being filled out incorrectly.

The Monacans didn't have to go about looking for trouble, trouble seemed always to find them. For instance, about fifteen or twenty years ago landowners in and around Amherst County decided to begin selling off their land. The orchards and tobacco farms had begun to be less profitable. Real estate was on the rise.

The landowners began to inform the Monacan tenant workers that they must find housing because the tenant houses would soon be torn down. The Monacans would still have work in helping build subdivisions, but they would not have places to live.

Gene Branham, Lucian Branham's son, and I usually spent a lot of time together. We were either involved in working on projects or fishing, both of equal importance. One day while sitting on the creek bank and casting out fish bait, I had a brainstorm. "Gene," I said, "we need to find some land we can afford."

Gene said, "Why?"

I said, "We need to build some houses."

We got real busy fishing for land. We found fifteen acres Mr. Burgess had put up for sale.

We had ourselves a powwow with Mr. Burgess and I told him, "Mr. Burgess, we don't have any money, but we intend to find out what grants might be available. We'll think of projects to make up any difference. We need to buy your fifteen acres that are for sale."

The land lay at the foot of High Peak Mountain and had lots of red delicious apple trees on it.

Mr. Burgess said, "Father, you're trying to help the Monacans find a place to live, right?"

"They need a place to call their own, but not a reservation, never that," I said.

Mr. Burgess said, "There's a forty-thousand-dollar delinquent loan on that land. Pay the loan off and the land is yours."

We went to Farmers Home Loans, Inc. They were interested in helping us. They explained to us how to put the package together. They also explained how to get the project financed. I had had some experience with this method. I had been involved in a similar subdivision venture before I came into the church army. In that deal, I had signed a contract for a half million dollars, but didn't have to pay any of it until each house was sold.

Farmers Home Loans, Inc., agreed to this premise for this project. The group we formed voted Lucian Branham in as treasurer. He would co-sign checks with Farmers. I think Lucian got a big kick out of co-signing those, to the Monacans' way of thinking, gold-plated checks.

Our cooperation is still in effect and Lucian can still sign checks. He just doesn't have an opportunity to do so anymore. The fifteen acres now has the number of houses, built and sold, allowed on that parcel of land. There are eighty-five acres at the top of High Peak Mountain that can now be bought and built on. The impediment is me. At my present age, I'm not sure I want to be involved in putting together another subdivision. Oh, we named this fifteen-acre project "Ridgecrest."

My understanding of the church history having to do with the Monacans in the 1800s is unauthenticated. The history has been handed down by word-of-mouth. It is said that early on and very seldom, some Methodist minister would ride in and preach the gospel message to the Monacans. Later on, circuit riding Baptist preachers came from time to time.

Then the Amherst preachers apparently developed a sense of concern. They began to come by to minister the word of the Lord. Then the Episcopalians came. The record keeping began with them when they sent in Arthur Powell Gray II. He came in as a student minister in the year of 1908. Arthur Gray was a responsible, dedicated young man. He took the plight of the Monacans to heart and encouraged them to build a church. He helped them in every way he could while also preparing himself to enter seminary. The Monacans and Gray built the back half of the church on solid rock—placed there by God Himself. That rock is for real. The Monacans carried much lesser rocks, although large, by hand, sled and wagons, down the mountainside. They used those rocks to form the foundation for the front portion of the church. When the little white painted church was finished, they named it St. Pauls Church. Gray ministered to the Monacans there until 1910. The church still stands and is still used in 2006. It is a beautiful, picture-perfect monument to God.

28
Rosemary Clark Whitlock

I am Rosemary Clark Whitlock. My parents were Frank Calvin Clark of Rock-bridge County and Dora Branham Clark of Amherst County. My maternal grandparents were Edmund Branham and Elena Willis Branham, both of Amherst County. Elena was Edmund's second wife. His first wife was Betty Ann Johns of Amherst County. My paternal grandparents were John C. Clark and Margaret Tyree Clark.

My maternal great-grandparents were Elisha B. Willis and Malinda Adcock Willis of Amherst County and also Richard and Christine Wise Branham. According to Edmund and Elena Branham, Edmund's paternal father, Richard was the son of old Ed Branham, who came from Scotland.

The Branhams are of English descent who married into the Monacan Nation.

The Clarks came from Ireland in the early 1700s and settled in the Blue Ridge Mountains. One particular mountain became mapped as Clarks Mountain. There is a sign on the Blue Ridge Parkway reading, "Clarks Gap, highest peak of the Blue Ridge." That is where my father was born and raised to manhood.

There were Cherokee Indian hunting parties in the mountain range from time to time, and some Monacans resided in the Natural Bridge area.

At my birth, I was christened Rosebud. It wasn't until many years later when I changed my name legally to Rosemary that I learned Rosebud is an Indian name.

I, myself, never experienced any prejudice growing up in the Allegheny County area. I have been told of two incidences in which my older siblings experienced rejection. This is their version of those experiences. They were living in Waugh in a house known as the Frenchman Place. Waugh is right next door to Big Island. Soon after moving to Waugh, on an early spring morning, Mama told the children they could attend the little white-painted church within walking distance. The children were so excited as they approached the church's open door.

19. Elena Willis Branham, the author's grandmother, whose trial testimony is included as Appendix D.

A deacon standing at the open door refused to let them enter. He told them to go back where they belonged. Some children loitering in the churchyard began throwing rocks at them. Heretofore, my siblings had not experienced the prejudice against Indians and other dark-skinned people. They entered a school for white children that autumn and the rock-throwing kids became their friends. All was well until 1930. I had joined the family and was now four years old. We moved to Longdale, Virginia. The other siblings entered school, a white school. All was well the first two years, then the children brought home a letter for Mama from the teacher. The letter stated the Clark children could not return to an all-

20. The wedding picture of Dora Branham Clark, author's mother, at age fifteen, in 1909.

white school due to a complaint from the Bureau of Vital Statistics. Well, Mama wrote Dr. Walter A. Plecker a letter of complaint. A copy of her letter is included here in her own handwriting (Appendix E). I am told by my older siblings this was the first of several letters Mama wrote which were ignored by Dr. Plecker.

My mama was a noncursing lady but she got to the point she needed something emphatic with which to refer to Dr. Plecker, so thereafter Mama referred to him as "Old Plecker."

Years later when I was in my early teens and Fred, my brother, was twelve years old, he became the focus of one man's prejudice. Fred was darker skinned than the rest of us. He had coal-black hair and deep-brown eyes. One thing of note was that Fred's coal-black hair was fine and silky. Apparently, the man he was about to encounter took notice only of the dark skin tone, but didn't notice the silky hair.

Fred had spent the day helping Clarence, his brother-in-law, rearrange some shelving in the shoe repair shop of which Clarence was manager.

When the town began to roll up the streets for the night, Clarence decided it was time to quit work and grab a bite to eat at the Main Street restaurant before it, too, closed for the night. When Clarence and Fred entered the restaurant, the owner looked up from his station behind the counter. He looked at Clarence, who was tall and slender with pale blond hair and blue eyes. He looked at Fred, who was short and dark-complected with black hair, and the owner said while pointing at Fred, "He is not welcome in here. I don't serve Negroes."

Clarence said, "He is not a Negro. He is my brother-in-law."

They argued back and forth for a few minutes, then the restaurateur said, "I have a Negro woman working for me in the kitchen. She can spot anyone trying to pass for white in a damned minute. I'll call her out here and we'll settle this once and for all."

He stormed into the kitchen and came back with the black lady and explained what he wanted from her.

The black lady nodded. She looked Fred over from head to toe and toe to head. Then she shook her head and said, "Mr. Boss Man, I don't rightly know what he is, but he sure ain't one of us."

The restaurateur's face turned a motley color and he shouted at her angrily, "Finish cleaning the kitchen. We are closed as of this minute."

Fred grew up and was inducted into the army as a white man, serving in Alaska and overseas. Fred played several instruments and sang, (sometimes told) a little too much like Hank Snow. Fred spent his two-year hitch as a member of an all-white orchestra. He wrote Mama a letter soon after entering the service. "While the non-musical soldiers are being jerked awake at early dawn by reveille's bugle call, we are just going to bed, having played or practiced music until dawn."

After being discharged from the army, Fred toured with a country music band and eventually ended up in California. He fell in love with California. He said, "California is the place to be. No one cares about anyone's race, color, or creed. Everyone is just simply, people." Fred could probably have gone far in music. He had talent and he loved music. He wasn't very motivated though to putting a lot of energy into anything. He drank alcoholic beverages more and more frequently. His health deteriorated and he died at age fifty-seven.

In 1946, a divorce court trial was held and our lineage was one aspect being examined. The records of the trial are open to the public, but I only want to include a few documents in this volume having to do with our family. This testimony, excerpted in Appendix D, of Grandma Elena Willis Branham, must have been traumatic for an elderly woman. My mother's heritage on the Branham side in particular was examined because it was charged that she was colored according to Dr. Plecker's records. After examining the documentary evidence and testimonies, the judge declared the Branhams were white and ordered the director of the Bureau of Vital Statistics to correct the birth and marriage records accordingly.

Appendices G, H, and I are copies of my parents' and grandparents' marriage licenses. Notice that on Edmund Branham's first marriage to Bettie Johns, they are listed as race: "col.," "Col," or "colored" meant African American. My grandpa Edmund couldn't read, having no schooling, and I believe Bettie Johns was also unschooled. This young couple would have objected had they known. Since the state of Virginia refused to acknowledge them as Indian, they chose to be accepted as Caucasian rather than Negro. The Negro race had a few more privileges than the Indians, but scarcely more.

Also used as exhibit was my grandpa Edmund and grandma Elena Willis's marriage license on which they are both listed as white (Appendix I). On my father Frank Clark's and mother Dora Branham Clark's marriage license, they are both listed as white (Appendix G).

In this same trial, the War Department's statement of my older brother Harry Clark's discharge from the army was entered as an exhibit (Appendix F). Harry served in an organization composed of white men. This was also entered as evidence of white rather than Negro.

My brother Harry was born in 1910 and my brother Fred in 1928. These official documents show they both served in the United States Army as white men many years apart.

My mother Dora Branham Clark's letter to Dr. Walter A. Plecker is also a part of the same court record (Appendix E). This inclusion is a Xerox of her letter written in her own handwriting.

Appendix C is a transcript from the *Times* newspaper in Richmond, Virginia, in 1896 that was used also in the trial of year 1946. It was used as Exhibit No. 8. Media coverage of the Monacan story is very informative. An Associated Press article in the *Roanoke Times & World News* on October 11, 1992, tells of the anthropologist Jeffery Hantman of the University of Virginia. Hantman, speaking after some of his digs were reported in the article, said, "Their past is hidden and they have been intensely discriminated against." Hantman was speaking of the Monacans.

It has been said of Indians that we were triads. After many, many years of persecution, some Indians began to intermarry with blacks and whites. Let's think this through logically. If Indians married whites and blacks, that means whites

and blacks married Indians. Intermarriage can't work just one way. Also from almost the moment the English and French came to American soil, they began to
get sexually chummy with Indians and women got pregnant. All Americans are
triads or at least duos.

Why is it some of us refuse to accept that fact? We can't pigeonhole people as
much as some people would desire to. What it all boils down to is that all of us
are Americans and we all need to get back to our Declaration of Independence as
stated in the second paragraph, part A. "We hold these truths to be self-evident,
that all men are created equal; that they are endowed by their Creator with certain unalienable rights; that among these are life, liberty, and the pursuit of hap-
piness."

From 1912 to 1946, Dr. W. A. Plecker insisted on persecuting not only the Indian race, but some other races as well. He had an all-consuming drive to elimi-
nate all mixing of races and determined there would be only white and colored
races listed on legal documents under his control as state registrar—and he alone
determined which was which. For years before the Racial Integrity Act of 1924,
Plecker, John Powell, and consorts had their narrow-minded dream of elimi-
nating racial mixing in Virginia.

In an October 4, 1935, response to a question about the status of a person from
the Philippines, Dr. Plecker answered: "In reply to your inquiry as to the racial
classification of a native Filipino, I beg to advise that they, as well as Asiatics, including Chinese, Japanese, natives of India, etc. are classed as colored and included
with the colored in compiling the statistics.

"Under the law of Virginia, Filipinos and other Asiatics are not permitted to
marry white people. The child will be classed as colored" (Smith 1993).

Dr. Plecker wrote many letters along these same lines, filled with hate and
prejudice.

When I was growing up, my mama many times evaded my persistent questioning about her childhood. She only answered with her stock answer, "Those
were hard times. We must look toward tomorrow. Yesterday is gone."

I could not understand why Mama wouldn't share her memories. I had no idea
of the suffering and oppression her people had been subjected to by Dr. Plecker's
big jar of bile. In recent years when I have interviewed my mama's people, once
in a while I have heard those same words uttered by elders in their reluctance to
speak of the past.

I want to point out to all black Americans that I most emphatically mean no
disrespect, no offense in this book when I refer to black Americans as "col," colored, Negro, or blacks. I use these terms to point out their usage by prejudiced
people in days gone by, just as my mama's people also hated being called issue,
which was meant to insult. We Monacans certainly understand. I recall a rhyme

children used to chant, "Sticks and stones may break my bones, but words will never hurt me."

That is certainly untrue. Words spoken to put down another, to the recipient, can cut to the bone.

The rightful meaning of words can be misunderstood and then when given the right twist, it comes out meaning thus and so. For instance, the word issue has many connotations. One terminology is a person's lineal descendants. That mean's a person's children, grandchildren, and on and on. Therefore, the more is-sue you have, the more gifts you get on Mother's Day, Father's Day, and Grand-parent's Day, too.

Issue is spelled "issha" in Hebrew and the word means woman.

A magazine in a series of magazines is an issue.

In the military one is issued supplies. I could go on, but these suffice.

One can twist a phrase's meaning, too. This is something I heard somewhere, sometime, but it fits. A group of Americans were sightseeing in Israel. Two Israel-ite guards were leading the group of Americans. It was a hot day. One American mopped his brow with his handkerchief and remarked to the man walking be-side him, "It's hot like hell here."

One Israelite guard looked at the other guard and said, "These Americans have been everywhere."

The Monacan's reply is, "Under Dr. Plecker as state registrar, our ancestors felt like they had been everywhere."

There was a replica of a Monacan wigwam in Explore Park at route 460W in Roanoke, Virginia. I visited there in 1996. The guide, Stanford Dean Ferguson, now at the Natural Bridge, Virginia, Monacan Village was and is an excellent guide.

The Monacan wigwams of old were built with wood from poplar trees. Pop-lar trees grow straight of trunk and have uniform, straight limbs. Other tree limbs are used to build the circular inner walls and to build the bed framing and attach it to the walls. The bed framing is usually covered with the hides of elk. The beds could be very uncomfortable. The tree limbs used were out-of-round, knobby, and not uniform in size. The framing is tied to the support poles securely with cordage made with dogbane. Dogbane is of the milk weed family. It makes very strong ropes almost impossible to break. It tolerates freezing temperatures very well. Dogbane is an edible plant. Indians learned much about edible plants from observing animals and their eating habits. Wild animals instinctively know which plants and herbs provide the nutrients and vitamins to meet their dietary needs. Wild animals also know the skins of white-tailed deer are pure protein. This and other reasons are why some animals eat all or parts of each other.

To get back to the wigwams after that little detour is to take another step back into time. The frame of the wigwam was covered with the bark from pop-lar trees. A smoke hole was formed in the center at the top of the wigwam to let the smoke escape from the fires burning in the center of the earthen floor. These indoor fires were only used in very cold weather or to smoke cure their meat, which was laid out on wood poles near the top of the wigwam. There was also a hatch door made of bark and cattails. The door hinges were made of hemp rope. The inside walls were covered with cattails to insulate and weatherproof.

Each wigwam could house ten people. The people slept head to toe on (no kicks?) the circular bedding.

Indians didn't worry too much about modesty in wigwam days as they didn't totally strip down anyway.

The wigwams were used as a last resort because Indians much preferred to live and sleep in the outdoors, thought of as the Great White Father's vast wigwam.

To build the replica wigwam at Explore Park necessitated cutting fifty grown poplar trees. To build the replica comparable in size of the wigwams once in use by Monacans according to researched measurements, it took two years and two thousand work hours.

Dean Ferguson said he would imagine it took the Monacans of olden days a much shorter period of time.

The Monacan Indian Nation was present in Virginia when the Treaty of Middle Plantation was signed in 1680.

A tale I once heard is an apt illustration of the steadfast goal the Monacans aim for. It goes like this:

The visiting preacher preached an emphatic sermon on mankind's need of Jesus. Then he gave a compelling invitation to all who would to come for-ward and find Jesus in baptism in the creek.
A man stumbled forward to the altar and said, "I want to find Jesus."
The preacher led the man out to Falling Rock Creek behind the little white church. The preacher said, "I'll dip you backwards into the water and you'll find Jesus as I baptize you."
When the preacher lifted the man's head back up out of the water, he said, "You found Jesus?"
The man said, "No."
The preacher said, "I'll dip you again and this time, surely you will find Jesus."
Again, as the man surfaced, his answer was, "No."
The preacher said, "I'll keep on dipping you."
After a few more dips, the preacher's arms were worn out. He said, "I don't understand. Why aren't you finding Jesus?"

The man was spitting and sputtering as he said, "I don't rightly know, preacher. Are you sure Jesus fell in right about here?"

This story is a good example of the Monacan Indians and their goal. Just as this man kept on getting dumped in the water, determined to find the Jesus he sought, the Monacans have kept on keeping on in petitioning the government of Virginia to grant them their rightful heritage. They have obtained state recognition after many trials and tribulations. The Monacans will continue this fight until they obtain their rightful federal recognition. The documents in the appendices give profound examples of the prejudice they have endured in their continuing struggle as Monacan Indians.

Appendixes A and B

These next two documents, A and B, are portions of the Term Reports of Bear Mountain Mission School, or the St. Pauls Episcopal Mission. The students' names are blocked for privacy. These reports indicate the number of miles the students had to walk to and from school, the courses taught, and statistics reported by the teacher concerning the students and the school. Note at right under building and grounds on A that the mission school is referred to as "Schoolhouse on a rock." In the lower right-hand corner of both A and B, the additional courses of sewing, singing, and drawing were taught in 1922–1923. Cooking was noted on the report, B, for 1924–1925. Notice that the teacher, Miss Ella Pier, who was white, noted the race of students as Indians in 1922–1923, but as Mixed Indian on the 1924–1925 report.

TERM REPORT

Division **Amherst** District **Court House** School **Bear Mountain Miss**

Teacher **Miss Ella Pier** Race **Indian** School Year **1922-1923**
(Mr., Mrs., or Miss.) White

NOTE—Under subjects below write fraction in proper space after each name, the numerator to show grade pupil is in for the current session, and the denominator the grade to which promoted.

	No. of months taught	**6**
	No. days school was open	**120**
	No. of days teacher present	**120**

	Boys	Girls	Total
1 Total enrollment	28	33	61
2 Average daily attend.			
3 Total days on roll	2084	2328	4412
4 Total days present	1193	1369	2562
5 Per cent attendance	57+	58+	58+
6 No. dropt grades 1—4	15	13	28
7 No. dropt grades 5—7	1		1
8 No. dropt grades 8—9	—		None
9 No. dropt grades 10—11	—		None
10 No. promoted grades 1—4	8	15	23
11 No. promoted grades 5—7			None
12 No. promoted grades 8—9			None
13 No. pro'ted grades 10—11			None

BUILDING AND GROUNDS

14 Material **Schoolhouse on a rock**

15 No. Rooms **2**

16 State of repair **Fair**

17 How ventilated **2 doors + 8 windows**

18 How heated **2 wood-stoves**

19 Toilets: **2**

(a) Character **sanitary**

(b) Condition **good**

20 Desks:

(a) Kind **Non-adjustable for height**

(b) No. **50**

(c) Seating capacity **55 or 60**

21 Blackboards: **7**

(a) No. sq. ft. surface **480**

(b) Kind **Boards and oilcloth**

(c) Condition **Very poor**

22 Size of school lot **About 50 sq. yds**

(a) How inclosed **not at all**

INSTRUCTION

23 Could pupils secure text-books at contract prices? **Books enough on hand.**

24 No. hours devoted to instruction in common school branches **23 hrs. weekly**

25 No. hours devoted to instruction in higher branches **2 hrs. weekly**

26 Have you graded course of study? **Yes**

27 Is there a United States flag on school-

Form T. No. 3- 7-18-24- 40M.

TERM REPORT ~~~~~ High Schools

Division **Amherst Co.** District **Court House** School **Bear Mt. Mission**

Teacher **Miss Ella Pier** — **White** Race **School Mixed** Non-School Year **Oct. 24 – May/25**
(Mr., Mrs., or Miss)

DIRECTIONS.—With ink write below in alphabetical order first the names of boys, and then the names of girls, giving in each case the surname first. Give in column two, age on September first. See the register for method of computing average attendance and percentage of attendance. Under school subjects below, write a fraction in proper space after each name, the numerator to show the grade the pupil is in for current session and the denominator the grade to which promoted; modify subject titles for high school use.

NAMES OF PUPILS	No. of miles from school	Age	Days on roll	Days present	Reading	Spelling	Writing	English	Mathematics	Community Study	Va.-Hist.	U.S.-Hist.	Civics	Geography	Hygiene	Physical Ed.	
	1	2	3	4	5	6	7	8	9	10	11	12	13	14	15	16	17

SUMMARIES FOR TERM

No. of Months taught **7**

No. of days school was open **139**

No. days teacher was present **139**

	Boys	Girls	Total
1. Total enrollment	18	25	43
2. Average daily attendance	4.86	10.96	15.8+
3. Total days on roll	1212	2149	3561
4. Total days present	746	1699	2345
5. Per cent attendance	.61+	.68	64%
6. No. promoted grades 1-4	4	11	15
7. No. failed grades 1-4	4	2	6
8. No. dropped grades 1-4	7	9	16
9. Total No. enr'd grades 1-4	15	22	37
10. No. promoted grades 5-7	0	1	1
11. No. failed grades 5-7	2	0	2
12. No. dropped grades 5-7	1	2	3
13. Total No. enr'd grades 5-7	3	3	6
14. No. promoted grades 8-9			No grade
15. No. failed grades 8-9			above 6th
16. No. dropped grades 8-9	—	—	—
17. Total No. enr'd grades 8-9	—	—	—
18. No. promoted grades 10-11	—	—	—
19. No. failed grades 10-11	—	—	—
20. No. dropped grades 10-11	—	—	—
21. Total No. enr'd grades 10-11	—	—	—
22.			

NOTE.—The totals, boys and girls, items 6, 7, and 8 above, will be the same as the total, boys and girls, item 9; in the same way the totals for items 10, 11, and 12 will equal the total for item 13; the totals for items 14, 15, and 16, will equal the total for item 17; and the totals for items 18, 19, and 20, will equal the total for item 21. The total of items 9, 13, 17, and 21, will equal the total of item 1. This careful checking of the above table shall be made before the report is turned in at the superintendent's office. The items of the above table must agree with the corresponding items in the age-grade distribution table shown on the other side of this sheet. Note the special instructions given under this table.

INSTRUCTION

25. Could pupils secure textbooks at contract prices? **Yes**

26. No. hours devoted to instruction in elementary school branches **21 weekly**

27. No. hours devoted to instruction in high school branches **None** { Music 1 Sewing 2 days Cooking 1 hr. }

28. Did you use State course of study? **Yes**

29. Is there a United States flag on school-house? **One large one in Schoolhouse; none on building** (OVER)

Appendix C

The following is a transcription of an evidentiary document, a newspaper article, used in the divorce trial that began April 11, 1946, in which the question of the race of the Clarks and Branhams was raised. Partial testimony from that trial is included as Appendix D. Dr. Plecker still served as state registrar of vital statistics at the start of the trial, but submitted his letter of resignation on May 27, 1946. As evidence in the trial, this article was used as an aid in ascertaining that the Branhams, Willises, and Clarks were Indian. Monacans at that time were assumed to be Cherokee, but these named families were clearly considered Indian. Titled as "William Henry Clark, Exhibit No. 8," it is an excerpt from *The Times,* Richmond, Virginia, Sunday, April 19, 1896, page 8. Original on file at the Clerk's Office, Alleghany Courthouse, Covington, Virginia.

Cherokee Indians.

In this county it is not generally known that we have had a settlement of Cherokee Indians for many years. A few, and a very few, of the oldest remain to tell the story and the younger portion, who know it only as a tradition, are passing from observation by the mingling of races, one of the results of the great upheaval produced by the war.

In that portion of the foot-hills of the Blue Ridge Mountains in Amherst County, known as the Tobacco Row Mountain, Bear Mountain, Stinnett's, and Paul's mountains, from five to eight miles southwest of the courthouse, a race of people exists to-day claiming to be Cherokee Indians, and not without satisfactory proof. The older part were typical Indians, a rich copper color, high cheekbones, long, straight black hair, tall and erect in form, stolid and not emotional like the African, but of as manly bearing as some of Buffalo Bill's best specimens. The original settlers came to the county at an early period. William Evans, a Cherokee Indian, first resided about the time of the Revolutionary War, on Buffalo River, in Amherst County. His daughter, Mollie Evans, married one William Johns, son of Mallory Johns, an Indian, sometimes called a Portuguese, who lived to an advanced age, said to be 114 years, and died at the house of his grandson, William B. Johns, in the "Indian Settlement" as it was then called, and by which it was known when I first knew them. There exists a tradition at this day, amongst these Indians, that Mallory Johns, William Evans, and John Redcross, all came from the South, and it may be that they belonged to the Cherokees of North Carolina, who found their way here in the visits of the Indians then made on foot along the air line from North Carolina to Washington to see the Great Father as they do now on the railroad, and that either in going or returning they stopped by the way and took up their abode here. Beyond the tradition I know nothing reliable, but my theory as to why they were here is doubtless the correct explanation.

An Interesting History.

About the year 1825 William Johns purchased of Landon Cabell, 500 acres of land on Bear Mountain, and on this tract, known as the "Johns settlement," he built a humble dwelling in a little cove making out from the east side of Bear Mountain, not far from where Mr. John Hamilton now lives a short mile west of Berkley M. E. Church, South, which is on the road leading from Amherst Courthouse to Pedlar Mills. Here he lived and died, a worthy and peaceable citizen, following farming as a business, and raised a large family of sons and daughters— dying about 1855. Some of his descendants moved to Ohio and West Virginia, but 258, by a count recently made for me, remain in Amherst at this day. They are engaged in farming in a small way, or working on shares with owners of adjoining lands. One of his sons, Tarlton Johns, married Eliza Redcross, a daughter of John Redcross, a well-known Cherokee Indian, and by Billy Evans, Mallory Johns, William Johns, and John Redcross, this colony was started. Two of them, William Johns and John Redcross, were known to the writer, who in early life held an office that brought him in contact with all classes of citizens. John Redcross died about 1861, at the house of Tarlton Johns, on the summit of Bear Mountain. Previous to the late war, these people were isolated and practically shut out from contact and intercourse with the outside world, owing to the fact that their color precluded intercourse with the whites, who were the land and slave owners, and they on the other hand held themselves above the slaves. In this way there seemed to be no place for them, and no provision in the law for such a race as to schools as there is now, and to some extent they were cut off from church privileges. The State Law forbid the assembling of colored people unless specially permitted by the county court, and under control of the whites, who had to be present. Indignantly rejecting the idea that they had African blood and scorning the term of "free niggers," but earnestly to this day claiming to be pure Indians, they could not enter the white churches and disdained to worship with the slaves, they became for the time, as they really were, a separate and distinct race and colony, and remained so until a few years before the late war. It is greatly to their credit that under such peculiar circumstances they did not become a settlement of thieves and murderers and their colony a hiding place for fugitives from justice. Shut out and hidden in the little coves of Bear Mountain, where hunting and fishing, gambling and drinking amongst the "bucks' was the Sabbath amusement, without schools and a gospel, and where "no Sabbath's heavenly light" ever came for 25 years, could anything else have been expected but heathenism? Strange as it may seem it was not the case, and a new era was about to dawn on them, for in the year 1858, the late Judge Samuel H. Henry, and Col. Thomas Whitehead, one a lay preacher in the Baptist Church and the other a class leader in the Methodist Church, South, determined to obtain from the county court of Amherst, permission to use the court-house on Sunday afternoons for preaching to the slaves, and using for that purpose one Addison Washington, an eloquent negro preacher, a slave, a born orator, gifted in prayer. They commenced religious services and had large and successful meetings, which soon were noised about. . . . Whitehead, of whom it was sometimes said by narrow-minded people of that day were moving ahead of the times in which they lived, received a message from the Indian settlement from an old woman, saying she lived there and had children living in the colony; that she was old and that her life was coming to a close; that she had not heard the gospel preached nor hymns sung for 25 years; she had been a member of the Methodist Colony at Rocky Seats (now Smyrna) from 1830 to 1835; that the white people had asserted that her people, the Indians, were "free niggers" and must sit with the slaves in seats provided for them. That this move offended the Indians, who left, vowing they would never enter a church again, but she felt a great desire to hear the gospel preached once more, and begged that singing and prayer be had at her house.

Heard the Gospel.

They complied with her request and appointed a day for preaching. A few days after this her son returned and said they had built an arbor with seats and a stand for preaching in the Indian reserve. He stated that many of them had never heard prayer, a hymn or the Scriptures read, because they steadfastly kept the vows their fathers had made. These men preached according to their promise, carried on their meetings, had revival services, buried the dead and established a joint church in which Henry procured a Baptist minister to immerse those who preferred that mode, and Whitehead brought the Methodist minister to those who preferred the Methodist Church, and thus it continued until the war carried the evangelists into the Confederate Army. Soon after the war the Northern Methodist Church sent them one E. W. Pearce, a preacher, who remained with them for one year, and after he left the Rev. W. C. Clements, of the Northern Methodist Church, came and remained three years, collecting a congregation and starting the building of a church, but his death from heart disease put an end to his labors. In the last two years the Rev. J. W. Johnson, of the Baptist Church, a colporter, has preached to them and in his work has been assisted by Mr. S. H. Walkup, an elder in the Presbyterian Church, and the teacher of the public school for them. It is evident that much good is being done by these gentlemen. Here is to-day an opportunity for the Indian school at Hampton, to accomplish great good amongst the 258 descendants of these original Indian settlers. There are a number of bright youths amongst them, who would gladly welcome the chance to get an education at the Hampton school, and who would in a few years return home to lift their people to a higher plane of moral and religious life. Let this good work begin at once, and let the neglect and the errors of the past, that were born of prejudice against these sons of the forest, be wiped out and forgotten.

Survivor 97 years old.

One of the sons of William Johns, Charles Johns, was a soldier in the war of 1812, and during the late war many of their young men were drafted and carried to Petersburg and Richmond, to work on the Confederate fortifications. From another son of William Johns, William B. Johns, born the 19th February, 1799, now living on the farm of Mr. Adolphus Coleman, I have been enabled to get much information about their history, and to verify much that I had already heard about them. On a recent visit to him, while I noted down his answers to my questions in my memorandum book, I glanced at this man of ninety-seven years, and as he stood before me with his well-defined Indian color and features, erect in form, with his white locks hanging down to his shoulders, a venerable relic of the past, standing on the threshold of the 20th century, a representative of a race soon to be "numbered with the things that were," I was forcibly reminded of (Thomas) Campbell's "The Last Man." [The last six lines of the first stanza of the poem.]

(Signed) Edgar Whitehead.

Appendix D

The following is an excerpt of the transcription of the testimony of Elena (Lena) Nora Willis Branham used in the divorce trial that began April 11, 1946, in which the question of the race of the Clarks and Branhams was raised. The trial ended on September 2, 1946, with the judge's decree that the Branhams were white, and he ordered that records of the state registrar be immediately corrected.

Exhibit pages 47–67 in the original, on file at the Clerk's Office, Alleghany Courthouse, Covington, Virginia.

Lena Nora Willis Branham, another witness of lawful age, being first duly sworn, testified as follows:

BY MR. ALLEN:

Q   How old are you, Mrs. Branham?

A   Sixty-seven.

Q   Do you know what year you were born?

A   Born in 1877.

Q   Mrs. Branham, where do you live?

A   315 Lafayette Street, Baltimore, Maryland.

Q   How long have you lived in Maryland?

A   Seven years.

Q   Who is your husband?

A   Edward Branham.

Q   When were you married?

A   1896.

Q   Do you remember the date?

A   September 23rd.

Q   Where were you married?

A   I was married at home.

Q   Where was your home then?

A   Lived on the mountain, just above John Hamilton.

Q   Where are you talking about? What county?

A   Amherst County.

Q   Who married you?

A   Preacher Wiley.

Q   Were you married by a colored minister or a white minister?

A   A white minister.

Q   Well, had you had a child before you were married?

A   Yes, sir, this oldest child of mine was born before I was married.

Q   Born out of wedlock?

A   Yes, sir.

Q   Who was that child?

A   You mean who was its daddy?

Q   Who was the child that was born out of wedlock?

A   Dora, the one that is here, Dora Clark.

Q   You married Frank Clark?

A   Yes, sir.

Q   Who was the father of Dora Clark?

A   Charlie Lee Hicks.

Q   Was he a white man or colored man?

A   He was a white man. You know Charlie Lee Hicks. You should know him because he lived up in that section.

Q   No doubt that he was a white man?

A   Yes, sir, there was no doubt of his being a white man.

Q   Well, did he ever propose marriage to you?

A   Yes, sir, he had been going out with me and had been for two years wanting me to marry him but he didn't want to ask for me and he wanted to run off and get married and that is the reason for why I didn't marry him.

Q   When was your daughter Dora, who is now Dora Clark, born?

A   She was born November 4, 1894.

Q   Whereabouts?

A   In Amherst County.

Q   You have stated that you were married about two years after that to Edward Branham.

A   Yes, sir, it was in 1896. That was not quite two years because I married in September. Wasn't quite two years.

Q   Why did she take the name Branham?

A   Well, I just took to writing it that way because my husband was Branham and we just wrote it like that. Of course, that was not the name but I just wrote it like that.

Q   Is there any doubt in your mind that Charlie Lee Hicks is the father of Dora Clark?

A   No, sir.

Q   Why isn't there?

A   Because it is not. I know it.

Q   Well, how do you know it?

A   Because I know he was her daddy. There wasn't anybody else to be her daddy.

Q   Well, did you ever have sexual intercourse with anybody before you had it with Charlie Lee Hicks?

A   No, sir, I never.

Q   Did he ever deny he was her father?

A   No, sir, he never denied he was her father.

Q   Now give the court something of your history. Tell the court who were your father and your mother?

A   My father was Elisha Willis and my mother was Ella Adcock.

Q   Who was Ella Adcock?

A   She was William Adcock's daughter.

Q   Who was William Adcock?

A   Well, he was a man from Culpeper. There was none of his people of that family there with him and that is all I know about him.

Q   Well, was he a white man or a colored man?

A   He was a white man.

Q   You remember him very distinctly?

A   Sure I do.

Q   Well, describe him.

A   He had blue eyes and his whiskers was between a brown and a red and they come way down and a many a time I have set on his knee and combed his whiskers and played with them. I was a child and I thought those long whiskers on his face was so pretty and his hair was about the same color as his whiskers.

Q   Did you ever hear of him having any negro blood in him?

A   No, sir, I never.

Q   What do you know about Elisha Willis?

A   That was Elisha Willis?

Q   Yes, Elisha Willis.

A   I know he was a white man. He was born white and he was always white, and we never went with anybody but white people and we never went with any children but white children. We have always attended the white church. And I have attended St. Thomas Church, about three miles this side of Bedford City. Preacher Pierce was the preacher. I went with Malcolm Griffin, who married Lila Tucker, Bishop Tucker's daughter.

Q   Who was Pierce, what church was he preacher of?

A   He was a preacher in the Episcopal Church in Bedford City and he preached at St. Thomas, too.

Q   Was St. Thomas an Episcopal church?

A   Yes, sir.

Q   Was that a white Episcopal church?

A   Sure.

Q   You say you lost a child?

A   Yes, sir.

Q   Where was that child buried?

A   St. Thomas.

Q   In a white cemetery?

A   In a white cemetery.

Q   Who preached the funeral?

A   Mr. Pierce, Rev. Pierce.

Q   Well, how long did you live with Mr. Malcolm Griffin?

A   About three years.

Q   About three years?

A   We went to church with him and his wife every Sunday to services. He took the whole family with him. We all went together and set together in the church.

Q   St. Thomas was an Episcopal church?

A   St. Thomas was an Episcopal church. It was the one Mr. and Mrs. Griffin belonged to. They moved their membership from Norfolk, after they moved, to St. Thomas.

Q   How were you treated in the Griffin family?

A   I was treated as nice as anybody could be treated. I ate at the table and never ate anywhere else with the people I visited. I never ate anywhere but with white people and never went anywhere but to white churches and white schools.

Q   Did you have any children in Bedford City that attended school there?

A   Yes, sir.

Q   What schools did they attend?

A   Ivy Grove and Big Island and Hunting Creek. The one named Sam went to high school in Big Island—Marcuse School. If you ever passed through there, you have saw it.

Q   Were they white schools, or colored schools, or negro schools?

A   They were white schools. There are no negro schools that I know of anywhere through there. If there are any negro schools it must be in Bedford City, somewhere on the back. I don't know of any anywhere.

Q Mr. Ja[c]quelin Ambler testified here some weeks ago that a man named Sell Branham was the reputed father of your daughter, Dora Clark.

A I never heard of no such a name as that.

Q Who is Sell Branham?

A I don't know. I never heard of such a man as that. There is not such a name that I know of, nobody by the name.

Q Did your husband have any brother by the name of Sell Branham?

A No, sir.

Q You don't know who Sell Branham is?

A No, sir, I don't know where he come from. I don't know anything about him, and Mr. Ambler knew nothing about me, until this child was a great big child. She had been going to school for three or four years before I ever saw him.

Q Did you ever live on the Ambler place?

A Yes, sir, I lived there three years.

Q Do you recall what years you lived on the Ambler place?

A 1908, 1909, and 1910.

Q Where were you living before you lived on the Ambler place?

A We were living on old Mr. John Hicks' place, Charlie Lee Hicks' father's. We moved from there to Jacquelin Ambler's.

Q When did Mr. Ja[c]queline Ambler first know your daughter, Dora Clark?

A He never knew her until he started teaching school. She had been going to school four or five years. She was going to Mr. S. H. Wachouph and he never knew us, or didn't know anything about any of us until he started teaching school.

Q How old was she when Mr. Ambler first knew her?

A Let's see. The children started to school then when they were five years old. She was ten years old when he knew her.

Q Now how far was the Hicks place, where you were living before you moved to the Ambler place, how far was that from the Ambler place?

A Oh, I don't know how far it was. It was either eight or ten miles around that mountain, something like that.

Q On the other side of the mountain?

A Yes, sir.

Q Eight or ten miles away?

A Yes, sir.

Q Well, you said your daughter Dora was born in 1894 and you didn't go to live on the place until 1908?

A   1908.

Q   So she was a girl fourteen years of age when you went to live there?

A   Yes, sir, that was her age, then. I might have it wrong there, but she went to school to him before we moved there. He was teaching school and she went to school to him two winters before we moved there and then she went one winter after we moved there, and then she was married. She was married, just a girl.

Q   Then how old was she when she was married. Do you remember?

A   She wasn't quite fifteen.

Q   Who did she marry?

A   Frank C. Clark.

Q   Where was he from?

A   He was from Rockbridge County and my husband's father fought in the Civil War. He wore his uniform home and brought his old musket and this child in here remembers his musket. He gave it to my husband when we was married and he kept that old army musket and then he gave it to one of the boys and the boys did something with it.

Q   Your husband's father?

A   My husband's father.

Q   What was his name?

A   Richard Branham.

Q   You say he fought in the Civil War as a soldier?

A   Yes, sir, he fought in the Civil War as a soldier.

Q   How long was he in the Civil War?

A   He was in there nearly three years, he always told me. Of course, I don't know. That is what my husband said. He said he remembered it as well when they taken him away and when he came back as if it was yesterday.

Q   How old is your husband?

A   My husband was born in '46 or '56.

Q   How old do they say he is?

A   89.

Q   That would be '56. He is living, is he?

A   Yes, sir, he is living.

Q   Is there any negro blood in your veins?

A   No, sir, there is no negro blood in my veins and I don't think that it is fair for somebody to come up and say that there is negro blood in your veins when they don't know it. Now it is up to them to prove where it came from. Let them come back and scratch up where any negro blood came from. That is an unfair thing.

Q   Can't you scratch it up?

A   No, sir, there is nothing to scratch up.

Q   Well, is there any negro blood in your husband's veins?

A   No, sir, there is no negro blood. Old man Ed Branham came from Scotland here.

Q   Who was that?

A   His grandfather. He was a Scotchman.

Q   He was a Scotchman?

A   He wasn't a very large man. He owned a big tract of land around on the
side of what they call Bear Mountain.

Q   How do you know he came from Scotland?

A   He always told me he did.

Q   And his son was Richard Branham?

A   Richard.

Q   And the son of Richard Branham was Ed Branham, who is your husband?

A   Yes, sir.

Q   And he is 89 years old?

A   He is 89 years old.

Q   Do you know when your husband's grandfather, Ed Branham, died?

A   Sure I do. I remember it just as well as if it was yesterday. I have seen the
man many a time before he died. He was old when he died and I know
just exactly how the tract of land run. He owned some negroes and that is
the way that mountain land was worked. Was rough mountain land and he
owned those negroes and he had them to work his place.

Q   That was your husband's grandfather?

A   Yes, sir.

Q   He owned slaves himself?

A   He owned slaves himself, my husband's grandfather did, and I can go today and show the old house where they stayed in. He had three houses on
his place, old Mr. Branham did.

Q   What became of your husband's grandfather's place?

A   Well, when he died, the children sold it. Jim Higginbotham bought the
main house and then Jim Grant bought on the back end, and then Jim
bought back the other way, adjoining Beverly Ambler, and they put up a
blacksmith shop there and Jim Grant built a store and opened a store there
and they started a Post-office by the name of Amy.

Q   Amy?

A   Yes, sir. You remember that Post-office, I know.

Q   Who bought the other part?

A   Jim Grant bought both sides.

Q   Just divided into two pieces?

A   Yes, it was just divided into two pieces.

Q What part of the county is that, Peddlar Mills?

A The old Peddlar Mills road, going towards the mountain. Amy is about five miles from Amherst, then you keep on and go about five miles more when you come to Tobacco Road Mountain and then you come to Peddlar Mills.

Q Is that near the city of Lynchburg?

A Yes, sir, just above Peddlar Mills, just roughly speaking.

Q What does Mr. Ja[c]quelin Ambler know of your ancestry?

A He don't know anything.

Q Why do you say that?

A Because I know he does not know it. They lived in Lynchburg until after he was a grown man and married and my husband helped move his father out. His mother bought this place out there and he helped move them out there and he knew nothing in the world about my people and my husband's peoples, either.

Q Was Dora born when they lived up there?

A No, he lived up there when I was about ten or twelve years old or something like that.

Q Now where was Dora born?

A She was born in Amherst County.

Q I mean whereabouts?

A Right up above where John Hamilton's place was, above Berkley Church.

Q How far was that from where Ja[c]quelin Ambler was then living?

A I don't know. Ja[c]quelin Ambler was living way down towards Monroe, down there. I don't know.

Q I know where they lived but the court don't know. How many miles would you say from where your daughter Dora was born?

A Where we lived when I was married, we lived ten or twelve miles from Mr. Ja[c]quelin Ambler and I never saw any Ambler and never heard anything about any Ambler.

Q Did you belong to the St. Paul Church that was founded up there by the Episcopal Church?

A Yes, sir, Bishop Tucker confirmed me when that church was dedicated.

Q When was that church dedicated?

A It was—let's see. I will have to look to tell you.

Q Have you got anything there that will tell you?

A Yes, sir, I have got something here that will tell me how it is.

Q You have got the thing in here?

A Yes, sir, there was fifteen hundred people there when that church was dedicated and Ja[c]quelin had what little he had to eat spread among the rest of the people and they were all together and enjoyed themselves. And Bishop

Tucker from Richmond, and old man Preacher Gay from Amherst Court-house and preacher Messick from Arlington.

Q   Arrington.

A   I know he was from down there somewhere.

Q   Was young Preacher Gay there?

A   Yes, young Preacher Gay, Old man Gay's son.

Q   That was the Mission that was established by the white Episcopal Church?

A   Yes, sir, and is still under the diocese of Sweet Briar, Virginia.

Q   Of the Episcopal Church?

A   Yes, sir.

Q   Well, do they allow any negroes to attend that church?

A   Why, no, there was never a negro in that church.

Q   Now a good deal has been said here about some people of Indian descent being mixed with negro blood. State whether or not any members of that church, anybody was allowed to join that church that has any negro blood in them, although they may be of Indian descent?

A   No, sir, they were not.

Q   Did you all ever have any negroes?

A   Not that I know of. I have been away from there thirty-three years. There was never any in my knowing.

Q   Well, why do you think Mr. Ambler would come up here and try to make it appear that you all had this negro blood in you?

A   Because he simply don't like poor people. His father didn't like poor people. When his father would have mechanics to thresh, he didn't allow the hands to eat in the dining room. They had to go down in the basement to a side table, to eat, and not sit with them. He said: "I am going to bring you down."

Q   Who said that?

A   Ja[c]quelin Ambler. He said: "I have got to do something another to get you all down, you all are getting up too high and you will have to be gotten down," and he said, he told them, "You never have gotten rich." We was poor people. He thought he was rich and he didn't have any-thing more than I had. His father had plenty one time but he didn't have it.

Q   Mr. Ambler testified, on cross-examination, when I asked him a ques-tion he said, speaking of your daughter, Dora, he said, "Well, now, it was accepted that her father was Sell Branham, who was a cousin of Ed Branham."

A   Ed Branham has got no kin people by that name. He didn't have any kin people except his brothers and sisters.

Q And he refers to your daughter as being of the "free issue" stock.

A Wonder where he got such stuff as that from? I never heard of such stuff as that.

Q He said he would explain it. When they had certain slaves they were of the free mulattoes, those people being "free mulattoes" or "old issues" and they resent that very much. What do you know about that?

A I know it is not so. I can't speak just what I ought to say about it, but I know it is not so.

Q Why can't you speak what you ought to say? I want to know the facts.

A I would have to say he told a lie and nothing but a lie and that is what I would tell him.

BY THE COURT:

Q Do you know anything about the free issue or old issue in Amherst County?

A No, I do not.

BY MR. ALLEN:

Q He said there was a notorious Captain Edgar Whitehead and Paul Cabell. Did you know Mr. Edgar Whitehead?

A Yes, sir.

Q Did you know Mr. Paul Cabell, anything notorious?

A No, sir.

Q What kind of people were they?

A White people.

Q How did they stand in their community?

A They were high-standing people.

Q Did you ever hear of them being notorious?

A I never heard of them bothering anybody.

Q Did you ever hear of Mr. Paul Cabell representing Amherst in the Legislature?

A Oh, yes, I knew that.

Q This separate school that was established there for you people was an Indian Mission School. When was that established, as nearly as you can remember?

A I can't tell exactly. It was around 1884 or 1885.

Q Who was the first teacher there, do you remember?

A Old man Wachauph. He taught school when I went to school and then my children.

Q He was a white man?

A Sure he was. He lived right there at Amherst Court House and owned land. He used to stay at our house a many a night. It was so far to walk that distance and he would go around with just one child and another and stay to keep from walking home when the weather was bad.

Q   Who succeeded Mr. Wachauph?

A   Miss Cornelia J. Packard. When he quit teaching she went to teaching and a woman by the name of Lucy Bloxton from North Carolina.

Q   Was she a white woman?

A   Sure she was.

Q   She taught at that mission school?

A   Yes, sir.

Q   Who did she marry?

A   She married my cousin, Pitt Adcock.

Q   She was a white woman?

A   She was there for five or six years and she said she had a home in New York and she went back there.

Q   Are you sure she was a white woman?

A   Yes, sir, I am sure she was a white woman. Miss Packard was from over here at Washington.

Q   Who succeeded Miss Packard, or do you know? Miss Bloxton?

A   No, sir, after Miss Bloxton went away, Mr. Ambler taught school for three years in one room and Miss Packard in the other and I moved away and I don't know who taught them. Dr. Sandidge's wife taught school there for six years.

Q   She still teaches there?

A   She still teaches there. That is what I have heard, she still teaches there.

Q   Do you know Miss Isabel Wagner?

A   I did know her.

Q   Now are you sure this school was established either in '84 or '85?

A   Yes, sir, somewhere along in there. I don't know just exactly when it was. Well, I will tell you I was a girl of fourteen years old when it was first established. Now you can tell the date yourself. I was born in 1877.

Q   How many years did you go to school there?

A   I never went to school but one.

Q   And that was to Mr. Wachauph? He came from Lexington originally?

A   He was an ex-Confederate. He told me he was born in a brick house right opposite to the R. E. Lee monument.

Q   Now Mr. Ambler says that you are a mixture of white and colored, what was generally known as a mixture of colored and white, is that true?

A   No.

Q   Where did he get that?

A He made it. He just made it. I never was accused of such a thing and there never was any colored blood in me, nor none of my ancestors.

Q Where did Elisha Willis come from, do you know?

A His father came from Louisa County and he was born next to Chestnut Hill Church, up next to Snowden.

Q In Amherst County?

A No, in Bedford County. Father was buried in Chestnut Hill Cemetery.

Q What was your grandfather's name?

A Jack Willis.

Q And he was buried in a white cemetery?

A Yes, sir, he is.

Q At Chestnut Hill Church?

A Yes, sir.

Q Do you know whether Elisha Willis had been married before he married the Adcock woman? What is her name?

A Ella. No, sir, he was never married but once and he is buried in the white cemetery at Staunton, Virginia.

Q Who?

A Papa is. Go ask Dr. DeJarnette and he will go and show you his grave.

Q How did he happen to go there?

A Well, his mind got kind of bad and they sent him to the sanitarium.

Q How old was he when he died?

A Eighty-two.

Q Eighty-two? And he died over there and was buried in Staunton?

A Yes, sir, he was buried there.

BY MR. MINTER:

Q That was your father, you say?

A That was my father.

BY MR. BUTLER:

Q Elisha B. Willis.

BY MR. ALLEN:

A I reckon it is known all over the world that nobody with negro blood in them goes to the Staunton Hospital. There is another place there for them.

Q I never thought about that. Everybody—they ought to know it.

CROSS EXAMINATION

BY MR. MINTER:

Q You say your father's name was Elisha B. Willis?

A Elisha B. Willis.

Q   How many children in your family, brothers and sisters?

A   There was nine of us, four girls and five boys.

Q   Did you have a brother named Bernard Willis?

A   Yes, sir, and one, my oldest brother was named Powell.

Q   Did you have a sister named Anne Elizabeth?

A   Yes, sir, she was Anne Elizabeth.

Q   Did you have a brother named Powell?

A   Yes, sir, I had one named Powell.

Q   One named Charles Howard?

A   Yes, sir.

Q   Will?

A   Yes, sir.

Q   And Clifton?

A   Yes, sir.

Q   That is you—Lena?

A   Yes, sir, Lena is my name.

Q   Did you have a sister named Emma?

A   I did have but she is dead. They are all dead. I have a brother named Bernard.

Q   You have a brother named Bernard?

A   Yes, sir, he is in Washington. He has been in Washington twenty-nine years.

Q   And there is only six names on this list here: Annie Elizabeth, Powell, Charles Howard, Clifton, and Will. Who are the others?

A   Lena Nora, Anne Elizabeth, Powell, Howard, William, Clifton, Emma, Homer, and Bernard.

Q   Lena Nora does not seem to appear on this list.

A   That is my name.

Q   Homer?

A   That is my baby brother.

Q   And Bernard?

A   Yes, sir.

Q   Do you know how the Bureau of Vital Statistics authorized that as being of the colored race?

A   No, sir, I don't.

Q   You don't know that?

A   No, I don't know anything about it.

Q   That is shown by Exhibit 11. Do you know how many brothers your husband had, that is Edmund Branham?

A   Let's see. I would have to count them.

Q   Did he have one named Blanford?

A   No, he had one named James and Chester and Willie and John and Joe.

Q   Who was Blanford Branham?

A   I don't know anything about him. He was none of his people.

Q   Well, your husband's father was named Richard, wasn't he?

A   Yes, sir, his father was named Richard and his mother was named Christine. She was Christine Wise.

Q   They have a record here showing a son Blanford.

A   He must have died when he was a baby. I don't know. There were several little ones that died when they was babies, they said, but I don't know anything about that.

Q   Now your husband, I believe, was married before he married you.

A   Yes, sir.

Q   Do you know who he was married to then?

A   Yes, sir.

Q   Who?

A   Bettie Johns.

Q   Bettie Johns, and he was married somewhere about 1890?

A   I don't remember. It was somewhere along there.

Q   About that time? He was a farmer, wasn't he?

A   He was always a farmer until he got so he couldn't work.

Q   Well, did you notice that certificate of marriage showed he was colored when he married Bettie Johns?

A   No, I didn't know it. His license was white license and I heard Papa say so, and he was married in the Episcopal Church at Amherst Court House.

Q   All I know is, where it shows "Race" it says "colored." He was twenty-five years old at that time.

A   About that, I reckon. I don't remember.

BY MR. ALLEN:

In 1890, he wouldn't be eighty-nine, if he was twenty-five in 1890.

BY MR. MINTER:

Q   You do know this record showed he was colored?

A   No, I don't know anything about it.

RE-DIRECT EXAMINATION

BY MR. ALLEN:

Q   Have you your marriage certificate when you were married?

A   No, sir, Wiley went off and never did turn the license in.

Appendix E

Exhibit 21 from the 1946 trial, letter written by Dora Branham Clark to Dr. W. A. Plecker, Special Agent, Bureau of the Census.

Exhibit #/

April 20th 1930
R 1 Bot 452
Long Dale Va

Dr W A Plecker
Special Agent, Bureau of the Census
State Office Building
Richmond Va

Dear Sir I am writing you
in regard to obtaining a certificate
of the History of my family Record
as to our race. My children
have Been deprived of the entire
last term of school here Through 1929 + 1930
a complaint from the
Bureau of Vital Statistics
(Over)   Richmond Va

I have my Children's Birth
certificate, A Legal Record,
Registered as (White) signed by
you. Dr. W. A. Plecker,
My Husband + I were married
under (White) licens.
all my four Parents were
married under (White) licens
So there is no. Just Law under
the sun to Prevent my children
from entering eny + all
White School's in the State
of Va, or eny other state.
as a white Race
So Please send me a certificate
of the History of my family Record
as to Its Race and color.
I have had trouble enough

in this matter. and therefore
I wish to have my Record cleand
up (White) as it should be
also please inform me as
to who made the objection
to my children entering the
Sharon School of Long Dale Va
Alleghany county.
My children attended the
said Sharon School of Long Dale Va
2 School terms before there was
eny objection made. they also
attended School in Selma Va
serveral terms. there was never
eny objection made there
we have always Been white in the Past.
so therefore we must be White
in the future. My children
(over)

4.

are intitled to an Education and
must have Education
                hoping to hear from
        you by return mail
        Cincerely Yours
                Mrs F. C. Clark
                R.1. Box 42
                Long Dale Va

Dora Branham - Author

Appendix F

Exhibit 4. War Department. AGRD-W-301, Harry L. Clark, used in 1946 trial.

WAR DEPARTMENT
THE ADJUTANT GENERAL'S OFFICE
DEMOBILIZED RECORDS BRANCH
HIGH POINT, N. C.

IN REPLY
REFER TO
AGRD-W 201 Clark, Harry L.
(18 Jan 45)

STATEMENT OF THE MILITARY SERVICE

of

HARRY L. CLARK
Army Serial Number 6 814 131.

The official records show that Harry L. Clark, Army serial number 6 814 131, enlisted 29 May 1929, at Richmond, Virginia, at which time he stated that he was born 8 February 1910, at Monroe, Virginia. He served with Battery D, 6th Field Artillery, an organization composed of white men, and was honorably discharged 23 July 1932, a private, Detachment, Quartermaster Corps, at Fort Hoyle, Maryland, by reason of expiration of service. He again enlisted 25 July 1932, at Baltimore, Maryland, and died 26 August 1932, at Clifton Forge, Virginia.

This official statement of service furnished 26 January 1945, to Mrs. F. C. Clark, Route 2, Box 6, Covington, Virginia.

By authority of the Secretary of War:

J. A. ULIO,
Major General,
The Adjutant General.

Dara Clark
Exhibit 4

Appendix G

1923 Marriage License of Frank C. Clark and Dora Branham. Used in 1946 court trial.

MARRIAGE ✻ LICENSE

Virginia, Amherst County _____ to wit:

To any Person Licensed to Celebrate Marriages:

You are hereby authorized to join together in the Holy State of Matrimony, according to the rites and ceremonies of your Church, or religious denomination, and the laws of the Commonwealth of Virginia Frank C. Clark ½ brother to John Henry Clark and Dora Branham

Given under my hand, as Clerk of the circuit Court of Amherst County this 8th day of February 1909

W. E. Dandridge Clerk

CERTIFICATE TO OBTAIN A MARRIAGE LICENSE.

TO BE ANNEXED TO THE LICENSE REQUIRED BY SECTION 2224 OF THE CODE OF VIRGINIA, AS AMENDED BY ACT OF FEBRUARY 8, 1900

Time of Marriage, Feby 10th 1909	Place of Husband's Birth, Amherst Co. Va
Place of Marriage, Amherst Co. Va	Place of Wife's Birth, Same
Full Names of Parties Married, Frank C. Clark	Place of Husband's Residence, Same
and Dora Branham	Place of Wife's Residence, Same
Color, White	Names of Husband's Parents, J. C. & Margarit Clark
Age of Husband, 30	
Age of Wife, 16	Names of Wife's Parents, Edmund & Lena Branham
Condition of Husband (widowed or single or divorced) Single	Occupation of Husband, Farming
Condition of Wife (widowed or single or divorced)	

Given under my hand this 8th day of February 1909

W. E. Dandridge Clerk.

Certificate of Time and Place of Marriage.

I, George H. Ray, a Minister of the Presbyterian Church, or religious order of that name, do certify that on the 10th day of Feb _____ Amherst Va, under authority of the above License, I united in Marriage the persons named and described therein.

Given under my hand this 7th day of Sept 1923

George H. Ray

Appendix H

Marriage License—1890, between Edmund Branham and Bettie Ann Johns.
Edmunds parents are listed as Richard and Christine Branham. Note that Edmund and Bettie Ann Johns are listed as "col," meaning Negro.

MARRIAGE LICENSE

Virginia, Amherst County to wit:

any Person Licensed to Celebrate Marriages:

You are hereby authorized to join together in the Holy State Matrimony, according to the rites and ceremonies of your Church, or religious denomination, and the laws of the Commonwealth of Virginia,

Edmund Branham

Bettie Ann Johns

Given under my hand, as Clerk of the County Court Amherst County this 18 day of Nov 1890

Chs L Ellis Clerk.

CERTIFICATE TO OBTAIN A MARRIAGE LICENSE.

To be annexed to the License, required by Acts passed 15th March, 1861, and February, 1866.

of Marriage, Nov 18 1890	Place of Husband's Birth, Amherst County
of Marriage,	Place of Wife's Birth, " "
Names of Parties Married, Edmund Bran	Place of Husband's Residence, " "
am & Bettie Ann Johns	Place of Wife's Residence, " "
Col⁴	Names of Husband's Parents, Richard and
f Husband, 28 Years	Christina Branham
of Wife, 28 "	Names of Wife's Parents, — Susan
tion of Husband, (widowed or single) Single	Johns
tion of Wife, (widowed or single) "	Occupation of Husband, Farmer

Given under my hand this 18 day of Nov 1890

Chs L Ellis Clerk.

MINISTER'S RETURN OF MARRIAGE.

I Certify, That on the 19th day of November 1890, Ascension Ch. Amherst C.H. Va I united in Marriage the above-named and described parties, under authority of the annexed License.

Arthur P Gray

Appendix I

Marriage License—1896. Following the death of Bettie Ann Johns, Edmund re-married Elena Nora Willis, and this time they were listed as "White." Used in 1946 court trial.

MARRIAGE LICENSE

Virginia, Amherst County _____ to wit:

To any Person Licensed to Celebrate Marriages:

You are hereby authorized to join together in the Holy State of Matrimony, according to the rites and ceremonies of your Church, or religious denomination, and the laws of the Commonwealth of Virginia, Edmund Branham and Elena Nora Willis

Given under my hand, as Clerk of the County Court of Amherst County this 21ᵗ day of September 1896

Wm Sandidge _____ Clerk.

CERTIFICATE TO OBTAIN A MARRIAGE LICENSE,
TO BE ANNEXED TO THE LICENSE REQUIRED BY SECTION 2220 OF THE CODE OF VIRGINIA.

Time of Marriage, Sept 23ᵈ 1896
Place of Marriage, Amherst Co. Vᵃ
Full Names of Parties Married, Edmund Branham and Elena Nora Willis
Color, White
Age of Husband, 28 Years
Age of Wife, 18 "
Condition of Husband (widowed or single), Widower
Condition of Wife (widowed or single), Single

Place of Husband's Birth, Amherst Co. Vᵃ
Place of Wife's Birth, Same
Place of Husband's Residence, Amherst Co. Vᵃ
Place of Wife's Residence, Same
Names of Husband's Parents, Richard and Christina Branham
Names of Wife's Parents, E. B. and Malinda Willis
Occupation of Husband, Farmer

Given under my hand this 21ᵗ day of Sept 1896

Wm Sandidge Clerk.

MINISTER'S RETURN OF MARRIAGE.

I Certify, That on the 23ʳᵈ day of Sept 1896 at brides home I united in Marriage the above-named and described parties, under authority of the annexed License.

J. L. Wiley

Appendix J

This is a copy of the content and provisions of the Racial Integrity Act of 1924, Virginia. The law was overturned by the United States Supreme Court in 1967 in *Loving v. Virginia*.

An Act to Preserve Racial Integrity

1. Be it enacted by the General Assembly of Virginia, That the State Registrar of Vital Statistics may as soon as practicable after the taking effect of this act, prepare a form whereon the racial composition of any individual, as Caucasian, negro, Mongolian, American Indian, Asiatic Indian, Malay, or any mixture thereof, or any other non-Caucasic strains, and if there be any mixture, then the racial composition of the parents and other ancestors, in so far as ascertainable, so as to show in what generation such mixture occurred, may be certified by such individual, which form shall be known as a registration certificate. The State Registrar may supply to each local registrar a sufficient number of such forms for the purpose of this act; each local registrar may personally or by deputy, as soon as possible after receiving said forms, have made thereon in duplicate a certificate of the racial composition as aforesaid, of each person resident in his district, who so desires, born before June fourteenth, nineteen hundred and twelve, which certificate shall be made over the signature of said person, or in the case of children under fourteen years of age, over the signature of a parent, guardian, or other person standing in *loco parentis*. One of said certificates for each person thus registering in every district shall be forwarded to the State Registrar for his files; the other shall be kept on file by the local registrar.

Every local registrar may, as soon as practicable, have such registration certificate made by or for each person in his district who so desires, born before June fourteen, nineteen hundred and twelve, for whom he has not on file a registration certificate, or a birth certificate.

2. It shall be a felony for any person willfully or knowingly to make a registration certificate false as to color or race. The willful making of a false registration or birth certificate shall be punished by confinement in the penitentiary for one year.

3. For each registration certificate properly made and returned to the State Registrar, the local registrar returning the same shall be entitled to a fee of twenty-five cents, to be paid by the registrant. Application for registration and for transcript may be made direct to the State Registrar, who may retain the fee for expenses of his office.

4. No marriage license shall be granted until the clerk or deputy clerk has reasonable assurance that the statements as to color of both man and woman are correct.

If there is reasonable cause to disbelieve that applicants are of pure white race, when that fact is stated, the clerk or deputy clerk shall withhold the granting of the license until satisfactory proof is produced that both applicants are "white persons" as provided for in this act.

The clerk or deputy clerk shall use the same care to assure himself that both applicants are colored, when that fact is claimed.

5. It shall hereafter be unlawful for any white person in this State to marry any save a white person, or a person with no other admixture of blood than white and American Indian. For the purpose of this act, the term "white person" shall apply only to the person who has no trace whatsoever of any blood other than Caucasian; but persons who have one-sixteenth or less of the blood of the American Indian and have no other non-Caucasic blood shall be deemed to be white persons. All laws heretofore passed and now in effect regarding the intermarriage of white and colored persons shall apply to marriages prohibited by this act.

6. For carrying out the purposes of this act and to provide the necessary clerical assistance, postage and other expenses of the State Registrar of Vital Statistics, twenty per cent of the fees received by local registrars under this act shall be paid to the State Bureau of Vital Statistics, which may be expended by the said bureau for the purposes of this act.

7. All acts or parts of acts inconsistent with this act are, to the extent of such inconsistency, hereby repealed.

Appendix (excerpt)

Alexander Francis Chamberlain, A.M., Ph.D., Assistant Professor of Anthropology, Clark University . . . says: "In some regions considerable intermixture between negroes and Indians (*Science,* New York, Vol. XVII, 1891, pp. 85–90), has occurred, e.g., among the Pamunkeys, Mattoponies, and some other small Virginia and Carolinian tribes." "It is also thought probable that many of the negroes of the whole lower Atlantic coast and Gulf region may have strains of Indian blood." This probably accounts for the increasing number of negroes who are now writing to our Bureau demanding that the color on their birth certificates and marriage licenses be given as "Indian." The Amherst-Rockbridge group is the most notable example.

http://www.vcdh.virginia.edu

A Note from the Interviewer

Amherst and Rockbridge counties are home to the Monacan Indians.

Appendix K

This appendix documents the interview questions posed in each interview, and the variations in wording. In all cases, those interviewed were encouraged to introduce topics of interest to them. While a standard list of interview questions was attempted, a formal, rigid structure was not applied during the interviews.

Chapter Two: Chief Kenneth Branham

Question: "Who are you?"

Question: "Did you believe the Indians were rejected by the people in Amherst or do you believe the rejection was caused by Dr. Plecker's influence?"

Question: "You filled out forms in public school, all of you, stating your race as white, but your teachers would mark through and write in colored, Issue, or mixed. Is that what they believed to be correct or were they afraid of Dr. Plecker's ruling?"

Question: "Do you believe the white students were prejudiced or do you believe their parents were prejudiced?"

Question: "Did your teachers want a better education for you as well as your parents?"

Question: "You didn't want to be a non-people, you wanted to be a people in your own right?"

Question: "Is there a government grant pending to help restore the old St. Paul Mission Schoolhouse?"

Question: "Now in the late 1900s, you Monacans are invited to speak and educate others about your heritage in universities, colleges, and graded schools. Is that correct?"

Question: "The powwows serve three purposes I've been told: Teach Indian heritage, entertain, and with the profits, buy back Bear Mountain piece by piece. Is that correct?"

Question: "Life is never all heavy stuff. Will you please share some of the fun and laughter and learning experiences of your growing-up years?"

Chapter Three: George Branham Whitewolf

Question: "Who are you?"

Question: "You came here to Amherst County from Maryland. What year was that?"

Question: "Do you know how Bear Mountain got its name?"

Question: "Do you know what the term Issue meant here in Amherst County?"

Question: "Why is it important to you to put your model sweat lodge on sacred burial grounds despite objections from other Monacans?"

Chapter Four: Danny Gear

Question: "What do you mean by the five Confederacies?"

Question: "Do you wear regalia dress exclusively for performances because it is no longer functional for daily use?"

Question: "Even today, Monacans are sometimes called Issue; is that what you're saying?"

Question: "Your ancestors did believe in God?"

Question: "Indians did kill and raid long ago, yes?"

Question: "Danny, I didn't know the word 'squaw' was derogatory. What was the proper word for 'wife'? Do you know?"

Question: "Can you spell the proper word for wife for me? To me it sounds like you are saying phonetically Ma ahn nay?" (Tutelo)

Question: "Can you tell me a few examples of Tutelo pronouncement of words?"

Question: "Are you going to tell me anything about the numbers and the meaning of certain numbers?"

Question: "Tell me about the drums and the music."

Question: "What does it mean to offer tobacco to God?"

Question: "Tell me about sweat lodges?"

Question: "What were sweat lodges constructed of originally?"

Question: "Are the skins of animals the same thing as hides?"

Question: "Why was it, according to your research, the state of Virginia did not acknowledge Indians as Indians?"

Chapter Five: Lucian Branham the Patriarch in 1997

Question: "Was the St. Pauls Mission School just for the Indians? Was there a school bus for that school?"

Question: "Do you feel you were robbed of an education?"

Question: "Could the windows be raised in those log cabins? I was wondering why you slept outdoors in the summertime?"

Question: "You said there were only three medical doctors in the Amherst area. How were your medical needs met?"

Question: "What happened if somebody died? How did you handle that need?"

Question: "There was no way to embalm a body. What did you do?"

Question: "Did they hold what people used to call a 'wake' in somebody's home?

Question: "Would some preacher come to conduct the service?"

Question: "Did the white kids call you names other than Issue?"

Question: What were some of the favorite foods your mother prepared for her family?"

Question: Author's note: No questions asked by the reviewer, only appreciative laughter as Lucian recalled his courtship of Ollie Johns and then his marriage to Cora Hamilton.

Question: "Diane Shields drove me to Morris Orchards. The clerk said I should take a picture of the very old log house just outside the packing shed. Do you know who used to live there?"

Question: "Lucian, do you recall any songs of your youth?"

Chapter Six: William E. Sandidge, Clerk of Court

Question: "Did you know Dr. W. A. Plecker personally?"

Question: "Could you have been put in jail if you failed to obey Virginia laws regarding Indians?"

Question: "Was it legal to send state-supported teachers to teach at an Episcopal Mission?"

Question: "The census takers had to obey the same laws you had to obey regarding Indians. Is that correct?"

Question: "I've been hearing a lot about a list of Indian names Dr. Plecker compiled called 'Plecker's Hit List.' Are you familiar with it?"

Question: "Do you not wonder how one man (Plecker) could have so much influence?"

Question: "I know the Monacans provided for themselves, but kerosene was a bought item. Did they make their own candles for light?"

Question: "Can you recall the brand names of the coffees of the early nineties?"

Question: "Do you remember any of the old superstitions?" Sandidge's answer recorded here, said with laughter, "No, I'm not a superstitious man."

Question: "You are now ninety-three years old and you say you still dance and drive your own car?"

Question: "Do you still use that Royal typewriter or is it still on your desk for memory's sake?"

Question: "Thank you. Is there anything else you want to say?"

Question: "Will you look at these marriage documents and explain the discrepancies?"

Chapter Seven: Dena Branham

Question: "What kinds of crops did people raise here on Bear Mountain when you were growing up?"

Question: "Where did you say babies came from?" (Asked with much laughter)

Question: "Did you feel sad when you found out there was no Santa Claus in a red suit?"

Question: "I've never heard of horehound tea. Was it used for a drink at mealtime or was it used for medicine?"

Question: "Was square dancing the most popular form of dancing when you were a youth?"

Question: "Well, let's see, what else can you think of to tell me?"

Chapter Eight: Jo Ann Staubitz

Question: "Do you remember your ancestors doing crafts and if so, what kinds of crafts?"

Question: "Some people have told me the two-room schoolhouse at St. Pauls Mission for the Indians had seven grades and some people say eight grades. Can you explain that?"

Question: "So, were there two or three grades per teacher in a two-room schoolhouse?"

Question: "Did you ever consider leaving Amherst County to live elsewhere?"

Question: "Did the wish to leave have anything to do with prejudice shown toward Monacans?"

Question: "Dr. Plecker seems to have concentrated on persecuting Indians in Amherst."

Question: "Everyone I've asked has told me they don't know how Bear Mountain came to be named Bear Mountain. Do you know any of the history of its name?"

Question: "Do you remember anything about the home remedies used for medicinal purposes?"

Question: "Did anyone play drums when you were growing up or what kinds of instruments and styles of music were popular?"

Question: "Did you have opportunities to continue your education in later years?"

Chapter Nine: Lee Branham

Interviewer's note: I asked Lee Branham several questions, but he was in pain from cancer and wanted only to tell me the names of crops and the piggishness of landowners.

Chapter Ten: Annie Johns Branham

Question: "Did you attend St. Pauls Mission School?"

Question: "Did you ever wonder why the state of Virginia let white people be white and black people be black, while doing a number on Indians, who were actually the first Americans?"

Question: "My mother referred to Dr. Walter A. Plecker as, 'Old Plecker.' Did you have a name for him in Amherst County?"

Question: "Do you remember who delivered Indian babies in olden days, doctors or midwives or both?"

Question: "What are some things you do like to talk about having to do with being Indian?"

Question: "Do you recall any of the crafts your people liked to do? Did they make jewelry or pottery or basket weaving or quilting?"

Chapter Eleven: Phyllis Hicks

Question: "Did Virginia's racial laws cause your people's records to be in error?"

Question: "What was the popular form of dance?"

Question: "Do you mean there were news reporters who came to interview the Monacans promising to help in your cause, but who betrayed you?"

Question: "Did any of you ever really understand what the word Issue meant?" Answer: A negative shake of the head.

Question: "Do you believe government laws or government officials caused the most persecution of the Monacans? Or, do you think the people of Amherst County were more responsible for persecution of the Monacans?"

Question: "Are you teaching these children of today to appreciate all St. Pauls Mission has done in the past for the Monacans?"

Question: "You said your grandparents told you that back before St. Pauls Mission Church in 1908, none of the other churches in Amherst County would allow the Monacans to hold funerals or weddings and if your people attended worship services you were made to sit in the loft or on a back bench. Is that correct?"

Question: "I've been told Monacans had problems with drugs and drinking. Is this true?"

Question: "Do you know anything about your people ever making jewelry or pottery?"

Chapter Twelve: Thelma Louise Branham-Branham

Question: "Have you lived in Amherst County all your life?"

Question: "Did you attend St. Pauls Mission School?"

Question: "Did your mother or grandmother make all your clothes?"

Question: "I understand there were only two white doctors and their offices were in the town of Amherst. Is it true your tribe had to depend mainly on midwives for medical care?"

Question: "I want a copy of your cookbook. I understand you and Lacie Branham are great cooks, having learned in early childhood."

(This particular recipe is not included in the Monacan Indian cookbook.)

Chapter Thirteen: Eugene Branham

Question: "Who are you?"

Question: "Were times good or bad here in Amherst County when you were growing up?"

Question: "Were you ever called Issue and if so, do you know the meaning of the word?"

Chapter Fourteen: Herbert Hicks

Question: "How were chiefs chosen before 1995 when Kenneth Branham became the first elected chief?"

Question: "Did you attend St. Pauls Mission School?"

Question: "What are your thoughts as to why the Europeans did such a number on Indians?"

Question: "Monacans never wanted a reservation. They just wanted the same rights as other Americans. Correct?"

Question: "Do you think alcoholic beverages are fire water only to Indians?"

Question: "What kinds of games did you play?"

Question: "This book I'm writing is all about what the heart wants to say. Is there a particular something you know you want to share?"

Chapter Fifteen: Karenne Wood and Diane Shields

Question: "Which of you wants to talk first?"
Question: "In your research, good is coming out of evil, right?"
Question: "Do you believe there has ever been a pure white race in America?"
Question: "Virginia has finally granted state recognition to eight tribes?"
Question: "There were once hard feelings between the Monacans who stayed here and those who moved away, true or untrue?"
Question: "I know you are Diane Shields and you have been sharing along with Karenne. What is your job title?"
Question: "What is your understanding of a pure white race according to the Racial Integrity Act?"
Question: "Please explain the marriage bond and why Monacans were hard put to pay it."

Chapter Sixteen: Sharon Bryant

Question: "I viewed the video *Reclaiming Our Heritage* for the first time the other night. Please tell me about it."
Question: "You said you had trouble at school with a little girl calling you Issue and you didn't know what she meant. Was that the only incident?"
Question: "Do you believe there is always some good in life, too?"
Question: "Why do you think your people stayed here under such poor conditions?"
Question: "So, you're saying Grandma Edy ruled the roost?"
Question: "What did your folks call Dr. W. A. Plecker?"
Question: "Tell me about foods."
Question: "What were some of your people's favorite superstitions?"

Chapter Seventeen: Brenda Branham Garrison

Question: "Where do you work and what do you do?"
Question: "Who refused to allow you to ride the school bus, the school authorities or the bus drivers?"
Question: "Did you have any trouble in public school with classmates slighting you because you were Monacan?"

Question: "Many have said St. Pauls Mission was central for all in your growing-up years, true?"

Question: "I've heard that nursing school is tough subject-wise? Was it more so for you being from a minority race?"

Question: "Times and attitudes are changing, right?"

Chapter Eighteen: Hattie Belle Branham Hamilton

Question: "Do you remember any of your schoolteachers at the Mission?"

Question: "Does it bother you knowing you have Indian blood?"

Question: "I've heard Dr. Walter A. Plecker referred to as 'Old Plecker.' What is your opinion of him?"

Chapter Nineteen: Bertie Duff Branham

Question: "Did you ever question why you walked to school as the school bus passed you by?"

Question: "Who paid the schoolteachers' wages?"

Question: "Where did you attend church, at St. Pauls?"

Question: "Did you have medicine men or midwives?"

Question: "Did women have a hard life as Indian women?"

Question: "I'm hearing a lot about basket weaving."

Question: "Please tell me about family superstitions."

Question: "Do you remember any of the home remedies?"

Question: "Sundays were always for church?"

Question: "Can you explain the meaning of the word 'hue bangies'?"

Question: "The census takers made serious mistakes?"

Question: "Hospitals obeyed Dr. Plecker's rules?"

Question: "What types of employment were open to the Monacans?"

Chapter Twenty: Cecil Hamilton Terry

Question: "Is there a particular reason your name is Cecil?"

Question: "Did you live in Amherst County as a child?"

Question: "Where did you go to school if not in Amherst?"

Question: "Why did you go to night school?"

Question: "You are saying you children didn't have time to play. What do you mean?"

Question: "Did your parents consent to your marriage at such a young age?"

Question: "How long did you live with your parents?"

Question: "In Bedford, and along the James River, were you ever treated differently because you were Indian?"

Chapter Twenty-one: Ella Branham Mays

Question: "Your children are a mixed breed because you married a white man?"

Question: "Do you know the meaning of the word Issue when used to address Monacans?

Question: "Your grandchildren are in public schools, as well as some great-grandchildren?"

Question: "I understand from earlier interviews that you had wonderful teachers at the St. Pauls Mission School?"

Question: "What about home remedies?"

Question: "I have not heard of bean dumplings before this interview. Tell me."

Question: "Oh, me, let's change subjects. What are some of the pranks you kids pulled? Remember any of those?"

Chapter Twenty-two: Betty Hamilton Branham

Question: "Did your daddy own the land he worked or did he sharecrop?"

Question: "So you couldn't attend school. It was too far to walk? You helped your dad work the fields?"

Question: "Did your parents talk to you children about Dr. Plecker?"

Question: "So you only went to school one or two years occasionally?" Note: "I'm sorry the cassette ribbon just ran out. Please go ahead and answer."

Chapter Twenty-three: Lacie Johns Branham

Question: "Tell me about yourself."

Question: "Did you attend school at St. Pauls?"

Question: "How do you spell your families' landowner's name? His name sounds foreign."

Question: "Were your parents paid wages or were they sharecroppers?"

Question: "I hear from others that you are what they call a born cook?"

Question: (Asked with laughter) "What is it your children are teasing you to share about babies?"

Chapter Twenty-four: Cammie Branham Johns (Deceased)

This chapter was written from viewing a video documentary titled *Reclaiming Our Heritage,* by Virginia Life Foundations. I also talked with Cammie's daughter, Lacie Johns Branham, and Cammie's grandson, Chief Kenneth Branham. Therefore, there is no question/answer format for this particular chapter.

Chapter Twenty-five: William Carson Branham

Question: "Who are you? How old are you?"
Question: "Who are your parents?"
Question: "Do you have any references to birth registrar Dr. Walter A. Plecker in your studies?"
Question: "Are you ever called 'Issue'?"
Question: "Tell me something about the dances as to what the dances signify."
Question: "Can you explain to me something about the drum beats?"

Chapter Twenty-six: Heather and Holly Branham

Question: "Ok to start?"
Answer: "I am Heather. Holly will introduce herself to you and then we'll both talk." "I am Holly. Our mothers are sisters who married brothers."
Question: "To either of you: Have people's attitudes changed toward Indians?"
Question: "About your schoolteachers now in the 1990s, are teachers less restricted?"
Question: "Powwows?"
Question: "The dances tell stories. Is that true?"
Question: "Any comments later from white or black students who attended the powwows?"
Question: "You haven't spoken of your grandparents." Interviewer's note: Heather and Holly talked intermittently. It was a joy to receive their youthful, but thoughtful input.

Chapter Twenty-seven: The Minister

Question: "Why did you choose this small parish?"
Question: "Did you fit in easily coming from the city of Baltimore?"
Question: "How did you advertise the event?"
Question: "Was St. Pauls dependent on the diocese?"
Question: "You felt empathy with them because of the curse they were subjected to?"
Question: "I understand you brought about a housing development?"
Question: "Do you know the history of this church?"

References

Bogdan, Debra

1973 The Amherst County Issues: Factors of Development, Existence, and
Persistence of a Rural Tri-Racial Group. Unpublished Master's Thesis,
Sweet Briar College, Sweet Briar, Virginia.

Cook, Samuel R.

2000 *Monacans and Miners: Native American and Coal Mining Communities in
Appalachia.* University of Nebraska Press, Lincoln.

Estabrook, Arthur H., and Ivan E. McDougle

1926 *Mongrel Virginians.* Williams and Wilkins Co., Publishers, Baltimore
City, MD.

Houck, Peter W., M.D., and Mintcy D. Maxham

1993 *Indian Island in Amherst County,* 2nd ed. Warwick House Publishers,
Lynchburg, VA.

McLeRoy, Sherrie S., and William R. McLeRoy

1995 *More Passages: A New History of Amherst County, Virginia,* 2nd ed. Heritage Books, Inc., Bowie, MD.

Smith, J. David

1993 *The Eugenic Assault on America.* George Mason University Press, Fair-
field, VA.

Treaty of Middle Plantation

http://ww.mariner.org/chesapeakebay/native/nam026htm/. (pertaining
to later date than 1680).

Wood, Karenne, and Diane Shields

1997 *The Monacan Indians: Our Story.* Monacan Indian Nation, Madison
Heights, VA.

Index